The Way We Played the Game

The Way We Played the Game

A true story of one team and
the dawning of American football

John Armstrong

SOURCEBOOKS, INC.
NAPERVILLE, ILLINOIS

Published by Sourcebooks, Inc.
P.O. Box 4410, Naperville, Illinois 60567-4410
(630) 961-3900
FAX: (630) 961-2168
www.sourcebooks.com

Library of Congress Cataloging-in-Publication Data

Armstrong, John.
    The way we played the game : a true story of one team and the dawn-
ing of American football / John Armstrong.
    p. cm.
ISBN 1-57071-941-1
1. Benton Harbor High School (Benton Harbor, Mich.)—Football—
History. I. Title.
GV958.I84 A76 2002
796.332'62'09496—dc21
                                                                2002003315

Printed and bound in the United States of America
DR   10 9 8 7 6 5 4 3 2 1

To the memory of Dick Kishpaugh

Contents

Prologue

The Way We Played the Game began as a speech delivered in 1965 at the Elk's Club in Benton Harbor, Michigan. The event was a high school sports banquet, and the evening's speaker was a quiet, unassuming old man who was unknown to all but a handful of attendees. Fletcher Van Horne was his name. His topic: old-time football.

While dessert was being served, Van Horne carefully climbed the stairs to the small wooden stage and positioned himself behind the podium. He lightly tapped the microphone and the crowd quieted, probably in deference to his age more than their expectations. He introduced himself as a 1905 graduate of their high school and said he had played football while he was there.

Van Horne began his speech by saying football was the only major American sport developed entirely by students. Although he gave the lion's share of credit to the collegians, he claimed great contributions were also made by high school players. As proof, he related the story of Gerritt Miller, a Boston high school student who in 1862 founded the nation's first football association. The Oneida Club, or the Oneidas as Van Horne called them, were composed of teams from five Boston high schools who played against one another for two seasons on the Boston Common. They created their own set of rules, which were adapted from rugby, and they introduced the idea of uniforms by tying colored silk scarves around their heads to differentiate their respective teams. The first college football game would not be played for another five years.

Van Horne claimed that up until 1913 high school and college teams routinely played against one another. He mentioned a number of notable games, one of them being the 1900 game between the undefeated University of Minnesota and Minneapolis Central High that ended in a 0 to 0 tie. Looks of skepticism on his listeners' faces caused the old man to pause and take a drink of water. But he regained their trust by relating a number of similar examples involving past teams from their own high school, complete with significant details and scores.

It was clear his audience wanted to hear about local football, so that's what the old man gave them.

He said football first appeared in their region, as in most of middle America, in the early to mid 1890s. High school boys quickly formed teams, and soon they were arranging games with other high schools, private clubs, or colleges. The players often improvised the rules and nearly always supplied their own uniforms—rarely was any control exerted by teachers or school officials. As the sport continued to draw spectators, gambling increased, both professionally and among the students. Grades and overall interest in academics suffered. Eventually, the mounting pressure to win resulted in an escalating rate of player injury and even death.

Van Horne claimed that the nation's first state organization to strike against the abuses of high school football was the State Teachers Association of Michigan. It happened in 1895 during the Association's annual meeting.

Shattuck Hartwell, principal of Kalamazoo High School, formally addressed the issue in his scheduled speech. Speaking on behalf of educators statewide, he focused on the growing problems associated with high school athletics, particularly football. By day's end, a committee of five had been appointed to formulate guidelines. At the following year's meeting, five rules were presented that specifically addressed player eligibility. A lively discussion ensued as to whether the committee should proceed with its reforms or if the Association should attempt an outright ban of football. The comments of Principal Frank Sage of Saginaw illustrated the hard reality the pro-football contingent faced.

Van Horne opened a book titled *Athletics in Michigan High Schools: The First Hundred Years* and read an excerpt from Sage's address as recorded in the minutes of the meeting:

> A game which, at best, leaves each player with every inch of his body bruised and sore, and many with faces so disfigured that they are not fit to be seen, seems to me to favor the prize ring and the bull fight, and equally to deserve our condemnation. I have personally noticed the accounts of the killing of three young men in football this season, and have been told of as many more. Teachers of the high schools of Michigan, I ask you if a game in which such things are possible is a game fit our boys?

Other principals presented opinions, some in support of reform while others favored abolition, but in the end the reform-minded members prevailed. The committee continued its work.

Michigan's State Athletic Committee, as it came to be called, was initially ineffective because high school teams were not required to comply with the guidelines and the Committee couldn't force them to do so. The Committee then established a football state-championship series with the stipulation that all participants sign a document requiring adherence to the established rules. The series ran from 1899 through 1905 and resulted in more schools signing, but overall policing of the rules continued to be difficult.

Van Horne's first year on the high school team was 1903, when the championship series was in full swing. He explained that 1903 was also significant nationally because it was the year mounting pressure forced the Intercollegiate Football Rules Committee to begin making changes that would eventually lead to the game we recognize today. At the time, the rules as defined by this committee were more or less the recognized standard.

Previous to 1903, the game's rules encouraged most of the ball movement to be concentrated within tight groups of players smashing headlong into one another. The forward pass was illegal, and only five men were required to be on the offensive line of scrimmage, which meant guards or tackles often lined up in the backfield and helped to push or pull the ball carrier forward. Most of the injuries occurred at the point of impact between the two teams. Some injuries were unintentional while others were quite the opposite. Players hidden within the concentrated mass could easily slug, gouge, elbow, and knee one another unseen.

The 1903 rule changes attempted to lessen the abuses by spreading the offense across the field.

One of the new rules stated that, when playing between the twenty-five-yard lines, seven men were required to be on the offensive line of scrimmage. And for the first time, the man receiving the snap was allowed to run forward provided he crossed the line of scrimmage at least five yards to the right or left from where he received the ball. But between each twenty-five-yard line and the end zone, it was business as usual. There was no five-yard rule and only five men were required to be on the line of scrimmage. Van Horne believed that portion of the new rule was its Achilles heel—it allowed the push-and-pull strategies to flourish. He told his listeners that the injuries among his teammates were still so numerous that his coach negotiated with a local physician to treat the entire team in exchange for a discounted rate.

Van Horne then explained some of the rules that didn't change that year but should have. A first down was still five yards in three attempts, and one player could be in motion while any number of other players could be in motion as long as they came to a complete stop prior to the snap. Tackling was not permitted below the knees, while hurdling was still acceptable. Hurdling was an offensive maneuver that allowed the ball carrier to be thrown or catapulted over the defense. Van Horne explained that most of the hurdling his teammates did involved the simple leaping over the opposing players or using a fallen or crouching teammate as a springboard.

The game was also much faster then, which caused unconditioned players to become exhausted and more susceptible to injury. A game consisted of two thirty-minute halves with a ten-minute intermission. The clock was stopped only when the ball was brought out for a field-goal attempt, a kickoff, after a fair catch, or when either team called for a formal time-out. All other stoppages were at the referee's discretion.

The old game was raw and primitive, this Van Horne admitted, but he also maintained that he and his teammates loved every minute of it. They counted themselves fortunate to have had the experience, both for the sheer fun and also for the opportunity to play under the guidance of their coach, Clayton Teetzel. Van Horne added that for every negative aspect of the game there were two positives, and Coach Teetzel was one of them. Van Horne believed he was a brilliant coach and one of the truly great men he'd ever known.

At the end of his speech, Van Horne fielded a few questions. One concerned uniforms, which he described simply as light on padding with almost no head and face protection. Another involved scoring. He said a touchdown counted for five points while the subsequent kick through the goal added one more. A field goal was worth the same as a touchdown, five points.

When the questions were finished Van Horne thanked his audience and they gave him a solid round of applause as he took his seat.

After the high school athletic director made a closing statement, Van Horne rose from his seat to leave but was quickly surrounded by a dozen attendees. More than half of them were young players eager to learn more about his football experiences. A few of the older men relayed vague childhood recollections of pre-1906 games, but they remembered them mostly as brawling affairs played in open fields or sandlots. Nothing could be recalled about rules or strategies. One of the boosters, a history professor, suggested Van Horne put his story to paper, an idea that surprised the old man until the professor remarked that the written record regarding early high school football was nearly nonexistent.

Van Horne thought long and hard on how to handle his football history and finally came to the conclusion he should relate most of the information by simply telling the story of his 1903 team from beginning to end. He organized his collection of yellowed newspaper clippings, brushed the cobwebs from his memory, and went to work. He spent a year reminiscing with pencil and paper, and then his daughter spent another three months typing the story into manuscript form. Not knowing what to do next, Van Horne offered the manuscript to the local historical society for publication.

The society was located in an old church and was staffed by volunteers. They were enthusiastic about the project, but no funds or volunteers capable of handling the task were available. But the Board of Directors recognized the importance of the manuscript and accepted it with good intentions. It was placed with the society's other documents in a metal storage cabinet in the basement.

And there it sat.

For more than thirty years, Fletcher Van Horne's manuscript remained hidden in the church basement where it endured the ravages of dust, humidity, and time, along with the fading memories of those who placed it there. It eventually survived even him—Fletch passed away in 1972. But its most serious threat occurred when the church was struck by lightning and burned to the ground. The document, along with hundreds of other papers and photographs, miraculously escaped the conflagration with minor water damage. It was during the restoration process that the old man's manuscript was rediscovered and finally published.

The Way We Played the Game is that manuscript.

The Way We Played the Game

The 1902 Season

Chapter 1

Clayton Tryon Teetzel brought the thinking man's game of football to West Michigan. He didn't start the game here, not in Benton Harbor anyway—the credit for that goes to attorneys Joe Terry and Alvah Cady in the year 1894. They encouraged the high school students to organize a program of athletics, and football was the first sport taken up. Cady was their volunteer coach.

At the time, football was already popular out east among the high school and college students, but serious inroads into the Midwest had been limited to the collegians. The Benton Harbor boys actually got their first taste of the game in 1892 when they bought a football and experimented on their own, but before a game could be organized, the ball was stolen and they couldn't afford another one. Cady, on the other hand, learned the game in college and was able to mold the boys into a respectable team.

The game in those days was very primitive, more akin to barroom brawling than the football of today. The playing was rough and unregulated. Rules often differed from school to school and could only be agreed upon through intense negotiations prior to the game. High school teams were usually organized by students and coached by one of the more experienced players or a volunteer from the community. In Benton Harbor the game prospered, despite the lack of formal organization. The biggest advance was the formation of a board of directors that raised funds for equipment and arranged schedules, but it did nothing to change the nature of the playing itself. That continued to be a rag-tag, bare-knuckles affair.

Football in Benton Harbor changed in a big way in the fall of 1903 when we hired Teetzel. Like I said before, he introduced us to the thinking man's game, which was based on his theory that a football team was like a machine. He believed each player was one part of the total, useless by himself, but functional when working together with all the other parts. Hiring coaches was against the rules back then. The State Athletic Committee declared all coaches should be volunteers from the community, but the rule was rarely enforced. Nonetheless, it was still a rule and we broke it.

The reason we paid top dollar for a coach goes right to the heart of this story.

It all began during the season of 1902. I was fifteen then and weighed 108 pounds—most players averaged around 140—which meant I wasn't big enough to make the varsity squad. Two of my classmates, both close friends of mine, made the team and I was happy for them. But that didn't mean I threw my hands up in frustration, no sir. I was determined.

You may wonder why a small fellow like me would subject himself to the physical abuses associated with playing so rough a game. Well, I shall tell you.

I watched my first football game in 1895 when Pa took me to see the high school team from Benton Harbor play Niles. It was a cool, sunny Saturday afternoon and the game was played in a nearby park. We walked there—I remember because of all the leaves on the ground. Only a handful of spectators showed up. A few of them were students, but most were tough-looking men who stood in groups smoking cigars and making wagers.

The setting was rough-hewn by today's standards. The sprawling field was marked with chalk, but there were no bleachers and the goals were simple wood posts with boards nailed between them—not much to hold a young boy's attention. But then the contest began and the entire scene was transformed into a spectacle that riveted me like nothing ever had or would again. It thrilled me to see the quarterback take the snap and make long tosses to one of his backs, who either ran with the ball or tossed it to another back. I especially liked it when the runner hurdled the line, and at one point a halfback ran so close to me I could see the fierce determination burning in his eyes. Their camaraderie was unmatched—I was moved by the way they collaborated to move the ball forward and then congratulated one another with handshakes or pats on the back.

At the time I was already playing baseball, but forever more that game would pale in comparison to football. The boys I watched that day had a fire in their gut I'd never seen before. In my imagination, they were like Greek warriors or Vikings—rugged adventurers of yesteryear I'd read about in school. The game was rough beyond belief, but I was hooked. I wanted to play football.

Against my mother's wishes, Pa bought me a football for Christmas and I actually slept with it that first night. The following day I took it outside and began kicking it around in the snow and almost immediately was joined by the neighbor kid. Within minutes, another boy discovered us and asked to share in the fun. An hour later, there were ten young gladiators furiously kicking my football up and down the street. Boys back then had a natural yearning to be outdoors running, jumping, and rough-housing. Toss a ball into the mix, add a few rules, and you had the makings of a dream come true. By spring, there were enough of us to make up two full teams.

Me and my two best friends—Cleve Lester and Mit Ludwig—formed the core of the group. We walked to school together, socialized, and went to all the high school home games, which at the time were limited to two or three per season, some years less. The team of 1896 disbanded when their game with St. Joseph exploded into a vicious brawl. By 1901, I had joined a neighborhood football club called the Little Giants, and in 1902 I was practicing with the high school team as a scrub.

The varsity team consisted of fifteen players. In all, there were about twenty of us scrub hopefuls—the numbers varied depending upon injuries, study time, responsibilities at home, and overall dedication. We ran through the same routines as the varsity and lined up against them for scrimmage practice, a damn rough job, but it had to be done if we wanted a shot at making the team the following year.

Our 1902 varsity players were an energetic bunch, but the over-all expectations for their success as a team were poor. They were an unlikely group, you see. Most came from the Benton Harbor neighborhoods while the rest were country boys who moved into town when school was in session to live with friends or relatives—the remoteness of their farmsteads made it impossible to travel daily back and forth to high school. Another teammate was an Ottawa Indian and two others were colored. No teams had colored players back then, at least none that we played against. But colored folks had been living in Benton Harbor since 1862 when the town was first built, working and living and going to church, and it was only natural they play on our sports teams. Some thought us unusual about that—I like to think we were ahead of our time.

Our roster was full that year but our coffers were not. We got almost no financial support from the community and none from the school. The team was run by a citizen board of directors and a manager. That was it. Every player, whether a team member or a scrub, supplied his own uniform and no two of us dressed alike. For footwear, some of the fellows even wore old work shoes with cleats nailed to the soles. The only coaching we got was from our team captain, a senior by the name of Hub Allen. Hub was a great player, but his knowledge of coaching was limited to the information he absorbed from talking to college players, gamblers, and armchair quarterbacks.

Our list of plays in those days was short and our strategy unso-phisticated—our basic game plan in 1902 involved a mass of play-ers trying to move the ball against another mass of players. We played to win, don't get me wrong, but most of the fellows simply wanted to have fun. That's why so many folks were surprised when we won our first games. And we kept winning until everyone from the poorest street sweeper to the highest society bridge club lady was talking about us. In fact, so many people began showing up to watch us play that by the end of the season there was no standing room along either sideline.

When it was obvious we were a team worth supporting, dona-tions from the community began trickling in. The team's board of directors recruited a medical student from Northwestern

University, a former football player, to provide us with some decent coaching. They slipped him a few bucks every Friday and Saturday when he came to town to work with us. His name was Bill Machesney.

With Machesney's help, we won the championship of lower Michigan, surprising the hell out of ourselves and a lot of other people, too. This feat set us up to play for the plum—the state title. All we had to do was show up in Ann Arbor on the day before Thanksgiving and beat the champions of upper Michigan. Back then, it usually worked out that the winners of Michigan's two peninsulas played for the sanctioned state championship. The 1902 champion of upper Michigan was Ishpeming.

And that was the rub.

Ishpeming was an iron-mining town located in the northern reaches of Michigan's upper peninsula, a cold, rugged part of the state bound up tight between Lake Michigan to the south and Superior to the north. Ishpeming was perched along the spine of the Marquette iron range and was heavily populated with immigrants—mostly from Britain and Scandinavia. The Ishpeming high school football players were mainly Swedes.

Back then, Ishpeming football was king of the heap. I don't know exactly how or why, but there wasn't a shortage of theories. Some said it had to do with the water they drank while others claimed the Swedes were a superior race of people. I was told by one of our supporters that their training included summer jobs working in the iron mines, which sounded reasonable to me, but in the same breath the fellow said they also used tree trunks for tackling dummies. For sure there was a lot of bullcrap flying, but certain facts about Ishpeming couldn't be denied. Foremost was the skill of their coach, George Sweetland.

Sweetland graduated from Hobart College in his home state of New York where he played football, baseball, and coached intramural sports. He graduated from the Grand Rapids Medical College before being enticed to take the Ishpeming coaching job. During the seasons of 1901 and 1902, he ran his teams against the best high schools, colleges, and sporting clubs in northern Michigan, Minnesota, and Wisconsin. They won all their games and captured the 1901 state title, Ishpeming's second in a row. In football circles, Sweetland was called the Wizard.

In 1902, few sports writers across the state gave us any chance against Ishpeming. Most believed Ishpeming already played their season's toughest game, which was against Escanaba for the championship of the upper peninsula. Before I go any further with my story, I must tell you about that dogfight.

We won the 1902 championship of lower Michigan a week before the winner of upper Michigan was decided, and that allowed us the luxury of following both Ishpeming–Escanaba games. The first game was played in Escanaba and ended in a scoreless tie. When the State Athletic Committee decreed a second game had to be played in Ishpeming, the Escanaba team balked because of the rough treatment they got there in 1901.

It was late in the 1901 game with Ishpeming ahead 11 to 0, when a couple linemen began fighting. Then both benches emptied and the two coaches even came to blows. The Escanaba players were holding their own until a throng of Ishpeming toughs, some armed with blackjacks, swarmed the field and joined the fray. The brawl would've been much worse for Escanaba if the police hadn't broken it up. When the referee called for the game to continue, the Escanaba players refused to play—said they feared for their lives. They walked off the field and Ishpeming was given the win. But that wasn't the end of it. A week later, a train carrying the team from Oshkosh, Wisconsin, stopped in Escanaba on its way to Ishpeming, and a handful of Escanaba players boarded to give them a warning. Said the Ishpeming crowds would mob and maybe even kill some of them if they didn't let the Swedes win.

Such was the bad blood between Escanaba and Ishpeming.

For the 1902 rematch, the State Athletic Committee made it clear to both parties that Ishpeming would be disqualified if their supporters interfered with the game. The Ishpeming's team management took the threat so seriously they built a fence around the playing field and arranged for a contingent of police officers to patrol the grounds.

The game was played, and Ishpeming won 11 to 5. We heard the results, first by wire, and then in more detail when we got our hands on a copy of the *Escanaba Journal*. The paper said "over three thousand rooters witnessed the fiercest and most exciting contest ever played on an upper-peninsula gridiron," a fact that was verified by Machesney. Yes, he was there.

The minute our team management knew we'd be playing for the state championship they contracted Machesney to prepare us. They also paid him to take the train to upper Michigan to watch the second Ishpeming–Escanaba match. He posed as a reporter for the *Milwaukee Sentinel* and was given a seat in the reporter's stand where he went to work filling his scratch pad with notes.

I'll never forget the days leading up to our 1902 game with Ishpeming. The town was excited beyond belief. A train was chartered for Ann Arbor and more than two hundred rooters signed up, not including the team members and the *News-Palladium* marching band, which added twenty-five more. The team even got new uniforms, all matching, courtesy of a local businessman and small-time gambler named Billy Harper.

We players felt good about our chances in spite of the negative news reports. That's because Machesney worked us hard and tutored us endlessly on the Ishpeming game plan, which he described as fast but otherwise pretty straightforward. I must have played especially hard that week because Machesney said I could go with the team as water carrier, which pleased the hell out of me. I'd have cleaned the horse stalls in every Benton Harbor livery for that opportunity.

Gamblers began arriving in Benton Harbor a couple of days before Thanksgiving—I knew who they were because of the hefty wads of cash they carried. The Ishpeming gamblers offered outrageous odds, up to eleven points. The Benton Harbor gamblers were uneasy over that kind of confidence, but they dug deep into their pockets to support us. I was proud of that.

I woke up well before sunrise Thanksgiving Day to find a hard morning. The grass was white with frost and the mercury in the thermometer had dipped to twenty-eight. I dressed, ate breakfast, and then walked to the depot to join some girls who were decorating the coaches with orange and black flags and banners. We also tied a broom to the front of the locomotive to signify that we'd swept the lower peninsula clean. Then the wagon arrived with our gear and I helped load it onto the train while the rooters boarded and claimed their seats.

We arrived in Ann Arbor just before eleven o'clock and immediately formed a parade line behind the band for the march to the university. The crowd broke for lunch while a fellow from the Athletic Department led us to our locker room. Shortly after one-thirty, we trotted onto the playing grounds beneath the gaze of nearly two thousand spectators.

The fellows were nervous, but their tension eased a bit when they saw the Swedes, which is what we called the Ishpeming players. That's because they weren't very big—Machesney said they averaged 135 pounds to our 154. At the time it seemed like a damn joke. But then the game started, and we got our first look at them in action.

The Ishpeming players may have been smaller, but the bastards were quick. Back then passing was illegal and huddles weren't used—the players simply got up after the play was whistled dead and scrambled back to the line while the quarterback called out his selection. Ishpeming did it so fast my head spun trying to keep up with them. They juggled fakes, runs, tackle-back plays, and old-style revolving mass plays that caught our players flat-footed. We played our hearts out but couldn't get a foothold on the Ishpeming game plan. At the end of the first half, the Swedes had already run nearly seventy plays. The score was an embarrassing 23 to 0.

In the locker room, Machesney coached us on Ishpeming's system, which was different from the one they used against Escanaba. He was baffled about that but was able to convince the fellows they could still make a respectable showing. I agreed. No one wanted to be a quitter.

By the time the second half started, a wet snow was falling and the field had turned to a muddy paste. Ishpeming made a quick touchdown that was followed up in short order by a touchdown of our own, carried across by our fullback Jacob Graham. Then the game really turned furious. The fellows played one battling round of football after another until the thing finally ground to a standstill in the middle of the slippery field. The Swedes attempted a place kick, but the ball went short and Hub Allen recovered it and made a good run. We moved the ball using a series of line bucks and Graham scored another touchdown.

Suddenly we were on fire.

We poured on the coal and did so well that the Ishpeming boys got agitated. They began to block with more ferocity, which our players returned, and then they began throwing jabs and elbows after the ball was whistled dead. That was all right with us—we could brawl with the best of them. But the officials didn't penalize Ishpeming for starting it. They penalized us.

Within the next eight plays, two of our players were thrown out of the game for fighting, and in the view of our rooters it was for nothing more than protecting themselves. I agreed, and I should know. I was watching up close from the sideline.

From that moment on, all gentlemanly conduct deserted the field. The players tore at each other like wild dogs, pushing, kneeing, and slugging at every opportunity. Soon they were smeared head to toe with sweat and mud, and as they gasped for air you could see their hot breath exploding into plumes of steam. Linemen on both sides were bleeding, mostly from bashed noses and split lips, and I saw several players spit loose or broken teeth onto the field. Even those who weren't injured had blood from other players splattered on them. Some degree of injury was normal, but this game had become extreme—the players looked like they'd crawled through the bowels of a slaughterhouse.

For the next few minutes, the boys continued to play hard and fast, but not much happened in the way of scoring until Ishpeming fumbled the ball and one of our ends picked it up and ran fifty yards for a touchdown. Our rooters went crazy until the referee called it back because of a penalty, and then they booed even harder. Just when we started to get the upper hand again, a great thirty-two-yard run by our halfback, George Bridgman, was erased by the same official because of another penalty. Those of us standing along the sideline howled our disapproval right along with the crowd.

In spite of the bad officiating, we were still in the game, at least until an Ishpeming player slugged Hub Allen in the face and broke his nose. Hub tried to stay in but couldn't. He was bleeding too hard and Machesney made him come out. Then it was over for us—Ishpeming ran in one more touchdown to make the final score 35 to 12. It was their third state championship in a row.

The university football enthusiasts who watched the game were impressed with Ishpeming's speed and timing and the variety of plays they used. They complimented us for our playing during the second half and argued we could have won if we'd played that well during the entire game. They said Hub Allen was one of the best high school quarterbacks ever to play the game in Michigan. But there was also a dark side to the commentary.

After the game, our fellows were sitting quietly in the locker room, most of them treating their swollen faces with ice wrapped in bloody, sweat-stained towels. Soiled, tattered sweaters and jerseys hung from open locker doors or were piled on the floor, puddled with muddy water and more blood. The air was pungent with the smell of perspiration and liniment and the wet-dog odor of damp wool.

Slowly the boys began to talk about the game.

They all agreed that one of the reasons we lost was because Ishpeming out-played us during the first half. But they weren't so sure about the remainder. A number of them believed we would have won the second half, perhaps the entire game, if not for the questionable officiating. Minutes later one of our board members came in and corroborated their suspicions—a rumor floating among our supporters claimed the referee had a fifty-dollar bet on Ishpeming.

The chill was immediate, the silence so penetrating I could hear water dripping from wet uniforms. Bridgman, our left halfback, finally broke the silence by quizzing the others for their opinion.

"Could the game have been thrown?" he asked.

About half of the fellows nodded in agreement, and then a rehash of the critical play calling ensued with those who weren't sure until every shred of doubt was eliminated. Skepticism turned to disgust and finally anger. Some of the fellows yelled while others threw things or kicked lockers. It wasn't pretty. And the more they talked about it, the madder they got.

On our way back to the depot we asked our team manager, Bert Burger, about the rumor. He said it was more than a rumor, that the official in question was a law student from the University of Michigan who was boasting publicly about his fifty-dollar windfall. Burger said he confronted the fellow, who bristled and insisted his calls were honest, but Burger didn't believe him.

The trip home was not pleasant, and it sure as hell wasn't quiet. There was endless talk about the officiating, but also about the ribbing we took from the Ishpeming crowd. Cracks about us being slow as pigs, complete with squeals, were interspersed with derogatory comments about our players having the physical characteristics of fat barmaids. After the game, a group of Ishpeming supporters told some of ours they'd never played against an African before, referring to Busby, and they were sure he was only on the team because he was fast. Doubted he could read let alone make it through high school.

The comments about Busby, along with the other taunts, banged around in my head for days. They bothered a lot of other folks too. But the jeering was legal and didn't affect the game's outcome like the criminal calls made by the referee. That was something we had every right to complain about.

Over the next few days, news of the injustice spread across Benton Harbor like wildfire, and it wasn't long before a group of local supporters asked Manager Burger and the team's Board of Directors to enter a protest with the State Athletic Committee. The Board held an emergency session but decided against it—said certain committee members were against us, which I'll get into later, and that one or two of them had also placed bets in favor of Ishpeming. They believed an appeal would fall on deaf ears.

After further discussion, the Board decided a rematch was our best recourse. They would arrange it themselves by baiting Ishpeming with money. The board members put the word out, and the Benton Harbor businessmen and gamblers who supported us chipped in and raised $5,000 to offer as a wager—winner take all. Burger sent a letter to Professor Scribner, Superintendent of the Ishpeming Schools, with the offer. Grand Rapids was suggested as a neutral location for the game.

While we waited for Ishpeming's reply, another home game was scheduled. It was arranged by Machesney to ready us for Ishpeming should they accept our offer—said it would be good practice. That was one hell of an understatement. I say that because the team he planned to run us against was the varsity eleven from Northwestern University.

Through the grapevine we heard the college boys bragged we'd never cross the goal line, which is how we and our supporters decided to measure victory. We felt the game would be a success if we could score once. One touchdown seemed possible even without Hub Allen. Hub wanted to save himself for the Ishpeming rematch, but judging from the way he looked even that seemed like a huge stretch—I couldn't see how he'd be ready to play for another two months. His nose and eyes were black and blue and his cheeks were swollen up like boiled tomatoes, which he claimed was caused by the repair. Told us how the doctor rammed an iron bar up his nose and pried it sideways until his nose was straight. But Hub said the pain was worth it to have another crack at Ishpeming.

Our game with Northwestern was played in a snowstorm with well over three hundred rooters there to support us. I didn't play, but I passed out towels and kept the water buckets full. The final score was 17 to 6 in favor of Northwestern, but our crowd was satisfied. We got our touchdown.

We weren't so lucky with Ishpeming.

The Swedes never responded to our offer for a rematch, which forced us to pack our pigskin away for the season. But we couldn't forget how we'd been denied a fair shot at the state title. And then, as if things weren't bad enough, the *Ishpeming Iron Ore* printed an editorial revealing Machesney was wrong to believe he watched the Ishpeming–Escanaba game undetected. Someone recognized him and informed the Wizard prior to the game. A group of Ishpeming toughs wanted to rough him up for spying, but the Wizard told them to keep it under their hats, that he had a better plan. During our game he suckered us by using a set of formations and plays that were completely different.

It was a masterful stroke.

The fact that we were bested in the spying game wasn't the

worst slap in the face—we played against the Wizard and lost. But the editorial in the *Iron Ore* didn't stop there. It referred to Machesney as a "lying little coach" and a "sneaking monkey," and it reported he wanted the rematch because his backers lost stacks of money when he predicted we would win. And there was more. The following is a direct quote from that editorial:

> Ishpeming could beat that crowd of fruit-filled chaps every day in the year for fun or money and it would be easy to raise $50,000 here in an hour to wager on the game proposed, but Ishpeming isn't in need of Benton Harbor's apple money. To take the few remaining pennies from the local hot sports would be criminal, as there is promise of a hard winter already before them due to the losses of last week. They are going without underwear and filling their shoes with corn husks, and couldn't raise $5.00 to bet against Ishpeming. The poor little coach can sneak in under our fence any time he wishes. We can give him all our signals and still shut his team out. There are a lot of poor washerwomen in Benton Harbor who will not be paid until late next summer, after the next fruit crop has been marketed. The sportsmen there shouldn't let their little coach run at large. He's foolish.

We were furious. That article became the consuming talk in the local pool halls, at the drugstore lunch counters, and practically everywhere else people gathered. And it was the reason we players and our board members pledged to organize a team the following year that would be the best ever to trample the sod of a Michigan high school gridiron. We knew Ishpeming would play for their fourth state title, and we promised to do whatever was required to take them on the following Thanksgiving. Vindication would be ours. And I, Fletcher Van Horne, was determined to be part of it. I promised myself I'd be on that field, spilling my own blood if necessary, to even that score.

In keeping with our pledge, one of the first things we did was search out and hire a full-time coach—the very best that money could buy. That's how Clayton Teetzel came to Benton Harbor.

A New Coach

Chapter 2

Teetzel was born in Chicago six years after the great fire. He grew up on the city's south side where he went to school and played sports at Englewood High. In 1893 he was a freshman on the Englewood football team and established himself as a player to watch. As a sophomore he was the team's undisputed star. They defeated their big rival, Hyde Park, and then Lake View to win the championship title of Cook County. The following year Teetzel attended the Orchard Lake Military Academy near Detroit, but he returned to Englewood to play out his senior season. Playing right halfback, he led the team to another Cook County championship.

After his senior season, the Englewood school newspaper praised Teetzel for his gridiron skills. He was described as a swift runner, a skilled dodger, and a ball carrier who could hit the line with overpowering force. By all accounts he was almost impossible to tackle. The article reported he was much praised, and even though he was skilled enough to play on any college team in the country, he never acted vain or conceited.

Teetzel was a high school star, no doubt about it, the perfect example of the gentleman athlete, but we heard he earned most of his feathers at the University of Michigan. He played with distinction for three years on the varsity eleven and set a couple of track records. He was also a member of the university's Interscholastic Committee, a student organization within the Athletic Department that organized intramural sports. They also worked in conjunction with the State Athletic Committee to conduct the annual state-championship game.

Teetzel graduated from the university in 1900 with a law degree, but he couldn't get the sporting life out of his blood and hired on as director of athletics at the state normal school in Ypsilanti. Ypsi Normal, as we called it, was a teacher's college less than a stone's throw from Ann Arbor. Teetzel stayed through the 1902–03 school year when his folks encouraged him back to Chicago to practice law.

We first heard about Teetzel from Carl McClelland, our high school principal. McClelland came to Benton Harbor in the summer of 1903, one year out of Ypsi Normal where he played sports under Teetzel. McClelland was a bright young man, cheerful and popular with the students, and he had strong convictions that athletics should be part of every student's education. Back then, most high school principals believed that sports were a hindrance to learning. When McClelland discovered the football Board of Control was looking for a good coach, he proposed Teetzel.

Most of the board members were businessmen with no formal connection to the high school, which meant they didn't appreciate school officials meddling in team matters. In fact, any official who tried to lend a hand immediately came under suspicion for trying to wrestle control from the board and place it within the fold of the school. McClelland had no obligation to the high school team nor did he have any responsibility to locate a suitable coach, but he knew if he remained silent, the board might hire a mucker or gambler, or worse yet, a proponent of the slugging strategies. He didn't want that. He wanted the best for his students. That's why he decided to offer his assistance and pray it wouldn't be viewed as a power grab. A week later, McClelland met with the board members at H.L. Bird's Drug Store to present his case.

Bird's was located off the lobby of our largest accommodation, the Hotel Benton, a blocky, three-story building that anchored the northeast corner of Main and Water streets. Behind the drug counter was the domain of the druggist, who I remember as forever busy working with spatulas, beam scales, and different sizes of mortars and pestles. Against the back wall was a long base cabinet and above it were shelves loaded with glass bottles, vials, and canisters. Most were labeled in Latin. There were also braces and wrapping cloth and even such oddities as sphagnum moss for dressing wounds. The store also sold newspapers, cigars, and post-cards, and was furnished with a full-service lunch counter. A half-dozen tables were positioned along the south window-wall with a clear view of Main Street. A lone slot machine stood guard to the right of the entryway, where a couple of young boys were busy dropping in nickels.

McClelland sat at the lunch counter sipping lemonade while waiting for the board members to arrive. Sitting with him was Bert Burger, the drug store's business manager who was also our team manager. The board selected him to run the team in 1902 and again in 1903. It was Burger who arranged the meeting and also told us later about McClelland's meeting with the board members.

Burger was a tall wisp of a fellow. I never realized how fragile he was until I once saw him walking along the sidewalk into a stiff headwind, bent over and swaying like a weed. Burger parted his hair in the middle and always wore a suit and tie with starched white cuffs and collar, the high, rounded type. He was well spoken and dictionary smart. By that I mean he used a wide selection of words, all of which suited him well in his position managing the drug store, which is where he could usually be found. Much of the team's business was conducted from his cramped office located in a small room behind the counter. He negotiated our schedule, arranged for transportation, purchased equipment, helped to settle grudges among players, and anything else you might imagine. And he did it without pay.

The first board member to arrive was Fossil Wilson.

Fossil's real name was Ernest, but we called him Fossil because he was damn old. His hair and Vandyke beard were white as snow and he walked with the aid of a dogwood cane. Fossil was a retired lawyer and a former superintendent of schools, but he didn't do much for the team—could barely hear anymore without the use of an ear trumpet—but he gave the board respectability. Fossil bought a lemonade, had a few words with Burger, and then took a seat at the furthest table.

Next in the door was Billy Harper. As I mentioned before, Harper owned a cigar business. It was called the Columbian Cigar

Company, although I never figured out why it wasn't called the Harper Cigar Company or the Benton Harbor Cigar Company. I suppose he thought Columbian had a more exotic ring to it. Harper was tough, and when he drank whiskey he could be mean and bullish and best to avoid. He was also a serious gambler. He gambled on the pacers and trotters at the local race track, which lots of folks did back then, but he also gambled on the killing games— cockfights and dogfights. And, of course, he gambled on us.

Monroe Morrow arrived next, and I can safely say he was probably talking and laughing it up with everyone he passed along the way. Monroe was a tall man in his early sixties, a foxy, backwoods sort of fellow who was part owner of a local grocery store. His partner was Charlie Stone, who didn't give a damn about football and thought we were all nuts. Morrow, on the other hand, was undeniably our best rooter. To show our appreciation, we dubbed him the Prince of Rooters. He also gambled on the team.

Before Monroe had time to sit down, Walter Banyon and Ben Curry came in together. Both were young men, former Benton Harbor football players. Banyon was a mail clerk at the post office and Curry was an advertising man for Young's Dry Goods Store. Curry was responsible for recruiting players, but it was also his job to turn out the rooters for our games. To that end he used posters, newspaper articles, advertisements, and word of mouth. And he wasn't above exaggerating the potential strength of our opponents when trying to convince our supporters we couldn't win without them.

When the board members were seated and comfortably smoking their cigars, Manager Burger led Principal McClelland over to the table and made a formal introduction. The way Burger told it, McClelland took a deep breath and immediately went to work. He began by talking about Teetzel's education and personality. Then he described Teetzel's coaching style and how it was patterned after the style of Fielding "Hurry Up" Yost.

Yost came to the University of Michigan in the fall of 1901 and coached the Wolverines to an undefeated season. Then he did it again in 1902. Both years the team averaged a point for every minute of play while no points were scored against them in 1901 and only twelve in 1902. At the end of the second season, Yost took his team to Pasadena to play Stanford in the first Rose Bowl game and won by a whopping 49 to 0. The country had never before seen football played like this.

Teetzel had already graduated from Michigan by the time Yost arrived. But because Ypsi was located so close to Ann Arbor, Teetzel was able to associate with the university's football players and enthusiasts, and to study firsthand the coaching strategies Yost employed to create his football phenomena.

McClelland's mentioning of Teetzel's interest in Yost was a master stroke. The way we heard it, the board members were nearly salivating over the prospect of hiring Teetzel. That's because colleges across the country were trying to hire former Yost players to coach their teams. The board members knew it would be impossible to get one of those fellows to come to a small town like Benton Harbor, as did McClelland, but he cleverly planted the seed that Teetzel would be the next best thing.

McClelland ended his presentation by telling the board members Teetzel was presently practicing law to please his folks but wasn't happy—football is what drove him. When Monroe asked if Teetzel would actually consider coming to Benton Harbor, McClelland said a moderate financial offer might be all the lure it would take. That's because Benton Harbor had a hidden advantage—relatives. Teetzel had an aunt and uncle living in town who would very likely give him reasonable room and board. A vote was taken and the decision was unanimous in favor of McClelland's proposal.

Manager Burger put the deal together and contacted Teetzel the following day by telegram. He offered him three hundred dollars to fulfill a contract that would run through Thanksgiving Day. Teetzel wired his acceptance two days later.

Teetzel arrived on a Wednesday morning in mid-September, a warm day as I remember. It had been arranged ahead of time for Doc to pick him up from the train depot. I heard Doc was there well ahead of schedule, pacing the platform impatiently, chewing on a half-smoked cigar.

Doc Bastar was a tall man, a bit on the heavy side and bald as a peach. His everyday uniform was a tailored suit and a derby, which he exchanged for a straw boater in warm weather, and he always carried a walking cane. He didn't need the cane but carried it anyway because it fit his style. He also wore a gold watch chain decorated with an elk's tooth fob draped across his vest. As he waited for Teetzel's train that morning, I'd have bet you ten bucks he snapped the cover off that watch every minute or so checking the time.

Doc was educated and refined in a small-town kind of way. He was also one of the busiest men I knew, always in demand for delivering babies, setting broken bones, treating colds, and such. That's why he owned his own horse and buggy, a fine rattan sided job with gold trim and a large folding top. In his line of work, it was a fundamental requirement that he be able to travel on a moment's notice and in any kind of weather. Gambling was Doc's passion, horses mostly, but he also gambled on high school football. We viewed that as his incentive to keep us healthy—he was our team physician.

Doc had never met Clayton Teetzel. He found him by looking for a young, well-mannered, well-dressed athletic type of fellow who was alone and also appeared to be looking for someone. The two of them talked and got acquainted during the ride to Doc's house on Columbus Street, where Teetzel met the Missus and ate lunch with them, which was most likely bologna sandwiches and beer—Doc's favorite. On his way back to work, Doc dropped Teetzel at his uncle's place on the corner of Empire and Broadway where he set up camp in the spare bedroom.

Doc told us later he and Teetzel talked over lunch about football, and that he also gave the new coach some advice regarding the local customs and prejudices. Said he wanted to prepare him for the folks who were suspicious of strangers, which was smart. Benton Harbor could be rough on anyone who found himself on the wrong side of the rumor mill.

Doc also told us McClelland was right about Teetzel—he was one fine fellow.

By the time Teetzel got to town, we were already into our second week of conditioning—one of the team's board members was coaching us. A fellow named Ben Curry. We drilled in a weedy sandlot located a few blocks from the high school known as the Old Athletic Field. Each day after class we walked there, unless we were lucky enough to catch a ride with a teamster driving an empty dray or orchard wagon. A big wagon pulled by a stout team of draft horses could handle fifteen or twenty of us.

The roster of returning players was pretty lean. Hub Allen, our star quarterback and team captain from the previous season, was in college. Some of the others were either too old to play or had graduated, while others simply quit school to get jobs. The only returning veterans were Cleve Lester, Fred Handy, Mit Ludwig, Dice Baushke, and Stub Winters.

Winters played quarterback. He was on the Benton Harbor team of 1900 but not the 1901 or 1902 teams because he refused to play second hand to Hub Allen. That's why we'd never met. The fellows who knew him said he was a good football player, but that he was better known for his steady hand with a pool cue. I got to know him during our first practices and found him an agreeable fellow. He was agile and had quick hands, and if I had to find anything wrong at all with him I'd have to say it was his size. He was a little on the short side. But he certainly wasn't the shortest man on the team. I had that honor sewed up tighter than a drum.

The rest of the players were new fellows. Most of them were young, a few downright green. Others came from the ranks of the neighborhood football clubs, groups that were loosely organized but good training grounds for boys who wanted to play high school football. Overall, there were about fifteen of us practicing the first week and twenty-five the second. The increased turnout was due in part to the board's recruiting campaign.

The campaign primarily consisted of us players finding and convincing good athletes to try out for the team. Personal contact was the most effective tool we had. But in 1903, the board added a new twist—recruiting cartoons—drawn by a cub reporter at the *Evening News* named Al Clark. On four separate days, Clark drew a different cartoon, each one depicting a test to be taken by candidates for the football team.

Clark's cartoons were comical, but there was more to it than humor. They stressed that only the toughest boys need come out for the team. Being seen as tough was exactly the kind of recognition we wanted, and the board members used that to their advantage. There was a certain mystique surrounding football back then and Clark's cartoons enhanced that image. Even I, small as I was, was ready to go out and look into the hooves of a mule, which was one of the absurd tests depicted in Clark's cartoons.

We were running drills at the Old Athletic Field when we first met Clayton Teetzel. It was a clear day, warm and dry with the feel of early autumn, and a large crowd of men had gathered to have a look at him. We knew who he was the minute he stepped from Doc's buggy. He was ramrod straight, tall with a medium build. His hair was brown, short on the sides and long on top, and he had a firm jawline. I'd say he was about twenty-five at the time, although he could have passed for younger. He was dressed in knickers and a sweater, which was standard garb for a football coach back then, and he was wearing a pair of orange socks. Our school colors were orange and black.

I remember hearing some of the players grumble when they first saw him. Said he looked too refined to be a coach, that he probably wasn't tough enough. And they weren't happy about the money he was getting paid. Most of them felt our training and play strategy wouldn't change regardless of who was coaching, so why dig so deeply into the team's meager funds?

Doc introduced Teetzel to Manager Burger and they shook hands. Then he met the five-man board of directors. After chatting for a few minutes, Burger waved us over and we gathered around him and stood quietly while the formal introduction was made.

"This is Coach Teetzel," he said.

"Gentlemen, the pleasure is mine," Teetzel replied without so much as a one-corner smile.

We all said hello in return but not as politely—some of the fellows replied with obvious skepticism in their voices while others rolled their eyes at his calling us gentlemen. But I knew better. Those five words were delivered in a way that was designed to convey professionalism and respect. He was already coaching us, and it didn't stop with his polite greeting. While Manager Burger continued to talk, Teetzel systematically examined each one of us. I watched curiously as he inspected our feet and legs, then arms, hands, neck, and finally shoulders. One by one the other fellows began to notice, too. We couldn't possibly have known what

Teetzel was thinking, but it was easy to imagine him mentally gauging what manner of conditioning each of us would require, what positions would benefit from our various physical attributes, and who would be easy to coach and who would not. His inspection was serious and thorough, that much was uncomfortably clear, but from that moment until the end of the season he never loosened his hold on us.

"And now I want to turn the practice over to Coach Teetzel," Manager Burger said.

The crowd of board members and enthusiasts standing behind him clapped along with some of us players, but ours was a smattering at best. That's because we were still intimidated by the thorough dissection we'd just experienced.

"Thank you, Manager Burger," Teetzel said. Still no smile. "It is useless," he began, "to begin constructing a successful football machine until the raw material has been thoroughly schooled in the fundamentals of the game."

Alright. That seemed reasonable to me.

"For that reason," he continued as he began pacing back and forth in front of us, his hands clasped behind his back, "each player must endure a thorough course in the rudiments of the game. He must be sure in kicking and tackling, capable in blocking, making holes, and running interference. He must be certain in his ability to catch the ball, carry it, and use of the stiff arm."

Teetzel continued to pace, alternately looking at us and then the ground, where he occasionally nudged pebbles or weeds with the toe of his shoe. The crowd was as quiet as the whispering breeze.

"That means hard conditioning," he added.

"Damn right!" a voice hollered from the crowd. "Drill them until their saddle-oysters fall off." It was Roscoe Farmer, the county game warden. The crowd laughed, but Teetzel didn't crack the slightest smile—he refused to even turn around and acknowledge them.

"But to believe hard conditioning is the only component required to build a capable machine is wrong," he continued. "And it is also wrong to believe that luck and brute force will carry the day. The other component, gentlemen, is strategy. Good, solid strategy is critical to a team's success."

"That's right," someone from the crowd shouted. "A strategy to bust as many asses as possible!" That elicited a chorus of "yeah"s and "amen"s and then more laughter, which caused Manager Burger to turn and face the crowd with his hands in the air to quiet them.

"Good strategy," Teetzel went on, "means every player must understand the team's signals, play formations, and the rules. And even then, excellence in all those areas still means nothing unless each man plays for the team and not for his own personal glory."

There was some agreeable clapping from the crowd. We players agreed too, sort of.

"In other words," Teetzel added, and then paused for a effect. "All players are stars, and each one should shine with equal brightness."

"It's Whitman himself come back from the dead!" Albert Decker, the horseshoer, hollered and the crowd laughed. Teetzel cleared his throat but still didn't turn around. His ability to ignore them was extraordinary.

"Who can tell me what this is?" he said after picking up the football that was laying on the ground in front of him.

"A pigskin!" Winters said.

"A bag of hot air!" Someone from the crowd cried out and everyone laughed, including most of us players. Teetzel stood silently and let it play out.

When all was quiet again he said, "This, gentlemen, is a prolate spheroid."

Prolate spheroid? I thought to myself. *What kind of coach refers to a football by its mathematical shape?* Then I looked around and saw the perplexed looks on the faces of the men, who were speechless, players too, most of them probably unaware of the term. One player, Cleve Lester, looked at me and shook his head in disbelief.

"Yes, a prolate spheroid," Teetzel continued, "an object composed of a rubber bladder encased in leather and laced with rawhide. It truly is nothing more than a device engineered to hold air, aesthetically unremarkable and absolutely worthless in every situation except for on the playing grounds. Then it becomes priceless for what it can do. The strategic handling of this item turns boys into men, followers into leaders, and it builds strength and confidence like no other athletic endeavor."

I have to admit I never thought of a football quite like that before. He paused to clear his throat.

"For the next three months," he added, "this ball will become your most valuable possession, the focus of your existence. It will be planted in your thoughts while you eat and sleep and study. It will be with you in school and at church—you will breath the very air that gives it its shape."

The crowd was dead silent. I think they were trying to figure out whether Teetzel was a fool or a coach with incredible vision.

"With that being said, I want to reemphasize one thing," he said, raising his voice for effect. "When one man takes this football, the other ten will work with all their might to help him advance. Depending on your position in the lineup, you may touch it frequently or only on rare occasions, but either way your task will be just as important as that of every other player. The runner may get all the praise, but in most cases he will have done the least amount of work."

That may sound basic today, but believe me, back then it was akin to parting the clouds for the sun to shine through. Unfortunately, few of those in attendance realized it.

"I still think you should make them eat nails!" Billy Harper shouted and was quickly rewarded with a smattering of crowd applause.

In spite of that comment and all the others, which were mostly made in good fun, Teetzel never deviated from his message of teamwork. He was a captivating speaker with a strong voice, and he exuded much confidence in himself. When his talk was completed the crowd broke up, most of the men and boys drifting away in pairs while a few gathered in groups to talk.

When Teetzel had us alone, he asked each of us our name and what position we played—I was probably best suited for end. There was no passing back then so height wasn't critical, but I crawled out on a limb and told him I wanted to play halfback. I expected him to laugh, at least to say something sarcastic, but he didn't, and I appreciated that. It made me want to work that much harder for him, which I certainly did, and much sooner than expected.

Within half an hour, we were on the field falling on the ball, tackling, blocking, and running back punts—Lester and Baushke handled the kicking duties. Then Teetzel tutored us on some basics, dwelling mostly on the proper way to position ourselves on the line. He instructed all players, including the backs, to crouch with feet spread and hands on the ground, as if starting a footrace. Previously, each player adapted his own style—some crouched but most simply stood and leaned forward. Next, he split us into formations of four to run rudimentary plays, which was a good way for him to observe our individual capabilities. After two hours of hard practice, he told us to jog over to the Pastime Athletic Club for rubdowns.

The Pastime Club was located on Pipestone Road one block from the downtown district next to the Wallace Brothers Sporting Goods store. Actually, the Wallaces owned the building, business too, but they hired a stout, middle-aged fellow named Joe Bourke to run the place. Joe was known to most everyone by the name Caully because of his severely cauliflowered ears, a payoff from a long, hard stint boxing on the armory circuit.

Boxing had not been kind to Caully. He was worn and grizzled beyond his years, a little simple-minded too, but yet he was always friendly and eager to please his customers. That's not to say Caully didn't run a tight ship, because he did. He was particularly adamant about enforcing the club's no-fighting, no-spitting-on-the-floor rules. Story had it he wrestled the last fellow who spit on the floor to his knees and forced him to clean it up with his tongue.

The club had a small gym for weightlifting and boxing, a locker room with showers, and four fellows on staff who performed double duty as attendants and rubbers from noon until closing time, which was usually around eight o'clock. There was a clubroom at the front of the building furnished with wood tables and chairs, a pair of slot machines, and a small counter where Caully sold beer, whiskey, and cigars. Most days he also served ham sandwiches and pickled items such as eggs, sausages, and pig's feet. The membership consisted of young men recently graduated from college, an assortment of policemen, firemen, and the occasional middleclass businessmen, but mostly it was home to gamblers and other members of the gaming set. Memberships would also be provided for the varsity football players once the team was selected.

"Hail to the champs!" Caully hollered as we stumbled through the front door, the entire mob of us exhausted and breathing hard from our jog over.

"Hear, hear!" someone else yelled. About a half dozen men sitting at the tables drinking and smoking cigars had turned to face us. Some of them tipped their glasses.

"Lookin a mite smudged are we?" Caully said with an affable grin. Then he made a sweeping gesture with his arm toward the rear of the room and added, "Carry yourselves to the back and have yourselves shined up proper. The boys are waitin for ya."

As we herded across the wood plank floor, our cleated shoes filled the room with a sound that was similar to a coffee can of nails being poured onto a tin roof.

We took long showers and then, while sitting along the benches in the locker room waiting our turn for rubdowns, Teetzel passed out copies of Spalding's *Official Foot Ball Guide* along with a packet of papers showing our basic play formations. He told us to memorize all the plays, which we expected, but then he told us to read the Spalding cover to cover and memorize those rules as well. That's when the dam burst.

"What's the deal, coach?" Dice said while a number of others moaned. Our faces were all reflecting looks of disbelief.

"The deal is to win," Teetzel replied sternly. "I wasn't kidding when I said all good football players must have a working knowledge of the rules."

"But most of us play sports to forget about school and homework," Mit added. I'd be lying if I said his sentiments weren't mirrored by every team member in that room.

"I was hired to help you beat Ishpeming," Teetzel replied as he stood up and began pacing again. "But before we even think about playing them I must turn you into a disciplined team. It will be no picnic...erase that thought from your minds...but we will have fun. Be aware, however, that your ultimate satisfaction will come only from winning, which means you will have to be dedicated and work very hard." Then he stopped pacing and looked around the room at each one of us. "Are you serious about winning?"

He was answered with a few tepid "yes sir"s, mine being one of the enthusiastic few. That's when I saw Lee shaking his head in doubt.

"Then read your Spalding and learn the rules. Expect a quiz a week from this Friday."

By the end of that first practice we'd pretty well sized up Teetzel's personality and football philosophy. Three things were clear. First and foremost, he was a thinking man's coach. He thought like a chess player. To master Teetzel's style of football a player had to understand the basics and have a good, working knowledge of the rules. I could already sense there was much more to football than I'd ever dreamed possible.

The second was his concern for our health, which was also revolutionary, at least in Benton Harbor. Teetzel said injuries must be kept to a minimum and that it was just as easy to stay healthy as it was to get hurt. He had two slogans relating to the prevention of injuries, the first one being "protect yourself." The other slogan was "when slugged, do not slug back," which for him was a polite way of telling us that our fighting days were over. Teetzel claimed slugging caused senseless injuries. And though I agreed with him on that, I almost laughed out loud when he said it. The other fellows, too. We knew the slugging game would be tough to stop, particularly since we had been taught from the very beginning that hurting your opponent was good football. And that didn't take into account the old scores that had to be settled or the needs of those players who weren't happy unless they finished the game with a fistful of bloody knuckles.

The nature of Teetzel's temperament was the third thing we'd learned about him. He wasn't a screamer. He was firm and professional and he calmly pointed out our mistakes without rubbing our noses in them. I liked that, even if I was sore about having to memorize all the rules. But I also knew there were others who thought his no-slugging policy meant he was too soft.

That could mean trouble.

Chapter 3

A dance was held in the Benton Harbor armory drill room the evening of Teetzel's arrival. The doors opened at nine, but when I got there at 9:15, couples were already dancing beneath the soft, amber glow of the gas lamps. I selected a glass of punch from the refreshment table and then glanced around the room looking for Cleve Lester. Lester was my oldest and closest friend.

The drill room was the size of a gymnasium, large enough to hold basketball and boxing matches on a regular basis. The crowd easily exceeded one hundred folks, and those who weren't dancing were primarily dispersed into large and small groups. The dim light made it difficult to recognize faces beyond twenty feet.

And so I strolled.

First I passed a group of high school boys leaning against a wall decorated with orange and black crepe who were shyly eyeing three girls gathered against the equally decorated opposite wall. It appeared to me the girls were trying to embolden them with playful giggles and looks of encouragement. Then I rubbed shoulders with a group of businessmen and their well-attired wives drinking coffee and nibbling on cookies and cake. It wasn't until I reached the back that I finally found Lester standing among a group of players watching Professor Null, our high school music teacher, as he directed the high school band. We considered the professor a friend—he played on the football team of 1895 and was still a strong football enthusiast.

Most of the boys who practiced that afternoon were at the dance, about thirty in all, and like me each one of them was cleaned and scrubbed and dressed in his best wool suit. The remainder of the crowd was composed of high school students, teachers, supporters from the community—many of them recent high school graduates—and parents. Thankfully, mine weren't among them. I was afraid their excitement over my trying out for the team might cause me some embarrassment, Pa with his proud, fatherly bragging and Ma with her confusing mixture of happiness and apprehension for my well-being.

The dance had all the trappings you'd expect at such a function. Plenty of food, drinks, music, people socializing and dancing, and enough chaperones to monitor a thousand high school kids. But most of the activity revolved around football. That's because it was a football party—a fundraiser—and hustling for funds by the board members was the event's primary purpose.

And for good reason.

No money was provided by the high school or the city, which meant all team funding came from the community. In those days, folks pinched nickels a whole lot tighter than they do now, and it was twice as hard to woo them when the money was for a crazy football team. But funding was a basic requirement for having a successful season, and thankfully the *Evening News* stepped up to the plate to help us. An editorial in that day's edition reported that the team already had a good crop of players with enough talent to win the state championship. All we needed was more funding. I say more because we already had some money.

Billy Harper started the fund two weeks earlier by donating a thousand cigars, which we sold for ten cents apiece to make a quick hundred bucks. But we had to have five-hundred more to pay for the coach and to take care of other expenses—things like footballs, bandages, traveling costs, and memberships to the Pastime Club. And even that wouldn't cover the cost of our uniforms and gear.

The board members provided us with one pair of pants, one jersey, a sweater, and a pair of socks. And let me tell you something, even the most expensive uniforms didn't give us much protection. Our pants were made of canvas or moleskin with cane strips and curled horsehair padding sewn in at the thighs. The cotton jerseys had a layer of felt padding in the shoulders, and the wool turtleneck sweaters offered no protection at all, but they did keep us warm. Back then you could get a decent pair of pants, jersey, and sweater for about ten bucks.

Our shoes were the ankle-high type. The best were made from kangaroo leather but they were $7.50 a pair, which meant we settled for calfskin at $2.50 to $3.50—still much better than nailing cleats to an old pair of castoffs. The running backs needed shin protection because they hit the line so hard, often made worse because they were usually being pushed from behind by two or three teammates. For $1.50 you could get a pair made of leather or moleskin with strips of rattan sewn into them. Some of us wore sleeveless canvas jackets that laced tight up the front and were useful in fending off the hands of a would-be tackler. We sometimes rubbed wax into the shoulders to make them even slicker. They cost forty cents.

Head protection wasn't required back then, but about half the fellows on the team wore a leather head harness, which looked like a small cap made with ear flaps. An adjustable chin strap held it in place. They cost about a dollar. Some of the poorer fellows simply tied a rag around their heads, which gave their ears some protection, but not much. And then there was the never-ending problem of protecting the nose, which is where Morrill's rubber nose mask came in handy. The nose mask was actually a combination nose protector, mouth guard, and torture device. The bottom was held in the player's mouth while the rest of the banana-shaped contraption covered up his nose from lips to brow where a head strap held it in place. I'm sure the damn thing prevented a lot of broken noses, but when you were bashed in the face it sometimes felt like your teeth were being ripped from your jawbone. For that reason I didn't wear one. But I did put my money on a head harness. I'd seen what happened to some of those players who were too tough to wear one—split ears and faces bathed in blood. I was in no hurry to be that tough.

There was one other thing we used for protection back then and it was free. Long hair. We let our hair grow during football season into a style called the chrysanthemum mop. Eastern college players started it in the early 1890s with the claim that it protected their heads, though by 1903 it was out of favor with them. But not so in the Midwest. We knew it didn't protect us, but many of the high school kids around here still let their hair grow as a badge.

Couples continued to dance and socialize as Manager Burger escorted Teetzel through the crowd making introductions. Football was all the talk, with most of the attendees eager to know Teetzel's estimation of our chances against Ishpeming. I think he was a bit surprised at the number of inquiries, but probably more so when he realized just how much venom we had for them. He refused to be cornered by the Ishpeming question, but he eagerly talked about training and strategy. He was also quite interested in education and politics and economics. And he didn't hesitate to sing the praises of President Teddy Roosevelt.

Teetzel seemed to be most comfortable talking to the men. He was a bit shy around the women, but he spoke to them politely about books and music. He even knew a little bit about the latest plays that were all the fuss. It was obvious he had a broad education, which was good. The women were pretty uninformed when it came to football, which meant most of them were unprejudiced about the game.

Emily Fitzgerald was the exception.

Miss Fitzgerald was our English teacher, a tall and proper young woman with thick auburn hair. She had green eyes and a small crop of freckles sprinkled across her nose. Quite pretty if you ask me, but headstrong as a banshee.

One of Miss Fitzgerald's crusades, of which she had many, was women's suffrage. Women couldn't vote back then, and that bothered her. Another of her crusades was football, which she opposed because of the violence. I was with a small group of men and boys talking to the coach when she came up and introduced herself. Lester was there, along with Walter Banyon and Ben Curry and a few others.

"And so, Mr. Teetzel," she said with a smile after they'd exchanged pleasantries. "Do I understand that you are to be the new football coach?"

"Why yes, I am." We all chuckled, but he didn't see or hear us.

"You have come to us well recommended," she continued.

"Well...I am very committed to sports. I believe that athletics should be a component of every young boy's education."

"And so do I, Mr. Teetzel. So do I. I think baseball and basketball are wonderful sports. In fact, I'm helping Principal McClelland this year with the young ladies' basketball program."

"Good for you." Teetzel nodded approvingly as he fell head first into her trap.

"But I must admit that football, in my opinion, is the most barbaric sport ever devised." Even from where I stood I could see her gaze turn cold as steel.

"I think I can..."

"And for the life of me I will never understand why the parents of this town allow their sons to go onto the playing field and risk their lives," she went on.

"Please, Miss Fitzgerald," Teetzel interrupted calmly, "you must realize that it's not as dangerous as it looks."

"How can you say that?"

"Because I know the game."

"Well, Mr. Teetzel," she continued without hesitation, "I know the game too. I know that for the previous two years, students have come to class with their faces so beat and swollen they are virtually unrecognizable."

"But if you..."

"And I can't tell you," she said, still gaining momentum as she continued undaunted, "how many broken noses, fingers, and even arms and collar bones there were, and how many times I saw boys walking on crutches with knee and ankle injuries. Most of them were the younger boys who didn't make the varsity but were allowed to practice anyway—some of them being no more than fourteen or fifteen. I believe they're called 'scrubs' and are used primarily for scrimmage fodder."

"Miss Fitzgerald!" Teetzel demanded, raising his voice as he straightened himself to full height. "Can I please address your concerns?"

"Please do," she said in a much lower tone of voice. Then she stood there with her arms crossed over her blouse and her eyes filled with victory. I think she was satisfied she'd made her point.

That's when Ben Curry elbowed me.

"I think all that lawyering experience of Teetzel's must have paid off." He was referring to the fact that she stopped talking. I didn't reply for fear of missing the rest of the conversation.

"Most injuries heal quickly, especially if the boys continue to exercise," Teetzel began. "The real source of the problem is not the game itself but the slugging. Many of those injuries you mentioned result from fighting during the games. I believe there is no room for such conduct in sports."

"Come, Mr. Teetzel. You must realize that any sport with as much violent contact as football is bound to encourage fights. How could it be any other way?"

"Yes, you are right…in part. But at the schools where honesty is valued, injuries are kept to a minimum. It requires officials who are willing to penalize a player for breaking the rules, which includes slugging."

She obviously didn't accept that argument. Teetzel had barely got out his last word when Miss Fitzgerald was again on the attack.

"You know as well as I do that few officials will issue a penalty against a player for fighting, particularly if both players are equally involved."

I had to hand it to her—she really knew her facts.

"Yes, Miss Fitzgerald," Teetzel responded. "There is much truth to your argument. But these problems can be remedied."

"How, pray tell?" she asked, shifting her hands to her hips.

"By education, and by the involvement of concerned citizens like yourself. Football is still a new sport, and at the moment it happens to be going through some rough times. We need to improve the game, not abolish it as the opposition has demanded."

"On this I will never agree with you, Mr. Teetzel, but I admire your stance on fighting. And I will respect your opinion regardless of its shortsightedness."

"And I will respect yours," he said with the faintest trace of a smile. "I just hope our future meetings won't be quite as contentious."

I think that last comment surprised her. She didn't respond. She didn't even smile—her face just got relaxed and calm and I could tell she was thinking about it. She continued to look directly at him until she finally gave in and smiled back. It was a very small smile, but it was there. I saw it.

"Perhaps we can continue this conversation another time," she said as she carefully held out her hand, which Teetzel took into his own and shook gently. "But for now I must visit with the other guests. It was nice to make your acquaintance."

"The pleasure was all mine, Miss Fitzgerald," he said with a courteous nod of his head.

Miss Fitzgerald disappeared into the crowd, which is when we broke out laughing. We knew how she felt about football and that she was actively agitating for our high school team to pull out of the interscholastic athletic agreement. Teetzel did fine with her, although we weren't so sure he knew it. He looked at us and shrugged his shoulders, and then he made the best quip of the night.

"You didn't tell me Benton Harbor has an anti-football movement." I can't tell you how hard we busted up over that one.

The athletic agreement was the document prepared each year by the State Athletic Committee that all high schools intending to play in the interscholastic series had to sign.

The series, as I said before, consisted of high schools playing against each other until the last two teams standing butted heads for the state championship on Thanksgiving Day. But back in those days, unbridled capitalism and rugged individualism were still the measure of a man's success, and for many enthusiasts the mere idea of an interscholastic agreement seemed ridiculous. Our board members saw it as a piece of paper used to sooth the guilty consciences of overly protective school officials. They didn't like it one bit, but because our high school teams wanted their fair shot at the state championship, the agreement was always signed. The lure of a state title truly was a carrot at the end of the stick.

The agreement was simple. Basically it required every member of the football team to be in school and passing his classes, that he not play for over five years, and not be over the age of twenty-one. Additions to the agreement adopted in 1902 also required each football player to pass a physical exam, have his parent's written consent to play, and sign a statement certifying he'd never played on a college team or for profit. It also stated that "the entire management of high school athletics be vested in students and teachers," which we weren't even close to following.

Miss Fitzgerald hated football, but she agonized even more over the fact that we were being managed by the likes of Billy Harper. In fact, she believed the entire Board of Control was corrupt, Doc and Burger included. Outwardly, she said we shouldn't sign the athletic agreement because we were being managed by an illegal board, but I suspect her real intentions were much more insidious. I think she believed student interest in football would dwindle if we weren't allowed to play in the interscholastic series.

She couldn't have been more wrong.

Supporters of football argued there would always be interest in the game, even at those schools where the agreement wasn't signed. They were right. In fact, more schools didn't sign the agreement than those that did, and for a number of reasons. At some schools the students still managed the team and didn't want the state telling them how to run their programs. It was the same for teams run by gamblers or local businessmen. Other schools didn't have enough players to make up a legal team and had to use boys who weren't in school. And just because a school signed the agreement didn't mean they obeyed all the rules anyway. Many just got better at cheating.

By the end of the night, most everyone at the dance had met Teetzel, or at least stood in one of the groups that had gathered to hear him speak. Everyone I talked with seemed satisfied that he was a good choice, but that opinion wasn't unanimous. The rest felt he was too refined and that he wouldn't be tough enough with us—board member Billy Harper was among their number. He was disappointed Teetzel hadn't screamed and threatened us at the afternoon's practice.

As the crowd was leaving, Teetzel came over to where I was standing and said he wanted to ask a favor of me. Even called me "Fletch," which surprised the hell out of me.

"Manager Burger tells me quite a few of the boys from last year's team haven't shown up for practice yet," he said. "Do you know why?"

"In fact I do," I answered cautiously. "Most of them are working."

"Do you think they'll come out as we get closer to our first game?"

"Maybe, but some of them are farm boys living in the country, and they're busy right now getting in their apples and peaches."

"What about the boys who live in town?"

"Sure…there are some good fellows here, too, but most will work up to the last minute. And some will want to play but won't sign up for school."

"That's a problem everywhere," he answered, shaking his head in disappointment.

"Sometimes they play without being in school at all," I offered.

"But that's clearly against the rules."

"I know, but the board members and school officials look the other way. Sometimes the players enlist during the fall semester and then quit when football is over."

Teetzel rubbed his right temple as though he was getting a headache. Then he said, "That's not good sportsmanship, Fletch. I don't want anyone playing on this team that isn't enrolled in school. There's enough interest here that I won't have any trouble finding fifteen good players, even though I'd prefer to have the very best available. Lord knows we're going to need them."

"Do you want me to talk to some of those fellas?" I asked, to which he replied yes.

Then I asked him if I should talk to anyone in particular, even though I didn't expect him to know who was who in Benton Harbor, particularly on the very first day of his arrival. But I should have known better.

"I've talked to Ben Curry about it," he replied, "and he said he's already been in touch with the folks at the *Evening News* about running more ads. That might drum up further interest. He's also met with Milton Ludwig and Leo Baushke about talking to some of the local fellows. But I would especially like to see Jacob Graham come out again, and I know he lives in the country."

"All the players would like to see Jacob come out," I said, trying my best to level with Teetzel, "but it might be a tough sell."

"Would you consider trying?" he asked.

"Can't hurt to try. I'll see if Lester wants to go with me." Ever since kindergarten, Lester and I had been through thick and thin together. "We can borrow my pa's rig and take a ride out there Saturday morning," I added.

Not many people had their own rig because of the expense, and I figured that was the reason Teetzel talked to me about going to the Graham place. A "rig" is what we called a horse and buggy back then. Burger probably told him my father had one.

"Oh…and one more thing, Fletch," he said as I started to turn away. "Do you have English with Miss Fitzgerald?"

I gave him a surprised look, which was real, and then I answered his question with a cautious "Yes."

"Is she always so outspoken?"

"Always."

He hesitated for a moment, but then he smiled and said, "Good luck with Graham." Teetzel shook my hand before turning to join Manager Burger and Ben Curry as they walked out the door.

I found Butts and told him about my talk with the coach. Lester's nickname was Butts. We called him that because of the way he blocked with his head, like a billy goat. He agreed that we needed Graham on the team, but I suspected he thought we needed Spud Wadsworth, too, but was considerate enough not to mention it.

Wadsworth was a farm kid from Twelve Corners who some-times played with us in pick-up games. He was a great quarter-back, which is why Burger and the board members tried to recruit him for the team the previous two seasons. He'd always begged off saying he didn't have the time, which pleased me. That's because he was a bastard—cocky and pushy in my view. He and I once came to blows over the way I tackled him during a game and we hadn't spoken since.

Butts and I left the armory and walked home along Pipestone Road beneath a sky filled with stars. It was so quiet that the tap-ping of our shoes echoed loudly against the cobbled brick streets while our voices floated high and easy over the neighborhood. We could almost hear people breathing in their beds. We talked about the dance and the girls we danced with and which ones looked the prettiest. Neither of us had a girlfriend, didn't know too much about girls, but knew that we really liked them. We liked the way they looked and smelled and teased us, and how they felt sorry for us when we got beat up playing football. But we also talked about Jacob Graham.

Graham was the most athletic fellow either of us had ever known. He was raw-boned to the core, a hard-muscled kid who was strong as an oak and agile as a prizefighter. He loved football, we knew that, but we were afraid he wouldn't sign up for classes. He hated school.

A lot was riding on our visit with Jacob. Neither Lester nor I, nor probably anyone else on the team, thought we could beat Ishpeming without him.

Chapter 4

The Paw Paw River wound a westward course along the north edge of town. Then it turned south and spilled into the St. Joseph River, which flowed a couple hundred yards further before cutting a muddy path into the blue waters of Lake Michigan. Across the St. Joe, which is what we called the big river, was a village of six thousand. The business quarter was situated on the crest of a high hill with a sweeping view of the lake beyond. St. Joe was a genteel old town and a lake port.

We were neither.

In 1903 Benton Harbor was a vigorous community with a population of eight thousand residents, give or take a few. We were still young, founded some forty years earlier by rough-hewn farmers who'd grown weary of being forced to cut bad deals with St. Joe's shippers. The lifeblood of the farmers, or growers as we called them, was their orchards. Using their fruit money, a group of these men financed the digging of a mile-long canal and then built Benton Harbor at its terminus. Access to shipping caused the town to grow like a weed. Over the years, a number of shipbuilding and manufacturing concerns located here, and by 1903 we had one of the largest cash-to-farmer fruit markets in the world.

In some respects, the Benton Harbor of my childhood was still a frontier town, a place where a poor man could still buy good farmland or start a business with little more than guts and hard work, but in other respects it had the amenities one might find in an old, well-settled eastern town. Brick buildings, paved streets, and hotels abounded. There was even an opera house and a library, and the schools were first class. Benton Harbor was serviced by two railroads, but because we had no deep water port, all lake steamers and schooners had to reach us through the canal. That was our only limitation, but on the positive side, it placed us over a mile from St. Joseph.

St. Joe was our big rival, you see. We didn't like them and they didn't like us, never had. From the very beginning, they referred to Benton Harbor as "Bungtown"—a name some enterprising wit made up as a wordplay off an item produced in our first factory, a wooden barrel-stopper called a *bung*. We didn't mind the name, in fact we used it all the time. We just didn't like it when they did.

The Graham place was in Hagar Township. To get there we had to cross the Paw Paw River and travel north up the Old Lake Shore Road. I needed Pa's permission to use the rig, which shouldn't have been a problem to obtain and wasn't, at least until I told him where we were going. Then he hesitated. He wasn't worried about me as much as Mattie, our chestnut mare.

His concern was with the roads.

All roads outside of town were rough back then, not much more than wagon ruts. That's because no one traveled by automobile—there were none—at least not around here. Everyone took the train, or steamship if they were going to Chicago, Milwaukee, or any other lake town. The only folks who used roads were farmers. In the end, Pa consented to let me take the rig if I promised to be careful.

Just after first light, I went out back to the carriage shed and fed Mattie, who seemed happy to see me. She was a damn good horse that Mattie—dependable. Ma always said to "treat her well and she'll be calm as honey." And so I did. After cleaning her stall and spreading a fresh layer of straw bedding, I went back inside and ate my own breakfast while Ma made sandwiches for my lunch.

"Now you be careful out there, Fletch," she said. "You know how your father worries about that rig of his."

"I know, Ma," I answered between bites of eggs and bacon. "There's nothing to worry about."

"He's right about the roads, you know."

"I know that, too. But it's a great day...clear and sunny...not a cloud in the sky. Nothing's going to happen."

"Well," she said as she placed the basket of sandwiches on the table beside me, "have fun and be home by dinner."

"Yes ma'am."

I was still chewing my last mouthful of food as I walked back out to the carriage shed where I fit the harness to Mattie's back and hitched her to the buggy, a small slat-bottomed businessman's model. I made the necessary adjustments to the hames and traces, and then I climbed into the seat. With a gentle snap of the reins, Mattie jerked the rig into motion and within seconds we were trotting briskly down the alley past the O'Reilly place. Mrs. O'Reilly was in the yard using a wire beater to pummel the dirt from a rug draped over the clothes line.

When I pulled up to the Lester home, I found Butts in the yard throwing stones at a mangy cur that he'd caught trying to kill one of the neighbor's chickens. I arrived just in time to see a sizzling toss to the mutt's ass-end that caused him to fart and then skedaddle with his tail tucked up tight between his legs. That was luck, and I don't mean the throw. It was luck for the dog. Lester was a great baseball hurler and easily could've delivered a lethal hit to the head.

"Want a good dog, Fletch?" he said with a grin as he sprung from the ground to the running board and eased himself into the bench seat beside me.

"You catch him first, then we'll talk about it," I said with a return grin. I snapped the reins and we were off again.

We drove through downtown Benton Harbor just as it was awakening to another day of commerce. The streets were already groaning with the wood- and iron-rimmed wheels of ice and coal wagons, drays loaded with groceries and barrels of beer, and with street trolleys nearly filled to capacity. Merchants were unlocking the front doors to their businesses while others were using long steel-handled cranks to winch down colorful awnings. Young boys were selling newspapers or hawking shoeshines while street cleaners were sweeping the previous night's horse droppings into large metal dustpans mounted on wheels. We drove one block over to Territorial Road where the growers were lining up their wagons filled with fruit for the wait to get into the market. We passed through them and were soon at the outskirts of town crossing the wood plank bridge over the Paw Paw River. Then we plunged into the wooded dune country where the trees were tall and shady and the air was cool.

For nearly half an hour we clipped along at a good pace chatting and enjoying the fine scenery until the road dipped into a ravine that bottomed out at a shallow stream crossing. I noticed the banks of the stream were soft and chewed up from the other buggies and wagons that had crossed, and I got a little nervous. I was about to pull back on the reins when Butts sensed my apprehension and hollered, "Give her hell, Fletch!"

Instantaneously, I put the whip to Mattie's back and she scooted into the water, doing fine until we were about halfway across and the wheels bogged into the mud. She struggled a bit then stopped and snorted and gave up.

"Damn!" I yelled, which started Butts to laughing. "And what's so funny?" I added angrily.

"That old nag of yours."

"She's not a nag. And what's more, she's more than you'll ever have." Lester's old man was a teamster, which meant his family didn't have much money. I shouldn't have implied that, but I was so put off I could've said worse.

"Yeah...but she's still a nag," Lester said. From the corner of my eye I could see him smirking.

That's when I gave him a hard elbow to the chest, which caused him to shove me. Then I shoved him back. Then he shoved me again and kept shoving until he pushed me right out of the damn buggy and into the creek, which made me mad as a bald-faced hornet.

By then Butts was laughing so hard his eyes were squinted tighter than a braided buggy whip, which is why he didn't see it coming when I jumped up, grabbed him by the shirt, and pulled him ass-over-apple-cart out of the buggy. Both of us tumbled into the water and started wrestling, yelling, and cursing with arms and legs flailing. Must have looked like two cats in a burlap bag.

We'd been tussling for nearly two minutes before I noticed an orchard wagon and a team of horses in the road. The wagon was set back a ways, parked beneath a shady oak on the north side of the creek. The driver was casually watching us with one foot propped up on the footboard, his forearm resting on his knee while holding the reins loose in his hand. A wide-brimmed straw hat sat low, just above his eyes, and a pair of suspenders covered a dirty, sweat-stained muslin shirt. The sleeves were rolled up tight to his elbows. Butts saw him at about the same time and we stopped fighting.

The driver studied us for a few seconds before speaking. "Nice day, wouldn't you say?" he called out as if nothing was out of the ordinary.

"Yeah," Butts answered sheepishly while raking his fingers through his straw-colored hair, which was dripping with muddy water. "Nice day."

The driver snapped the reins and eased his team up to the creek's edge while we stood there, soggy from head to toe looking like a couple of idiots.

"Going to market?" I said noticing the baskets of peaches stacked in his wagon, each one covered in red netting. I was trying to occupy him with small talk, hoping he wouldn't ask us what the hell we were doing.

"Yep…finishin up with the peach crop," he said as the horses stamped in their traces. "Say…how's the line today?"

"Long," Butts said. "Five, six blocks each way out Territorial Road…and Pipestone, too. The buyers are swarming."

While Butts chatted with the stranger, who was actually a young man of about twenty, I tried pushing the buggy again but got nowhere. Butts finally waded over to help but to no avail. The stranger watched us struggle for a few minutes, but he must have tired of waiting because he jumped from his wagon and walked to the edge of the creek to have a look. As he stood next to me I was a bit intimidated by his size—seemed big as a mountain.

"Let me give a hand," he said while wading in. He was wearing a pair of worn leather boots that reached nearly to his knees, but the creek was deeper than they were tall and the water poured over the tops. He didn't seem to mind—hell, he acted like he didn't even notice.

"One of you fellas lead the nag," he said with a mischievous grin, "and I'll push from behind."

I was no longer in the mood to argue with anyone who called Mattie a nag, especially with the stranger, being the healthy-looking fellow he was. I grabbed her by the bridle while Butts and the stranger pushed. It still wouldn't budge.

"She's sucked tight into the mud," the stranger said. "We'll have to rock her out."

The stranger palmed one of the wheels and began rocking the buggy, putting so much of himself into it that the veins strained across his neck and the muscles swelled his forearms. Butts pulled on the other wheel but the stranger broke the rig loose by freeing his side first. I led Mattie and the buggy from the creek.

"What's your name?" I asked gratefully, wanting to know who'd saved me from having to face Pa with the news that I'd busted up his buggy.

"Name's Lathe…Henry B. Lathe."

"I'm Fletch Van Horne and this is Cleve Lester, Butts for short. Say, what's the *B* stand for?"

"Stands for nothin. It's just B."

"It's a pleasure," Butts said and we shook hands all around. I noticed his strength again—his grip was like an iron vice.

"Pleasure's mine," Lathe said. "Hey…I'd like to chew the fat with you fellows a bit but I've got to get goin. But first let me show you how to get across when you come back through."

Lathe dragged two long wood planks from the bushes and laid them across the creek. "We growers use these. Just put em back when you're done and no one'll mind that you used them."

Then he climbed up into his seat, emptied the water from his boots, and eased his wagon across the creek. The planks went under the water from the weight of the wagon but didn't break. We offered to put them back in the bushes, and he tipped his hat in appreciation before giving the reins a quick snap and was off. We washed some of the muck off our clothes, climbed back into the buggy, and continued on our way little worse for the wear.

"How do you think he'd do at football?" I said as Mattie pulled us at a snail's pace up the long hill.

"He's plenty strong," Lester replied while wringing water from his shirt, "but hell, I'd be surprised if he's ever seen a game, let alone played in one."

"Maybe so, but I'll bet it wouldn't take much to turn him into a respectable tackle."

"Don't kid yourself. He probably doesn't even know what a prolate spheroid is."

"Did you know?" I said.

"Hell no, did you?

"Of course."

"Bullcrap."

"Lathe may not know anything about a prolate spheroid," I continued, "but with his big hands he could easily turn one into a prolate griddlecake." We laughed like hell, both of us.

"Seriously," Butts answered once we'd calmed down. "You know damn well he couldn't remember the plays."

"Fifty cents says he could."

"You're on," he said and then offered his hand to seal the agreement. While we were shaking he added one of his famous Lester stipulations. "Just remember this, Horn-boy. You won't get one red cent from me until he plays with us in a real game."

"Wouldn't have it any other way. But you don't collect either unless he gets into a game and forgets two plays in a row."

Butts hesitated, but then smiled and said, "Fair deal. That would be an easy eight-ball in the side pocket." Then he mussed my hair.

I knocked his hand away and we laughed some more, but at the same time I was already trying to figure out a way to contact Lathe and convince him to come out for the team.

Beyond the creek-bottom was a high, flat plain populated with working farms and orchards. There were fields of wildflowers and peppermint, which was grown for its oil, but for the most part we passed through orchards, miles of them. Apple, pear, and peach were the most common, with peach being the most common by a long shot. And they were ripe—the air was filled with their sweetness. I especially remember the way their smell was mixed with peppermint, and tinged with the fragrance of honey emanating from beehives scattered about the countryside. Everywhere we saw men, women, and children in the groves picking, and when we passed a boy loading a wagon just off the road, he smiled and tossed two peaches our way. Lester caught both of them, hollered thanks, and handed me one. Lake Michigan was less than a mile to the west and we could feel its cold breeze through our wet shirts, but the sun was warm and we felt fine as we talked and ate those juicy peaches.

It took another half hour to get to the dusty, one-block farming settlement of Riverside. I pulled to a stop at a small clapboard store to let Mattie rest and have a drink from the horse trough while Butts and I went inside. Butts bought a boiled egg from a sallow-looking kid working behind the cluttered, unvarnished wooden counter while I asked for directions to the Graham place. He told me we were almost there and I thanked him. Then we strolled into a grassy field next to the store, removed our shirts, and hung them in the spreading branches of a maple tree. We sat warming in the sun and ate our sandwiches while Mattie grazed. When our shirts were dry, we climbed back into the buggy and continued on our way.

Beyond Riverside the country got hilly. We continued to see orchards, but now they were interrupted by wooded ravines, rolling sand hills, and pond bogs. Some of the farmers still lived in log cabins built when they first cleared the land twenty or thirty years earlier. Two more miles or so and we were at the Graham place.

The house was a small two-story clapboard structure with a good-sized barn in back and a few outbuildings. The homestead was surrounded by woods on one side, peach orchards on the other, and in the rear was a small paddock with a couple of cows. There were chickens in the yard and a pig in a pen. I steered the buggy up the driveway and a dog came out barking. A lady in the backyard hanging laundry saw us and called for the mutt to leave us be.

"Mrs. Graham?" I asked after we'd introduced ourselves.

"Aye," she said in a gruff Irish brogue. "That's who I am."

I had never seen Mrs. Graham before. She was a severe-looking woman—the hardness of the years cut like furrows into her face. She wore a billowy, flowered blue dress that was well worn, almost threadbare in spots, and a white apron tied around her waist. Her gray-streaked hair was pulled back so tightly it turned her tired eyes into slits.

"We're friends of Jacob's," I said. "Is he home?"

"No." She replied, wiping her brow with a weathered hand. "He and his brother are workin at the Kingsland place today. The lads are buildin a barn…with their father."

When she mentioned their father, her voice was barely audible.

I knew about the trouble the Grahams were having. I'd heard it from my pa, who knew lots of personal things about people on account of his being a lawyer. When I'd told him I was going to see Jacob Graham, he advised me not to ask his mother the usual questions about how the family was doing. Said she wouldn't stop talking about it once you got her started.

Mrs. Graham gave us directions to the Kingsland place and we thanked her. I snapped the reins and we were off again.

"What was wrong with Mrs. Graham?" Butts asked as we turned from the drive onto the road.

"Word has it that Jacob's old man moved out and joined the colony."

"The House of David?" Butts asked as he placed his open hand over his eyes to shade out the sun.

"Yep, I hear he's working on their new headquarters building…at least when he's not working his own jobs."

Hutcheon Graham was a contractor. Farming was a part-time occupation. Lots of men were trying their hand at growing peaches back then, even those with other occupations, and they did it because of the big money peaches were bringing at the Chicago markets. Mr. Graham was a great builder but not much of a grower. I heard he lost money because of his meager harvests.

"I knew the old man was religious," Butts said. "But I didn't think he'd do something like that…joining the colony. That's a strange deal, isn't it?"

"Yeah…it is," I answered.

"I wonder if he'll let his hair and whiskers grow like all the men there?"

"They say he already has…that he's looking pretty shaggy."

"What I really wonder," Butts said, "is if he believes all that bullcrap about never dying?"

"Don't know…can't believe he would. But that's a strange deal, isn't it?"

"Yeah…a strange deal," Butts said, shaking his head. Then he spit, which we both did often because of the dust.

Dice Baushke's folks were also members of the House of David. In fact, it was his father and his uncle's donation of money and land that encouraged the colony to locate here. Dice never talked about it and I never asked. That's why I never knew much about the colony until they got popular a few years later with their park and bands and baseball teams. They eventually made the best ice cream in West Michigan and had a great beer garden, too. All colony members followed the beliefs taught by their leader, a man named Benjamin Purnell.

Purnell was a traveling preacher from Kentucky who convinced his followers that he was God's messenger. He told them they could live forever if they'd follow his teachings, which included things like not cutting their hair, eating or touching meat, or having relations with the opposite sex. Members gave their money and property to him and worked without pay to support the colony. In return, Purnell supplied them room and board.

In later years, the colony farms, businesses, and amusement park became an important part of Benton Harbor's economy. The Israelites, as they called themselves, were pretty much accepted by then, at least until the big scandals of the 1920s. But in the beginning it was all very mysterious.

Butts and I recognized the post-and-beam skeleton of the Kingsland barn long before we got there. The freshly hewn wood caused it to stand out like a beacon in the distance. Ten minutes later we pulled into the yard and were quickly driving past the house and into a barnyard dotted with small outbuildings. Then we curved around a large fruit-packing shed, passing through a cluster of orchard wagons before beelining toward the barn, which was set back against a patch of woods.

Gathered in a circle next to the barn was a group of men who were highly excited about something. I could tell from their shouts, which floated loudly over the field on the wind, but also from their wild gesturing amid rising clouds of dust. As we drove closer, I didn't see Jacob's old man but figured some of them were his crew—the rest were probably pickers or workers from the packing shed. It looked like they were watching a wrestling match. I halted the rig near some other horses, and Butts and I jumped out and ran over to investigate.

It was a wrestling match all right—and Jacob was in the middle of it.

Chapter 5

The men gathered around the wrestling match were a breed long since vanished. They were no-nonsense country folk, coarse in their bearing and tough as leather from working long hours outdoors. Most of them were wearing heavy cloth pants, frayed at the cuffs and knees and held up with sweat-stained braces that looked like cousins to those Lathe was wearing. Threadbare shirts and soiled, wide-brimmed hats made from felt or straw rounded out their outfits. I knew they were probably a good-hearted lot, but I still felt a little intimidated being among them. I think Butts did, too.

After one good glance at the combatants, I realized Jacob was fighting someone we recognized. The fellow was from a farming village north of here called Allegan, but at the time he was working on a fish tug out of South Haven. We'd seen him in Benton Harbor a few times when his boat put in for the night. His name was Geordie Bell, but we called him the Gill because of the fishy smell he carried with him.

The Gill was tall, well muscled, and mean—looked about twenty years old. And he was a two-fisted brawler. One night I saw him and a rangy looking fellow with scabbed knuckles clear out Conkey's pool parlor when they'd both been drinking. After that I always gave him a wide berth.

Jacob was a bit shorter than the Gill—a couple inches under six feet. He had a trim waist, but he was broad at the shoulders and powerfully built with big arms. His hands were the size of small hams. He had a thick shock of curly brown hair and one of the largest jaws I'd ever seen. Baseball and basketball didn't seem to interest him, probably because those sports weren't exciting enough, but he loved to box and wrestle and play football. Jacob was mostly a quiet fellow, non-boasting except when he was impressing his friends with his strength. He could bend twenty-penny nails in his bare hands, climb a rope without using his feet, and walk on his hands like a circus acrobat.

Without question, the Gill had his hands full.

As I inspected the two combatants, I quickly determined they'd been going at it for some time. Both were stripped to the waist, and rivers of sweat made watery trails through the dirt that covered their chests and arms. It was also obvious they were serious, but I couldn't tell if it was a grudge match, money fight, or both. Money had been wagered, that much was clear. Some of the men were holding stacks of bills in their hands and waving them in the air as they shouted. Jacob's younger brother Hectar, who we called Heck for short, was shouting with the loudest of them. Each time Jacob and the Gill went down, Heck went down with them, yelling and pounding the dusty ground with the flat of his hand.

We saw them hit the ground at least four times, rolling over and over trying to pin one another without success. The last time they went down, the Gill was on top with a knot of Jacob's hair twisted into his fist. I thought it was over until Jacob managed to break away and spring to his feet. The Gill immediately rolled over and was up at about the same time, the only trophy for his near victory being some wisps of hair still clamped between his fingers. He shook the hair from his hand, but before it floated to the ground he and Jacob were crouched and moving in a circle, both looking for another opening.

The Gill was spitting mad. I gauged his anger by the way he stared at Jacob, which was with the eyes of a wild animal. But Jacob remained firm. There wasn't the slightest hint of surrender in his eyes. It was then the Gill made a desperate lunge, which was a bad decision because in one swift move Jacob grabbed his arm, tripped, and pinned him. I'd never seen it done any smoother. The men who'd bet on Jacob howled like a pack of beagles who'd just caught the scent of a cottontail.

Jacob stood up breathing hard and someone handed him a jug of water. He tilted his head back and tipped the jug, allowing water to wash over his face. Then, just as he was preparing to have a drink, the Gill came to his feet, grabbed a broken piece of axe handle, and started toward him.

"Watch out, Jacob!" I hollered instinctively. A few others also yelled something or other.

In two or three strides the Gill was upon Jacob preparing to bust him in the head with the axe handle. Jacob, who had already turned to face him, immediately dropped the jug, took a quick step forward, and grabbed the Gill's shoulder with his left hand. That kept the handle from striking him. In the next instant he balled his right hand into a fist and drove it so hard into the Gill's gut I thought it might kill him. The Gill made a sickening groan as he dropped the handle and fell to his knees heaving.

At that point there was no question in my mind the fight was over. But this time Jacob didn't walk away. He stood and watched as the Gill, still on his knees, made a miserable attempt to compose himself but failed. Two men finally helped him to his feet, and while he was getting his balance he stared at Jacob, eyes burning with hate. He wiped his mouth with the back of his hand and shook the slop off.

"Graham..." he scowled. "This ain't over yet."

"Afraid it is," Jacob said. "Unless you're up for another round."

"I owe you," he threatened, "and be warned you haven't seen the last of me."

"Come on, Geordie," one of the men interrupted. "We got work to do."

"Count your days, Graham," the Gill said, grabbing his shirt and then limping into the woods between the two men.

Butts and I walked over to where Jacob was standing among a group of men and boys. He'd already put his shirt on and was working the buttons.

"Nice job," Butts said respectfully.

"How you doin, Butts...Fletch?"

"Hey...if it ain't the city boys!" Heck hollered. He walked over leading a large buff-colored Morgan that was harnessed up with a whippletree and a loggers chain and hook. "Guess we showed him, didn't we?"

"You showed him all right," Butts said sarcastically.

Heck was feisty and a bit of a braggart. He was smaller than Jacob but would fight anyone, anytime, and any excuse would do. Fortunately, he knew Butts well enough to let the comment pass.

"For a minute I thought I'd have to get in there and put me own fists to work," he said while the Morgan snorted impatiently, quivering its side-flesh to keep the flies away.

"Heck....I need another log for hewing. Do you think you could favor me with one?" Jacob was making beams for the barn.

"You betcha." He led the Morgan toward the woods, then shouted from over his shoulder, "You holler if that thunderin' jackass of a fish face comes after you again." He didn't wait for an answer.

"What's the deal with the Gill?" I asked.

"He's been needling me for a week now...mad because I beat him out of five dollars throwin axes."

Most farmers liked to play horseshoes, but in Hagar Township throwing axes was more popular. The fellows who were good at it could stick an axe into a tree at twenty paces or more.

"He's a mean-looking cuss," Butts said. "What's he doing out here anyway?"

"They threw him off the fishing tug for fighting, so he's been working with a couple other fellas clearing land for Charlie Root. I guess he couldn't get over the way I beat him. His partners lost money on the deal and they pushed hard for some kind of rematch. He finally couldn't stand it any longer and challenged me to a fight. I told him I'd fight, but it would have to be a square deal...no knives or billies...and with the others watching. You saw the rest."

"Yeah," Butts said. "We saw you almost get your head bashed in."

Jacob shot him a hard look, but instead of going into it further, he changed the subject. "So," he said, "to what do I owe the pleasure of this visit? I know you didn't come all this way just to talk about my health."

"Football's started," I said with an encouraging smile. "And we need you."

He stared at me in silence for a long time and I stared back, looking for the least sign of encouragement in his weathered face. He'd already seen more hard work than I would in a lifetime. "Can't do it, Fletch," he said shaking his head. "You and the fellows are gonna have to lick your wounds without me."

"But we can take Ishpeming," I said, doing my best to ignore his reply. "It's for certain with you on the team."

He looked up at the sky and took a deep breath. "Now that's some unfinished business, ain't it?" That's when I knew I'd hit a nerve.

Jacob started talking about the previous season, and Butts and I joined in and had a long reminiscence. We didn't stop until Heck came back leading the Morgan dragging a big log. He unwrapped the chain and tossed it aside while Jacob picked up a ball of bark-stained string and began unraveling it.

"Grab the line, Heck," he said after he'd nailed down his end, "and tighten it down to give me a guide."

"That fella's a jackass," Heck muttered under his breath, still thinking about the Gill as he stretched the line to the end of the log and secured it with another nail.

"We have a new coach, Jacob," I added hopefully, "and he's good....you'd like him. He asked me to come out here and talk with you."

"Wish I could, fellas...but I just can't." He started making cuts along the log with a large broad axe, every six inches or so. "I've got to help support my Ma now that the old man's left her."

"I'm off for another log," Heck said to Jacob as he steered the Morgan back toward the woods.

"Good. We've got to have four more of these hewn before the old man gets back!"

"Hey," I said in an effort to lighten the mood. "Do you know a fellow by the name of Lathe?"

"Yeah...I know the whole family. They live just down the road a piece."

"Henry pushed our rig out of a mud hole this morning somewhere between Benton Harbor and Riverside."

"That'd be Henry B," Jacob said with a chuckle, "with the *B* that stands for nothin. He's a good fella…and strong. We call him the Iron Man."

"Fletch thinks he'd make a good football player," Butts added.

"Oh yeah?" Jacob remarked and then stopped chopping and stood upright. He rested the axe head on the log and folded both of his hands over the end of the handle and gazed off toward the woods.

As Jacob was contemplating Lathe's athletic ability, I noticed a large gash in his left hand, stitched with black fish-line, the bristled ends protruding like tiny porcupine quills. I could tell he'd sewed it himself. Country folk tended most of their own cuts back then. All they needed was a splash of iodine or whiskey, a needle, a strand of twine or thread, and a bit of nerve.

"He likely would." Jacob finally agreed. "I don't think he's too agile, but he'd probably make a good tackle or guard."

"All right, Butts. You can hand over the fifty cents now," I said, thrusting out my open palm.

"Not so fast," he replied as he swatted my hand away. "We agreed I have to see him play."

"How can we get him to come out, Jacob?" I asked, fishing for clues I might use in my recruiting efforts.

"Likely there's nothing you can do. He's probably too busy with the farm…but I suppose anything's possible."

"If we see him on our way back," I said, "I just might have a talk with him. But Jacob, it's you we really need."

"Don't see how," he muttered under his breath as he continued chopping along the length of the log, the veins in his neck and arms bulging every time the steely blade bit into the wood. It was obvious he was torn.

"But what about our revenge? We're going to get it just like we talked about. And you need to be there." I was almost pleading.

"Hey!" he growled and then stopped chopping to fix me with those hard, pale blue eyes of his. "I just don't see how." He went back to chopping, then after a moment of silence he added, "But thanks for stopping by."

When he said thanks I knew it was time to leave. Jacob wasn't much at explanations. He was a fellow of few words, but he made those words understood by his tone of voice or facial expression. Wasn't hard to read him.

"Keep your chin up," Butts said.

"You too," he replied, stopping to wipe the sweat from his brow. "Both of you."

It was after three o'clock in the afternoon when we reached the Territorial Road and drove alongside a line of orchard wagons waiting to get into the market. They were stacked up for three blocks, maybe more, their horses standing patiently while bidding their time between dozing and shooing flies with their tails. Some of the growers stood in groups talking while others sat in their wagons dozing or reading newspapers. A few drank beer, Germans mostly. Men and boys browsed the sidewalks in front of the farm-supply stores looking at ladders, sprayers, baskets, and a hundred other items shrewdly placed there to tempt them. The merchants knew well it was payday for the growers.

We found Lathe at the front of the line standing next to his wagon while three different buyers swarmed over his peaches. I pulled Mattie to a halt, draped the reins across my knee, and waited.

We sat and watched as one of the buyers came over to make Lathe an offer. They dickered a bit, and finally the buyer produced a big roll of bills and counted the payment into Lathe's open hand. Then a couple of stout colored fellows began unloading the wagon. It was their job to transfer the baskets one block over to the canal where the peach steamers were moored, waiting with their boilers stoked and fired for the next trip to Chicago or Milwaukee.

The steamers worked twenty-four hours a day during the peach and apple season carrying fruit to the big cities. Throughout the summer and early fall, their steam whistles could be heard blasting throughout the day and night as they steamed in and out of the canal, stacks spewing huge clouds of black smoke. We heard those whistles blasting for miles around, even while lying in bed during the middle of the night.

While Lathe's wagon was being unloaded, Butts stood up, cupped his hands around his mouth, and yelled, "Hey Iron Man, you're a rich man now!"

He saw us immediately and walked over to where we were parked. "Ain't gonna do you no good. And how do you know to call me that?"

"Graham," I said as I reached down and shook his hand again. "We've been out to see Jacob Graham…about playing football."

"That's his game, ain't it?"

"Yep…that's his game all right. You ever think about playing?"

"Don't have the time," he said as he fidgeted with his suspenders.

"That's right, Fletch," Butts interrupted. "He doesn't have the time."

"Don't listen to him, Lathe. He bet me fifty cents that you wouldn't be any good at football."

"That so?" he asked, looking at Butts, his big arms crossed defiantly across his chest.

"Yes sir. But I still want you to come out. You have to prove it or I don't get my money."

"I could smash you like a shitfly."

"Lathe," Butts said sarcastically, "we don't play football like that anymore. We have a new coach…a gentleman…and we'll be playing a gentleman's game from now on. No slugging."

"Well…" Lathe mumbled as he rubbed his stubbly chin and thought about it. "Then what's the use in playing?"

"Winning?" I said. "There's more to playing football than knocking the other guy's teeth out, you know. Besides, we're going to win the state championship or bust, and anyone who's on the team will be in for a lot of glory. Just think of the attention you'll get from the girls."

"But you'll have to sign up for school," Butts added.

"I'm already planning to do that. My old man wants me to graduate so I can go to the agricultural college in Lansing."

"We practice at three o'clock every afternoon," I said.

"You say there's no slugging?" he asked again.

"That's what the coach says."

"Well…I just don't see what fun that could be."

I dropped Butts at his house on Superior Street and went home, where I tidied Mattie's bedding, fed and watered her, and then gave her a good curry-comb brushing. I walked in the house just in time for supper. Though I hadn't been successful with either Jacob or our new friend, Lathe, the day wasn't a total waste. I'd had a damn good time and the folks wanted to know all about it.

I talked about football all through dinner and then thought about it for the remainder of the evening, so much, in fact, that I had trouble getting to sleep. I knew Teetzel would be running us hard on Monday, which I was apprehensive about, and on top of it all I was worried I might not even survive the cut. We were yet to be told the names of the chosen fifteen. It was also a good thing I didn't know about the game Teetzel had scheduled for us for the following Saturday or I'd really have been anxious.

As I would soon discover, we'd be playing against a team fielded by a Chicago sporting club that was composed of players much older than us. And it wasn't until just before the match that Teetzel would spring the best surprise of all—most of them were former high school and college stars.

Chapter 6

Teetzel's first full week of coaching began on Monday, September 21, which is when the rest of the eligible veterans from the 1902 team finally showed themselves. Throughout the weekend, Mit Ludwig, Dice Baushke, and Stub Winters, along with most of the board members, worked hard to convince the holdouts to sign up for school, and shake the mothballs from their togs. Tall and agile Bob Busby was one of them—the colored boy I mentioned earlier.

Busby's family went back further in Benton Harbor history than most anyone I knew. Someone told me his grandfather was a former slave who in his younger days could run like the wind, which is how he eventually gained his freedom. He outdistanced the bloodhounds right up to the banks of the Ohio River. And then he had enough energy left to swim across the damn thing. Everyone said the Busby boys got their ability from him, especially Frank.

Frank was Bob's older brother. He was also the first colored fellow ever to play sports at our high school. There's a photograph to prove it—the football team of 1895—of which he was one of the better players. But then the sport killed him. During the last game of his senior season, he was hit in the gut and died from an internal rupture. The entire school showed up to his funeral.

Bob Busby continued to play the game in spite of his brother's tragic death. He played end on the team of '02, but he also did some punting and even kicked an occasional goal. Drop-kicking was one of his fancies, but he wasn't consistent and struggled constantly to improve his percentages. Few teams had colored players back then, at least none that we played against, and that was a shame. Overall, Bus was one hell of a nice fellow.

William Ossignac, who was called Joe by most everyone, also showed up that Monday, thanks to Stub Winters. Ossignac was an Ottawa Indian, a swarthy-faced fellow who was big in size but small in presence. By that I mean he was quiet, which was a deceiving personality trait. He played on the team of 1902 and was a vicious, sledgehammer of a tackle. His old man worked as a ship carpenter on the Benton Harbor canal and was teaching Joe the trade, which was the reason he nearly didn't sign up for the team. His old man didn't want him back in school—viewed it as a waste. But Stub did some persuasive talking and the old man finally gave in. That was a close call—we needed Joe to beat Ishpeming.

Wilbur Cunningham and Arthur Lee were two more veteran players who showed up that week. Cunningham was tall but lanky and a bit of a goody-two-shoes. But he was strong and a good runner. Lee, on the other hand, was tall, muscular and mean-spirited— he wore a scar on his upper lip that would've made a Prussian colonel proud. We called him Biffy. I don't know who gave him that nickname but it didn't fit. He'd tear your head off for looking at him wrong.

Another one who showed up was our famous halfback, George Bridgman. I say he was famous because everyone in town knew him, partly because his dad was a judge but also because he was boisterous and funny as hell. Practical joker wouldn't begin to describe him. He played on the teams of 1901 and 1902 and was our greatest open-field runner. Football back then was mostly played in tight formations, not much to look at, and that's why the rooters went wild whenever Bridgman made a dazzling run to the outside or a hair-raising line hurdle that was often followed by a blistering romp through a confused defense. He was a born showman.

It was great to see Bridgman walk onto the field that Monday, laughing and spouting his usual stream of wisecracks. Some of the fellows even cheered him. But the best was yet to come. We were still laughing it up with Bridgman when the fellows suddenly began to get quiet. I turned around to see Jacob, hands full of gear, walking across the field toward us. Heck was with him, swaggering along like he was ready to take on the world. I'd be lying if I said I wasn't surprised. I stood frozen in my tracks along with Teetzel and the rest of the fellows, no one saying a word. Even Bridgman shut up. The Grahams walked up and Jacob nodded. And there we stood, speechless.

"What's wrong with you thunderin jackasses?" Heck hollered. "Let's play ball!" We all cheered, and then we started shoving them and slapping them on the back.

Seeing Jacob was a real boost. And having Heck try out for the team was also good. Seems Butts's and my recruiting effort got Jacob thinking about how much he enjoyed the game—and how badly he wanted to have another whack at Ishpeming. He and Heck talked it over with their ma and she agreed to let them play. Said the neighbors would help her with the farm for the three months they'd be in school. Jacob told her he'd get a part-time job to help out with the bills, and his two older sisters, Eva and Lila who both lived in Benton Harbor, also promised to send her some money. Early that morning, Jacob and Heck hitched a ride in with a neighbor and set up camp at Lila's house.

Heck wasn't the only new player to try out for the team—there were probably twenty others. Most of them cut their teeth playing for the Never-Sweats, Little Knockers, or any of a half dozen other neighborhood football clubs. Charlie Jones came to us from the Windjammers, a name Ma wanted to believe was a clever reference to the area's maritime heritage. When I told her it was actually a boast by the players regarding their ability to jam the wind from an opponent's lungs, she threw her hands into the air and said, "You boys are hopeless." The one who didn't come from a club team was Iron Man Lathe, who surprised me to hell and back when he ambled onto the field midway through Monday's practice looking like a scarecrow with his straw hat and old-fashioned clothes. Everyone laughed except Teetzel, probably out of politeness, but maybe because he recognized the potential.

The only player we hoped to see who didn't show up was Arthur Baushke. His little brother, Leo, the one we called Dice, came out early but Arthur couldn't afford to give up his paycheck.

That was one hell of a sour note. He played halfback in 1902 and was one bruiser of a ball carrier.

In the end there were around thirty-five of us practicing that Monday. On Thursday, fifteen players would be chosen to represent the team, which didn't give us much time to show our stuff. Of those who weren't selected, some would drop out while most would continue to practice. Some of them would show up only occasionally while others would be very dedicated, hoping to replace any team member who might become injured. These fellows composed our first and second scrub teams.

Monday's practice is also when Teetzel really got down to business. We began with conditioning routines followed by more fundamentals—starting, blocking, tackling, and opening holes, followed by more work in formations of four. Butts and Busby practiced punting and drop-kicking while Jacob and Ossignac worked on place-kicking. Teetzel spent some extra time with Lathe teaching him fundamentals and rules, and he promised to get him some formal playing togs before the next day's practice.

Tuesday and Wednesday's sessions were worse than Monday's— I'd have to say they were the toughest days I'd ever lived through. The conditioning routines and play formations were now followed by some serious signal work. We weren't used to that kind of training. Some of the fellows had to drop out because of injuries, mostly twisted ankles or wrists, and we lost one with a wracked knee. There were stomach problems from all the running—lots of heaving. Even I coughed up my lunch. But after two days, the worst of it seemed to be over for everyone except Fred Handy. He was a bull of a player, a farm kid from Sodus, but he threw up every day. At least twice. You could've set your watch by it.

By mid week, we survivors were nursing shin splints, heat cramps, and a myriad of muscle aches and bruises, but as a team things seemed to be moving along fine until Winters made a block during a drill and got injured. At first we thought it was a dislocated shoulder, but after a visit to Doc Bastar's office, Winters reported his collar bone was cracked and that he was out for the season. Teetzel seemed calm about it, but I find it hard to believe he wasn't anguished over who would be his replacement.

Far as I could tell there was no one capable.

The board of directors met Wednesday evening to elect a team captain and to talk about replacing Winters. After the meeting, Butts, Mit Ludwig, and I walked over to Burger's house where he told us Jacob won the team captain position hands down—picked, he said, because he was the oldest member of the team and the most experienced. Seemed reasonable to me. Burger said they also liked him because they knew we'd respect him as a leader and because he'd help hold the team together when the going got rough. They were right about that, too—back then dissension caused the breakup of a lot of teams. We asked about replacing Winters and he said a decision hadn't been made.

When I got to school Thursday morning, I went nervously to Principal McClelland's office to have a look at the list of names pinned to his door—Teetzel's chosen fifteen. Some of the other scrubs were standing around, all of them quiet or talking in hushed voices. I brushed passed them, searched for my name, and found it. The excitement was too much for me and I whooped. Our positions were also named, and when I saw "quarterback" written by my name, my mouth fell open in disbelief. The secretary came out and threatened me for whooping, and I apologized.

"Don't believe it," someone muttered from the group of boys gathered behind me after the secretary went back into her office.

"A damn sophomore," someone else grumbled.

They were talking about me and for good reason. Teetzel's choice wasn't the obvious one, you see. I believed I was worthy of a position on the team, but being selected to play quarterback was a very different story. I'd gained sixteen pounds over the summer to put me at one-eighteen, which meant I was still considered a featherweight, and my height was only five-foot, two inches. On top of it, I was still a sophomore—in other words, not very experienced. Without saying a word, I turned and walked away.

I barely paid attention during classes I was so excited about making the team. But by afternoon my excitement had turned to apprehension. Why the hell did Teetzel choose me to play quarterback? I would have welcomed the opportunity to play backup, but leading the entire team was a frightening prospect.

"Thanks, coach, for keeping me on the team," I said cautiously at the field just before practice was to begin. The rest of the fellows were milling about, talking or kicking the ball back and forth.

"You've earned it," he replied evenly.

"But why quarterback?"

"Last night I talked with the board members who watched you practice throughout last season. They said you were determined and played smart, which was also my gut feeling from what I've seen of you so far. Plus you're too small to play effectively anywhere else."

That comment angered me. I considered it backhanded whenever someone referred to my size, but I swallowed hard and forced a smile.

"Well," I said, puffing up my chest. "I'll give it my best shot."

"Playing quarter is a big job, Fletch," he replied with a look of concern that immediately deflated me. "Giving it your best shot may not be good enough, in fact this might be the single most difficult challenge you'll face in your entire life. It will take every ounce of stamina and endurance you can muster and then some to lead this team to victory. Are you willing to do what it takes?"

He looked at me hard and waited for my reply.

Without a doubt I wanted to lead the team—it was a dream come true. But fear was all around me, working its black fingers of uncertainty into my heart, begging me to give it up. It would have been so easy right then. No one would have held it against me—no commitment had been made, no commitment broken. But then I thought about the terrible embarrassment of the Ishpeming defeat and the holy hell our players had gone through to win the games leading to it, not to mention the disgrace they lived through afterwards. I thought about the commitment I'd made to myself to do whatever it took to help even that score. Could I ignore that? Yes—no one knew about that commitment but me. It would have been so easy to decline the position.

That's when my better judgement began to muddy. I thought about competition and honor and about the glory our supporters would bestow upon me. I thought about the admiration I would get from my fellow students, how the girls would fawn over me

while the boys would be green with envy. It would be so grand—
I would be popular and everyone would know my name, even if
they weren't serious supporters. That's when the veil of fear began
to fall away to reveal a thrill the likes of which I'd never felt before.

"Yes, sir," I said, desperately trying to exude confidence. "I'm
willing and able to do whatever it takes."

"Good," Teetzel said and then smiled. "I know you can…that is
why I selected you. Be positive and dedicated…and remember…there are fourteen other players depending on you."

Braced by Teetzel's words of confidence, I jogged over to where
Jacob was forming the fellows up for conditioning routines and
boldly joined them.

While running drills, I continued to think about my conversation with Teetzel. I considered the challenge I'd accepted and was
pleased, but soon the black fingers came back. This time they
caused me to think about Hub Allen and how he was recognized
as one of the best high school quarterbacks ever to play the game
in lower Michigan—made me wonder if it was possible to fill even
one of his shoes. Hell, I'd barely mastered the art of shaving with
a straight razor yet, at least so my face didn't look like a plucked
chicken every third or fourth time. And there I'd be, in command
of maulers like Ossignac, Lee, Lathe, and the Grahams—guys who
could eat me for breakfast without the slightest burp.

If I was to have any chance of being a successful quarterback, I
realized it would require every ounce of courage I possessed. I
would also have to rely on my good physical condition, faith in
God, and the fair amount of horse sense Pa said I was lucky to have
for a boy my age. And there was another important necessity. I
would have to put my trust in Teetzel, which meant I would have
to believe his newfangled playing strategy truly was superior to the
one we'd always used.

Back then new ideas were accepted about as fast as a sick kid
agrees to drink cod liver oil.

Before Teetzel took charge of the team, there had never been
anything fancy or innovative about the Benton Harbor offense.
For the most part it consisted of simple runs through the line with
a few end-around plays mixed in for variety. First downs came

hard, which meant there was a lot of back-and-forth punting, and the yardage we did get was mostly due to our out-shoving the other team. In other words, brute force. We quickly discovered that our standard plays in some form or another would remain as the backbone of our offense, but new twists such as spinners, laterals, and double laterals would be added. We were surprised to learn the greatest component of Teetzel's new strategy wasn't the plays themselves so much as the manner in which they were executed.

In a nutshell, Teetzel's offensive strategy was based on Fielding Yost's hurry-up principle, a game philosophy emphasizing quickness and speed. The objective was to get the game started again as soon as possible after each play was whistled dead. From the beginning it was pretty clear Teetzel's strategy could have a huge payoff for teams proficient in its use. Being proficient meant two things. Neither were easy.

First of all, every member of the team had to know the plays inside and out—rules, too. That's why Teetzel gave us each our own Spalding rule book. Second, he had to be in better shape than Pheidippides, the ancient Greek runner we studied in history class. We quickly learned that the strength and endurance required to run even the most basic form of hurry-up offense was extraordinary. Because each man was required to play both offense and defense, there was almost no time for rest—fat lineman did not survive for long in that style of football. Players had to be lean and fast and filled with wind. The team that was caught flat-footed or unconditioned to defend against the hurry-up offense was usually doomed from the first sounding of the official's whistle.

But not always.

The hurry-up pace could be slowed down by stopping the game, and believe you me, attempts to achieve that end were made all the time. Kicking or throwing the ball out of bounds was sometimes tried, but few officials considered that a good reason to stop the clock unless the ball was not quickly retrievable. Better luck was had by faking an injury, with the best performances by those boys who fell to the ground at the end of a play twisting and howling in apparent pain. Some players simply pretended to be knocked unconscious. But since the officials were aware of these tricks, the act had to be convincing enough to make them call time. Some bought the tricks, usually the over-cautious, but most did not. Most officials refused to call time unless the circumstances involved serious fighting or injury, and I do mean serious. Fighting had to involve more than a couple of punches while legitimate injuries required profusions of blood or broken bones. A concussion wasn't considered genuine unless the player was lying on the ground with his eyes rolled into the back of his head.

That's why rooters from the opposing side were habitually suspicious of any player who went down with an apparent injury, often voicing their displeasure with raging taunts and ridicule. That kind of response could be quite disheartening to the player who was truly hurt.

The hurry-up style was the theory of the day, with some of the better college teams being so proficient they could run more than seventy-five plays a half. But they were the exception. Few college and fewer high school teams were sufficiently skilled or conditioned to execute it with that degree of competence. From the very beginning, Teetzel made it clear we would be one of them. He said we would strive to run his hurry-up offense at breakneck speed, each game from beginning to end, but that we would have to work damn hard to reach that level of competence. Explained why he worked us like dogs. Teetzel believed the level of speed we developed would ultimately make or break our season. The muscle was already there.

While our play execution was to be unusually fast and flawless, the actual types of plays we ran were fairly straightforward. Because there was no passing, the fullback, quarterback, or one of the halfbacks typically ran with the ball. Ends carried the ball, too, but not as much. We also used a single tackle-back option, one that evolved from the tackles-back and guards-back offenses of the mid 1890s, which was the greatest offensive weapon of the day. In 1903 we used a single tackle-back formation between the twenty-five-yard line and the end zone where only five men were required on the offensive line of scrimmage. The tackle often carried the ball, but he could also act as a decoy or a blocker. But that didn't mean he didn't carry the ball between the two twenty-five-yard lines either, because he did. He simply started from his normal position on the line. But regardless of where he started from, most plays where he carried the ball were steamroller plays—mass plays.

The mass play has been in the grave for a long time, but believe me, back then it was the most powerful weapon available. And when I say power, that's exactly what I mean.

Mass plays were composed of a ball carrier surrounded by a number of his teammates running next to him, pushing or pulling or simply holding him up. Instead of massing behind the line of scrimmage as was done with the earlier flying wedge and the other traditional mass-momentum plays, where more than three players could be in motion before the snap, the play would be timed so the various players met at or near the line of scrimmage at the same instant. They would then plow through in a knot. One man usually went through first as a blocker, then came the ball carrier with men running on either side to help hold him up. Finally, another player, maybe more, would follow the group and push from behind. The players would be moving fast, and when they crashed into the opposing team they literally formed a human battering ram.

We used mass plays all the time, but we also weren't adverse to using end runs either. While eastern football relied almost exclusively on plays that ran the ball straight at the opposition, in the Midwest the end run was popular and used often. It allowed for more offensive options and subterfuge, and it peppered the game with unexpected flashes of wide-open playing the fans loved.

Our plays, whether a mass play, line buck, or an end around, were called by the quarterback. They were his decisions and his alone. In fact, the entire operation of the team while on the field was his responsibility.

That worried my mind like you cannot imagine.

My baptism under fire happened that Thursday afternoon with our first scrimmage game. We lined up against the scrubs with me at quarterback, me and my total arsenal of eight plays. I managed to keep my butt out of the fire by using the same ones over and over and by listening to Jacob's recommendations whenever he sensed my frustration. The lineup was the one Teetzel planned to use Saturday against the Chicago sporting club. It was composed of the 1902 team veterans with the addition of Heck, Iron Man Lathe, and yours truly.

As opposed to my mediocre performance, Heck played surprisingly well and so did Lathe at right tackle. I let the Iron Man carry the ball a few times on tackle-over plays, and he smashed the line to pieces so convincingly that afterward I made Lester cough up the fifty cents from the bet we made. He didn't even balk.

Friday night we met Teetzel at the Pastime Athletic Club for our quiz. He asked us an endless stream of questions culled from the Spalding football guide and we answered them pretty well. That was something new to the Benton Harbor style of football— knowing the rules inside and out. Lee thought it a waste of time, and so did Heck and Dice Baushke and some of the others, but I took it seriously. I had to. Back then the rules didn't allow coaching from the sideline unless it was at halftime or during a time-out. I would be running the entire show without the benefit of Teetzel's help. Finally, we were lectured about the benefits of eating well and getting enough sleep and warned against drinking, smoking, or getting into fistfights.

Teetzel was serious about his no-slugging policy. Some of the fellows still thought it was a stupid demand. Most, in fact. I don't even have to tell you who they were. Pick any name and you'd probably be right—mine included—but I knew we'd find out soon enough if he'd gotten through to us. Saturday's game would tell the tale.

The game Teetzel scheduled for that Saturday, September 26, was against the Kershaw Athletic Club, a private organization from Chicago with sports as its focus. Its membership was mostly composed of high school and college graduates wishing to continue with their game, whether it be baseball, basketball, or football.

We heard they were damn good, and that made me nervous as hell.

Chapter 7

The mayor arranged for a pair of trolleys to carry the rooters to the playing grounds. One trolley was normal for that route, but another was added to handle to the overflow crowd that was expected. By two o'clock there was an incoming stream of bicycles, rigs, people on horseback, and growers driving orchard wagons, some pulled by prized teams of draft horses—Suffolks and Percherons were our most common breeds in those days. All the traffic made for a lot of dust, especially up front by the ticket shack where the rooters tethered their horses to trees and hitching posts.

It was a great afternoon for a football game. People sat in the sun and ate picnic lunches while kids played and wrestled and climbed trees. From every direction, I heard laughing mixed with the loud hollering of vendors hawking roasted peanuts, apple cider, popcorn, and ice cream. Men were selling Bald-Head and Ed Shaw cigars for five cents apiece while a local dentist named Lowry was advertising painless tooth extractions. For those needing immediate attention he had a tent and dental chair set up beneath the spreading branches of a chestnut tree. Above it all floated the loud cries of the gamblers calling out odds.

As the three o'clock kickoff time neared, hundreds of rooters began to gather along the east side of the field, some of them in groups, some singles, but mostly in clusters of two or three. At least a hundred were students. Many held long, thin, wooden sticks with orange and black ribbons tied to the ends, but ribbons were also pinned or tied to jacket lapels, hats, and walking canes. Women even tied them to their parasols. A large number of rooters had megaphones.

We were playing at a place called Eastman Springs, a woodland park located about a mile and a half east of town. We didn't have our own field, so that's where we played all our home games.

The park was privately owned by Colonel Harry Eastman, a grizzled old man with long white hair and beard and an appetite for cheap cigars. Eastman was a Civil War veteran, an attorney, and he often bragged he was the first elected mayor of Green Bay, Wisconsin. I couldn't say one way or the other. Gardening and writing poetry were his passions. Most of the locals viewed him as peculiar because of the way he sometimes recited verse in the midst of everyday conversation.

Of all the Colonel's interests, the park was his shining jewel.

Eastman Springs was centered around a wooded ravine whose shaded slopes were covered with vines and wildflowers. Walking trails traversed hillsides that were interspersed with clearings where visitors could sit on rustic benches, some of them covered with gazebos made of tree branches and bark shakes in the Adirondack style. A long suspension bridge stretched across the ravine and the small stream that drained the overflow from nearly twenty springs. It was the springs that brought Colonel Eastman to Benton Harbor in the first place.

The colonel read about the springs in a pioneer journal, booked passage on a steamer, and came across Lake Michigan to inspect them. He liked what he saw and bought the damn things. Soon after, he moved his family here and went to work building his park.

The Colonel gave each spring a name and posted signs listing their mineral contents. He claimed the Indians used the water to cure sickness long before the arrival of the white man. I can't say if they did or not, but it was a good sales pitch. And selling water for medicinal purposes was how Colonel Eastman made most of his money. Doctors prescribed the stuff for all manner of aches and pains and diseases, and even healthy folks drank it as a daily preventative. Hundreds of families in Chicago were among the Colonel's customers while local drug stores dispensed it by tap. The Colonel swore the success of our football team was due to his water, because we drank it. We actually didn't drink it that much except for when we were at the park for a game, but he used our good fortune of 1902 as a testimonial.

The football field was located toward the back of the park, between the edge of the ravine and an apple orchard. A cow pasture would be a fitting description, 110 yards long, with rickety wooden goal posts planted at each end and crude field lines. There was a lot of talk among rooter and player alike over the checkerboard pattern that marked the field between the twenty-five-yard lines. The new lines were laid out parallel to the sidelines to assist the referee when judging whether the runner crossed the line five yards to the right or left from where he received the ball. The benches for the teams were wood planks, weathered and sagging in the middle, nailed across rough-sawn tree trunks. Bleachers were nonexistent. Everyone simply crowded along the sidelines and moved along as best they could with the playing. As you can imagine, folks got pretty bunched up during a game's most exciting moments. A short pig-wire fence was all that kept the rowdiest of them from spilling onto the field.

In those days, nothing was more exciting than an afternoon football game. For the true enthusiast, a family reunion or a day at the lake couldn't compete—hell, a good game even topped an afternoon at the circus. And everyone dressed for the occasion.

Most of the men wore coats and ties and carried walking canes while the women dressed in full-length cotton or wool dresses. Corsets were still an important undergarment. And almost everyone sported some kind of hat. The women fancied big ones with nets and feathers and horticultural items while the men preferred derby bowlers, straw boaters in the summer. The wide-brim style of hat traditionally preferred by the growers was still popular here, even among the town folk.

The rooters socialized as they waited for the game to begin. The students gathered together in their own separate groups while the women gathered up the same way, men too. The members of the gaming set were also well represented, and they too preferred the company of their own kind. They smoked cigars and nipped from pocket flasks filled with whiskey or homemade apple brandy while discussing football strategies and the latest odds. Pa told me later that most of the talk centered around our chances of winning, pure speculation, and that most of the men felt we'd do well to hold the Kershaws to two touchdowns. They also agreed it didn't matter much if we won or lost since the game wouldn't count in the regular season. Some even thought it might do us good to get hammered.

They were the ones who believed humiliation was good medicine.

When a reporter from the *St. Joe Herald* asked Teetzel about the game, he said its purpose was to identify our strengths and weaknesses under fire. Our supporters were anxious to have a look at us for the same reason. Most of them felt we were untested.

Reading between the lines was easy. Being untested meant the team was playing without Hub Allen at the helm. It wasn't said in my presence, but I know there was doubt about my ability. I couldn't blame them—I had doubts, too.

The game was delayed when three o'clock rolled around and the Kershaws still hadn't arrived. The rooters turned restless, and to prevent them from leaving, Manager Burger ordered us back on the field to entertain them with a few more signal practices. The instant we ran out they exploded into wild cheering, shaking their ribboned sticks fast and furious above their heads. That was my first experience being cheered by a large crowd and it was thrilling, but it also scared the hell out of me. We hadn't played one game yet and already they were about to bust themselves open with excitement. I suspected they felt good about us because of the way we looked in our uniforms. If that was the case, I had to agree with them.

Over the course of my years playing high school football, I learned that uniforms do strange things to a boy. From the moment he puts one on until it comes off again, he feels special. He feels smarter, stronger, and more in control, at least if the initial attention doesn't make him shy away.

As we ran through our routines, I thought about policemen and firemen and how brave they looked in their uniforms. Maybe they weren't brave, but for me their uniforms gave them that appearance. That's when I wondered what the rooters thought when they saw me that afternoon. Did I exude bravery? Did I appear confident? Did I even look the part of a capable quarterback? With luck I appeared bigger than normal—I could only hope so. Maybe they noticed me because of the sleeveless jacket I was wearing. As a team we were wearing tan moleskin pants and black jerseys with orange socks—none of us were wearing wool sweaters because of the pleasant weather. But I was wearing a sleeveless canvas jacket, tightly laced, to prevent the opposing players from getting a firm grip on me. Would that give the crowd reason to regard me as chicken? Or a trickster?

In the end I decided I felt damn fine in that uniform, same as the rest of the fellows. The board members knew we would, and that's why they warned us we had to do more than look good, that the local businessmen must be convinced we were winners before pledging more money. But as I look back to that moment when I first wore a real uniform and was cheered for it, I can honestly say I wasn't thinking about finances. I was praying I wouldn't spoil my dapper appearance by making a fool of myself.

In an effort to keep my mind off the game I began to jabber with the fellows. I talked about anything that came into my head, but mostly I was trying to be funny. It was Bridgman who put an end to my little game.

"Need more padding in those shoulders?" I said jokingly while squeezing the shoulder of his meagerly stuffed jersey.

"If I need padding anywhere, Fletch," he said with a wide grin. "I need it in my pants." The fellows within earshot roared and that's when I shut up.

The Kershaws finally arrived at 3:30, and we immediately noticed how tall and athletic they looked and that they had and obvious age advantage over us. But by then the fellows didn't care—they were anxious to get on with it. The Kershaws were given twenty minutes to run through their routines, and then the referee summoned Jacob to the center of the field to meet with the captain of the Kershaws, a tall, beefy fellow named Vaughan.

We watched as the referee made the introductions. Two officials worked the field back then—the referee and one umpire. The captains shook hands and then negotiated and agreed the game would consist of two thirty-minute halves. The coin was tossed and Vaughan won. He chose to kick the first half.

"Bastard," Jacob said under his breath as he rejoined us.

"What'd he do?" Lee asked.

"Tried to crush my hand when we shook."

"I'll get him," he scowled.

"I will too," Heck said. There were similar nods and comments from the other fellows.

"Come on, men!" Teetzel yelled, clapping his hands together as he spoke. "He's trying make you lose your concentration. That's the oldest trick in the book!"

The fellows were using anything, any excuse to get fighting mad, and it was working. They were whipped to a fever pitch. I acted like I was whipped up too, but it was mostly a ruse. I was so nervous I could've wet my pants.

The rooters started cheering as we formed a semicircle around Teetzel and listened to his last-minute instructions. He told the backs to stay low when they carried the ball, and he stressed that everyone needed to play fast and smart, and then he reminded them I would be in total control while the game was in progress. Back then, any coaching from the sideline by Teetzel or by a substitute player was an automatic penalty of five yards and ejection of the offender from the playing grounds.

I wished he hadn't said it—made me all the more anxious.

"And remember. There's to be no slugging," he said, his voice rising up strong. "Now let's play ball!"

We trotted onto the field and took our positions. Baushke was playing right halfback and Bridgman was playing left. Lester and Busby were at the end positions while Handy and Ossignac were guards and Lee and Lathe tackles. Jacob was playing fullback and Heck was my snapper.

While waiting for the Kershaws to get into position, I stood quietly with my hands on my hips. I probably looked calm, but my mouth was dry as cotton and filled with the gunpowder taste of fear. Most of the rooters were pressed tightly along the east sideline jockeying for positions close to the center of the field. The rest were strung out on our side between the team benches and around both end zones. Shouts rang out above the rising tide of crowd noise and the deep bellowing of a ship's horn two boys had rigged to a forge bellows. Some came from the gamblers, who continued to holler out their odds, while others came from crowd members calling out the names of their favorite players. Mine was not one of them. That should have bothered me but strangely enough it had the opposite effect.

Not hearing my name was actually a relief. I took a deep breath and my muscles loosened. After more deep breathing my mind began to clear of everything but the job at hand. I could still hear people shouting, some whose voices I recognized, but there was also the distant sounds of children laughing and horses nickering. The smell of apples drifting in from the nearby orchard was suddenly overcome by the pungent scent of horse dung mingled with women's cologne, cigar smoke, and the burnt odor of raw whiskey.

Then my fear was gone.

The game began with a strong kick. The crowd cheered as Dice Baushke caught it and advanced ten yards before a pair of Kershaw players tackled him. In keeping with Teetzel's instructions, I called out the first play while the fellows were scrambling to take their positions.

The crowd had yet to stop cheering, and to be heard I was forced to bark the signals. On cue, the ball was snapped and twenty-two men slammed hard into each other with a collective groan. I ran a few steps to the left before tossing the ball to Bridgman, who stampeded wide for a magnificent ten-yard gain with Dice and me running interference. The crowd went into a frenzy, cheering even louder than before as they waved their hats and ribbons. I tried to ignore them as I wormed myself from beneath the pile, my mind frantically seeking a logical play based on the Kershaw's defense strategy, which of course I couldn't possibly have known after only one play. I seized the first play that came to me and hollered the appropriate number.

The fellows crouched and Heck snapped the pigskin the instant after the official put it down, and I dropped it. The ball was larger back then, more like a basketball with slightly pointed ends. Because of my small hands I constantly struggled to maintain solid grip. Being sweaty didn't help, and neither did Heck's powerful snap.

The crowd groaned but I fought hard and made the recovery.

For the next play, Jacob whispered his recommendation as we were picking ourselves off the ground and I called it out. Heck snapped the ball and I held tight as the lines crashed together again with a roar. I spun around and handed off to Baushke, who shot past the left end for a great fifteen-yard run and a first down. That was my first as quarterback, and I was elated. With rising confidence, I ran some good plays for gains before my signals became predictable and the Kershaws held us for downs.

Three minutes had passed and already we were oiled with sweat and gasping for air. And so were the Kershaws, only worse, which is why it took them a long time getting the ball into play. On their first down, we stood firm and stopped them cold. We stopped them on the second down, and the third, and then they lined up to punt. At the snap, Baushke broke through the line, made the block, and the ball shot straight up.

I was deep man back, and I watched as the ball fell into the swarm. At that point you would have thought pigskin was worth its weight in gold the way those players pushed and elbowed one another in their struggle for possession. The players finally collapsed, and when the officials untangled the pile, Heck had the ball, but he also had a patch of sod ground into the side of his face and a split lip. He stood up and ran to the sideline where he grabbed a patch of gauze from Mit. He clamped it between his lips to stop the bleeding and then ran back out.

If Heck had been pulled, his playing for the day would've been over—the rules didn't allow a player back in the game once he'd been taken out.

I ran another series of plays with Jacob advising me in brief, hushed commands which play to call. He used the same basic ten or twelve plays, but I listened and was able to muscle the fellows down the field using very simple line bucks and end runs. Our strategy may have been elementary, but the playing was hard with lots of elbowing and jabbing and throwing of forearms. The slugging was minor, and what little bit there was happened during the piling on.

We finally planted the ball on the five-yard mark, where the crowd was bunched up so tightly on both sides of the field I could almost feel their hot breath. I could see faces of people I knew and hear every word they hollered. "Let Jacob carry the ball!" or "Give it to Bridgman!" were some of the more civil remarks. Those who knew more about the game called out actual plays while others screamed like devils for us to "Kill the bastards!" Their bloodlust was unnerving, but I ignored them as I struggled with a new set of options.

We were now in the zone where the old rules applied. The offensive team was only required to have five men on the line of scrimmage and the five-yard limit did not apply, not that I planned to carry the ball, mind you. Teetzel told me not to run in that zone—said the defense would chew me to pieces.

This time Jacob simply whispered, "Give it to me," and I obeyed.

I called for one of our tackle-back formations followed by an appropriate play selection—a mass run through Lathe's right tackle position. The team immediately lined up with Ossignac taking a position to the rear of my left shoulder. I barked the signals over the noise of the crowd, which was the loudest it had been all afternoon, and the lines crashed together hard. I handed the ball to Jacob as he shot to the right. Moving fast, Bridgman and I ran along with him, one on either side with Ossignac pushing from behind. We charged up behind Lathe and followed him through the line as he blasted his man out of the way. A few seconds later, the five of us tumbled into the end zone for the season's first touchdown. The rooters went wild, shaking sticks, walking canes, parasols, and anything else that was tied up with orange and black ribbons.

I can honestly say that was one of the greatest moments of my young life, to reap so much glory in the company of such fine fellows. Jacob kicked the goal and the score was 6 to 0.

Like a snake, the knotted crowd then loosened and spread itself along the sidelines again, many of the them still clapping and cheering. Sometimes I swear they were cheering for the two field officials as much as for us. Tom Logan was the referee, a tough little fellow who was well known among Benton Harbor's sporting crowd. That afternoon he was wearing knickers, a tweed coat and tie, and a newsboy's cap. The minute the play was stopped he'd fearlessly muscle his way into the pile to secure the ball's proper position.

Caully was the game's umpire and the best showman. He too didn't hesitate to get into the thick of the fray, only he thought nothing of dashing time after time with his umpire's horn into the thrashing mass of arms and legs, sometimes disappearing completely from view before the play was whistled dead. But even then he always emerged unruffled with his cigar clamped safely between his teeth.

After our touchdown, we lined up for the kick—Jacob was the kicker, Heck the holder. Jacob booted a long one and the Kershaws advanced fifteen yards. They ran a series of plays but couldn't even make a first down.

After that I was feeling more confident.

With the smell of blood in our noses, we took the ball on their forty-five-yard line and really went to work. First I gave it to Jacob and then Baushke, both of them making end runs that finally planted the ball on the eleven-yard line. On the next play, Jacob charged up the middle, dragging a pack of Kershaws with him for another five points. He missed the goal and some of the rooters groaned, but most of them didn't seem to mind at all. They came to the field expecting the Kershaws to run up the score.

As we lined up for the kick, Handy bent over, put his hands on his knees, and heaved twice. The rooters cheered.

The game continued without much happening until just before the half. Bridgman took the handoff on an off-tackle play and grabbed hold of a strap on the back of Jacob's belt. Together they plowed into the end zone for another touchdown, and Baushke kicked the goal.

When the clock ran out the half, the score was 17 to 0 in our favor.

Using tin dippers, we scooped furiously into the water buckets. "Rinse and spit!" Teetzel hollered. "No one should drink more than half a dipperful!"

No one listened.

I remember rinsing at first, which was hard enough because I was gasping so hard for air. And my lungs burned the same as if I'd been breathing smoke from a brush fire. But soon I was gulping like a plow horse, desperate to irrigate my parched throat despite Teetzel's repeated admonitions that too much water would give us bellyaches. We splashed water on our inflamed faces and used towels to wipe away layers of sweat and field dirt, then we took turns visiting the privies. Wood and tarpaper shacks is what they were, and both of them had long lines. The fans graciously let us players go ahead so we could get back to our bench and Teetzel's analysis of our playing.

"The Kershaw linemen are sluggish," he said after we finished our pissing and were sitting on the grass listening to him. "And their backs are running too high with the ball."

"Yeah," Jacob said, "we've managed to get the jump."

"And we've surprised them," I added and a chorus of voices agreed with me. "The speed work we did last week is paying off."

"We are off to a good start," Teetzel confirmed, "but we have to be faster." Then he looked around at each of us and began to point out our mistakes. "Handy," he said, "you must get into the play quicker when the ball is snapped. You too, Lathe…and the rest of you on the line. Open those holes like you mean it! And Fletch…make sure to spread the work out among all the backs evenly so you don't tire any one of them too soon. Their right tackle is getting tired. Exploit that! That's the kind of weakness you need to look for. Busby, Lester…!"

On and on he went, talking at a pace that would have made an auctioneer proud, with hardly a break in his stream of instructions. Teetzel concentrated on our mistakes, which according to him were so numerous you'd have thought we were the losing team. A group of boys gathered around to listen, and Teetzel continued talking as if they weren't there. Nearby, two drunks got into a fistfight, probably over a bet, and he ignored them too.

Teetzel had ten minutes to get everything in and he made the most of it.

During the second half, Jacob let me call most of the plays to increase my confidence, at least until he sensed my confusion, and then he would whisper for me to do one thing or another. He even stopped using numbers when referring to his play choices, leaving that up to me, which was good, but the further we got into the second half, the more exasperated I became. Sometimes we were already lining up before I remembered the correct signal, if I remembered it at all. Not good. An effective hurry-up quarterback called out the proper play almost without thinking.

The ball continued to change hands without much happening until Jacob carried it across for our fourth touchdown—Baushke kicked from a wide angle and missed the goal. By that time we were midway through the second half and Teetzel began making substitutions. It didn't surprise me that I was the first to go—Mit Ludwig took my place. Then Biffy Lee was replaced by Cunningham while Jones went in for the Iron Man.

The three of us were cheered as we walked from the field.

I would never have admitted it then, but I was angry about getting pulled from the game. I was physically exhausted for sure, and I was even worse mentally. My mind was fatigued from trying to remember the best plays and when to use them, not to mention the signals that would appropriately inform the team of my intentions. But I wanted to stay in and keep working. I wiped my face with a towel and then half threw it on the ground. I was fuming as I sat down and watched the remainder of the game. The fellows scored three more touchdowns before Teetzel pulled Handy from the game. He was dog tired, and when he heaved again Teetzel mercifully sent him to the bench and he sat down next to me. Made me feel worse, sitting next to a puker.

There were no substitutes left, so Teetzel went in for Handy. Near the end of the game the Kershaws punted the ball and it went to Teetzel, who fielded one of the nicest catches I'd ever seen. Then he made a dodging run that was pure poetry. The rooters agreed, judging from their enthusiastic cheering, which they kept up even after he was tackled. In my opinion, Teetzel wanted to show Bungtown he was more than talk, that he was the real deal, and it worked. Everyone seemed damn impressed. I certainly was.

The game ended less than a minute later with the score pegged at 40 to 0 in our favor.

The rooters gave us a long ovation as we shook hands with the Kershaws. The congratulating part was embarrassing for me since they knew Jacob told me most of the plays to run. Thankfully, none of them said anything about it. A couple did say, "Nice game kid," and that didn't make me feel much better either. The "kid" reference rubbed me the wrong way.

After the congratulations were exchanged, the crowd began leaving the park along with the Kershaws, who had to make a six o'clock train. But Jacob and Bridgman, along with the rest of the fellows, weren't quite so eager to abandon the battlefield. They gathered along the sideline by our bench and continued talking about the match. A group of students and parents joined them, gamblers too—Jacob's old man was even there. I stood present but didn't say much, even after some of the fellows congratulated me. I was beginning to feel funny, like I'd failed—I could feel it in my bones. Why else would Teetzel have pulled me midway through the second half?

Where the rest of the fellows were filled with pride, I was empty. The black fingers began to tighten their grip on my heart again and I was simply too spent to fend them off. The darkness hovered. My disappointment grew, and finally it became so strong that I decided to have a talk with Teetzel on Monday. I planned to tell him I simply didn't have the skill or the mental capacity required to be an effective quarterback.

Either he would give me another position or I would have to reconsider my association with the team.

Chapter 8

I walked in the door and went directly to my upstairs bedroom to remove my shoes and socks. Blisters, both feet—they'd bothered me in the game and ever since. From the drawer of my nightstand I retrieved a spool of white worsted and a needle and sat down on the edge of my bed to fix them. After threading the needle, I carefully drew the worsted through each blister and clipped both ends. I would leave them that way until the skin peeled off—Jacob's remedy. I gave my cuts and scrapes another dose of iodine before limping back downstairs and into our small dining room to face my folks and little brother, Charlie, at the dinner table.

I was getting stiffer by the minute and they could tell. Ma said something about my swollen face and lips, but I refused to talk about it. She must have thought I was giving her the "tough boys don't fret about their injuries" routine because she then congratulated me on my playing, which did nothing to lift my spirits.

"Yes sir, Fletch," Pa chimed in as he spooned mashed potatoes onto his plate. "It'll be a long time before those Chicago boys forget the thrashing you gave them."

"Oh, I don't know about…"

"Yes it will," he interrupted. "And no small thanks to you."

"But I didn't have that much to do with it. I didn't even score a touchdown."

"Didn't have to, by God." Pa used his fork to pick roasted chicken from the bones and was eating the pieces one at a time as he talked. "It was you who decided which of the fellows would do the scoring. I saw it with my own eyes."

"Yes, Fletch," Ma added. "We thought you were magnificent."

"Appreciate it," I said without further comment, eyes down, staring hard at my plate. They finally understood that I didn't want to talk about my playing and let it drop.

After we'd finished with dinner, Pa got up and went into the parlor to read through some papers relating to his work. Charlie went outside to play, but when I tried to leave, Ma asked me to stay.

"I'd like you to help me clear the table, Fletch," she said. I didn't reply, but I didn't ignore her either.

When I had the dishes stacked, I carried them into the kitchen where I found the late afternoon sun smoldering like a warm smudge through the back door window. The east wall was bathed in soft orange light, but it was dark enough in the nooks and crannies for Ma to have already lit the kerosene lamp mounted on the wall opposite the sink. I found her feeding some sticks of wood into the cook-stove to fuel the fire for heating the water reservoir.

"Pump some water for me?" she said referring to the iron handled pump mounted beside our sink.

I primed the pump with a glass of water and began to pump until the water gushed out and half filled the sink—we would fill the rest with hot water until it was at the proper dishwashing temperature. Ma punched down a pile of dough that was rising in an earthenware bowl on the counter to let it rise one more time and then covered it with a towel. The dough would become bread for the following day's sandwiches.

"You know, Fletch," she said as she leaned back against the counter and then wiped her hands on the apron that covered her ankle-length cotton dress, "No one should expect to play perfectly in their very first game."

"What do you mean?"

"I know you're not happy with your playing." When I didn't say anything she added, "Am I right?"

"We won, and that's the important thing."

"Yes, and I thought you did a wonderful job leading the fellows."

"But I didn't."

"Of course you did." She seemed to be fishing for something, whether it was a concern or a confession I couldn't tell.

"Winning had nothing to do with me," I finally said. "The fellows are good football players. They could have won that game with you playing quarterback. In fact, Jacob told me most of the plays to use."

"That may be," she said. "But you are only a sophomore, and this is only your first high school game. You can't expect to know everything in just three days."

"It was embarrassing," I argued while nervously nudging the stove leg with the tip of my shoe. "And I don't know if it will get any better. I may never learn the plays, and even if I do, I still wouldn't know which ones to use and when. It's like going to school, which is not why I play football."

"I know," she replied. "You play because it's wild and adventurous and fun. But maybe there's more to it than having a good time. Maybe it's part of growing up, of learning to have responsibility."

"Please, Ma." I protested.

"I'm serious," she said, looking me straight in the eye. "You wanted to play on this team more than anything in the world, and now you've got your wish. Look to your father for inspiration. You know how hard he works for his clients and how often he stays up at night preparing for his court appearances. He never gives up."

I was immediately offended when she said the part about not giving up and said so. "I'm not a quitter," I bristled.

"Of course you're not," she said. But she was right—I almost was, at least until that very moment.

The word "quitter" stung like a hard slap in the face. Then a firestorm of shame surged through my body followed by a feeling of regret for planning to have Teetzel remove me from the lineup. At that moment I understood how wrong that conversation would have been. Never, in a thousand years, could I have lived it down.

"But I want you to think about one more thing," she continued. "I was close enough to see how you looked following the game today, you and the rest of the fellows, and it concerned me. I hope you realize that your cuts and bruises and rattled bones will hurt even more in the morning, and even then it's probably the best you'll feel until after Thanksgiving."

"Oh come on Ma," I said. "I practiced all last year with the fellows, and this year too, and I think I know what it's like to be sore."

"But that's different than playing against someone who's trying to hurt you, whether it's deliberate or not."

"No one was trying to hurt me," I argued.

"That's not the way it looked to me."

I walked over to the stove and fed a couple pieces of wood into the fire box. Ma continued to watch me, hands folded and resting gently over the front of her apron, but there was no attempt on my part to reply. That's because I knew she was right.

Sunday morning found me so damn sore I could barely get out of bed. Ma was right—my entire body felt like an ugly, purple bruise. I eased my legs out from under the covers and let them dangle over the edge of the mattress while I tried to rub the hurt from my thighs. The game was still swirling through my mind, at least until the strong odor of black coffee and bacon sputtering in the fry pan drifted upstairs and pushed my thoughts toward breakfast. I put on a pair of pants, socks, and a moth-eaten wool sweater that had long since been dedicated for house duty during cold weather. Downstairs, Pa was in the parlor reading the *Evening News*.

"Good print, Fletch," he said. Then he looked up and gave me a proud smile. "There's a fine article in the paper about the whupping you gave the Kershaws."

"That so?" I asked.

"Yes sir. And it was penned by Barratt O'Hara himself, apparently in town visiting his fiancée this weekend." O'Hara was a local fellow who worked sports for the *Chicago American*, but while visiting he occasionally wrote articles for the *Evening News*.

"Does he say anything about my fumble?" I added, hoping he might have seen fit to leave it out.

"Not much. Just that it happened. But he does relay much of the play-by-play action of the contest…which is a definite cut above most of last year's articles."

He handed me the paper and I began reading. Pa was right—O'Hara's play-by-play writing was first rate. In fact, it was so good I actually visualized myself replaying the game. And he didn't mention my other mistakes. Suddenly I was bursting with pride to be part of such a great team, but then I was saddened to think I might not be up to the task of leading them. Pa noticed.

"I know you feel bad about your playing yesterday," he said.

"Yes sir...and for good reason," I answered respectfully, even though I was in no mood to hear it again.

"But don't forget it was your first game," he continued. "And you'll only get better with practice."

"Maybe. But I'm not sure there's enough time. We play our first interscholastic game next Saturday and I'm not prepared."

"What exactly do you need to learn that you don't already know?" he asked.

"Signals," I said. "I need to learn the signals that will tell the fellows what play to run...and I need to learn them so well that I can call them in my sleep."

"Maybe we can help."

"Excuse me?" I said with an expression that surely reflected my skepticism. But before he could reply, Ma mercifully ended the conversation by calling for me to go outside and get Charlie, for breakfast. He was taking care of Mattie—Sunday was his day.

I went back upstairs to get the pisspot from beneath my bed. Then I went outside and dumped the night's offering into the privy before hollering to Charlie that it was time for breakfast. He mumbled something to Mattie before coming out and latching the door behind him. We walked into the dining room and found Ma and Pa sitting at the table talking about one of our gossip-mongering neighbor ladies. We prayed and then began eating our traditional Sunday breakfast of eggs, bacon, hot cakes with syrup, and coffee. Charlie and I drank milk.

"You didn't tell me what we could do to help you prepare you for next week's game," Pa said, determined to keep the subject alive.

"Nothing," I said respectfully, even though I wanted to scream for him to stop badgering me. "There's nothing you can do."

"We could help you with the signals," Ma said.

"What do you know about signals?" I asked. I wanted to growl at her but didn't out of respect.

"I watched you play yesterday, remember?" she said while passing me the platter of bacon. "And every evening when I go into your bedroom to tuck Charlie into bed I see your play booklet on the night stand."

"A good way to start," Pa added, "would be for you to explain just what signals are and how they work."

"Sir?" I said incredulously.

"Signals," he said. "The best way to test your knowledge of any subject is to teach it to someone. If you can teach it, that proves you understand."

"Why that's a great idea," Ma said enthusiastically.

Further protestation would have been futile, so I gave in and told them about signals over breakfast. Frustration must have been apparent in my voice, at least in the beginning, but soon I began to feel more confident about my knowledge and became increasingly animated.

I explained how signals were called by the quarterback, often while the fellows were still getting up from the previous play, which meant they had to be transmitted in a way that was unintelligible to the opposing side. That's why numbers worked best. The numbers we used were grouped in a series of three, but only one number meant anything—the other two were dummies. I told them it was determined ahead of time which of the three numbers identified the proper play. And if the quarterback suspected his signals were being unraveled by the opposing team, he could simply call for a timeout and change the live number to another position.

The important thing about the signal system was that it enabled a team to play very fast. But to be effective, the players had to be drilled until the signals became a part of their very being. When the quarterback called out a number, each player should know instantly what play it was and how he should line up.

"Teetzel believes," I said, "that we will never have the machine-like quickness and precision required to play championship football until we master his system."

They understood. I could tell by the looks on their faces they also empathized with me over the task I faced. And I knew why.

No American sport had ever been developed with so many rules or was played with such precision and split-second execution.

"Can you give us an example of a signal?" Pa said.

"Alright. The plays Teetzel taught us this week are very simple. One number means one play. For instance, number three means that the left halfback cross-bucks outside right tackle."

"Cross-bucks?" Charlie said, giggling.

"Yes," I replied. "That means he crosses from left to right, and as he passes behind me I hand him the ball. Then he rams, or 'bucks,' the opposing line to the right of the tackle."

"But what's a buck?" he continued.

"A buck is a technique used by a running back to advance the ball."

"Then what's a bucker?" He was serious, and Ma and Pa were openly laughing at his inquisitiveness.

"Alright Charlie," I said. "I can see you won't shut up until I explain this so listen carefully. I'm not going to tell you again. Understand?"

"It's a simple question, Fletch," he added.

"A bucker must be strong and a very quick starter because he has to reach full steam almost instantly. He runs very low with his head down, but even then he must be able to peer out through his eyebrows to see where he's going."

"What if they're bushy like Uncle George's?" he interrupted.

"Listen, will you?" I growled impatiently as he sat there grinning. "You got me started, now let me finish."

"Please continue," Pa said. I could tell he was genuinely interested.

"When the bucker reaches the line he doesn't try to knife through, unless of course his lineman have opened a hole for him. Instead, he rams through. The instant before he hits the opposing players he dips his head to allow the top of his skull to become the arrowhead that pierces the mass."

"Oh my." Ma said under her breath while Pa cleared his throat. Charlie sat there wearing a look of astonishment.

There was a long few seconds of silence. "Yes, I know," I finally said. "Only the toughest players can do it. Jacob Graham is the best line bucker I ever saw."

"I suppose number four tells the right halfback to cross-buck outside left tackle?" Pa said, getting back to the subject of signals. "Exactly."

I explained how the number five called for the right half to run straight ahead and six demanded the same for the left half. Seven called for the fullback to buck center on the right while eight sent him left. They thought that was simple enough, until I explained that we already had fourteen plays and three formations.

"What's a formation?" Ma asked. I took a deep breath and fortified myself for another round of instructions.

First I described formation A, which was our standard lineup with seven men on the line and the three backs balanced behind the quarterback. Then I told them that formation B called for the right tackle to be positioned a couple steps back of the line while formation C called for the left tackle to be back.

"We can run any number of plays using the same formation," I added, "which doesn't need to be called out before each play unless it changes. And if I want to change formations, I must holler it out immediately after the preceding play is whistled dead so the fellows know how they're to line up before taking their positions."

"Must admit," Pa said while shaking his head in awe, "Mr. Teetzel is one whale of a coach to think up a system like that."

"He sure is," I said. "But he learned it from Hurry-up Yost, and it gets more complicated yet. In two weeks he wants us to…"

"Excuse me, dear," Ma interrupted. "I'm still not sure how the formations relate to the numbers."

I sighed and prepared to begin again when Pa interrupted. "Wait," he said. "Why don't you show us?"

"Sir?" I answered, confused as to what he had in mind.

"Charlie. Go upstairs and get Fletch's football. We'll let him line us up in the backyard."

Ma protested at first, but then laughed and agreed it might be fun. By then the situation had become so ridiculous even I had to chuckle at the suggestion. Charlie came back and we went outside, leaving the dishes on the table to be cleaned up later.

Our backyard was typically small and bounded at the rear by an alley. Between the alley and yard was a four-foot high, wood-planked fence lined with thick plantings of hollyhock and blackeyed Susan. The carriage shed occupied the left corner of the yard while the privy anchored the right corner, its sunny side crawling with honeysuckle vines. The space may have been small, but there was enough room for what Pa had in mind.

"Okay," I said. "There are just enough of us to play in a formation of four. Charlie will be my center. Ma, you take the right half position while Pa takes the left."

I gave Charlie a quick lesson on snapping the ball and then positioned Ma and Pa back on either side of me. Ma took off her apron but still looked woefully out of place in her long, flowered dress with puffy sleeves. The skirt covered her feet, which was customary in those days, and her brown hair was brushed up and loosely pinned to the back of her head. I showed her how to stand at the ready with her hands on her knees, of which she did a fair job—Pa took to it right off. He actually crouched with his hips low and his knuckles on the ground leaning forward.

"How do I look, Fletch?" he said proudly. "Good as Jacob Graham?"

"Yes sir," I answered, praying none of the fellows would happen by and see us. "Almost."

"Call the signal, dear," Ma said. "I need to know the play. I'm getting tired of leaning forward."

"Okay," I said. "Here goes. Middle number is live—first and third are dummies." Then I hollered, "Ten–six–four! That means you, Ma…straight ahead."

Matty stuck her head out of the barn window and watched curiously as the four of us prepared to execute our first down. I imagined she was wondering what the hell we were trying to prove. Frankly, so did I.

"You can be our rooter, Mattie!" Pa hollered, and she snorted.

I got up behind Charlie and told him to snap the ball, which he did. Then I spun around and handed it to Ma and she pulled it deep into the folds of her dress, which swished loudly as she trotted past me. "Good show!" I hollered. For the next play, I called Pa's number and he took the ball on a cross-buck to the left. I thought two plays would be enough, but they wanted more.

We spent a good half hour running plays, going faster and faster with each succeeding series. We didn't actually run much or very far, which meant I had to call the next play almost immediately after Charlie made the snap. It didn't end until Ma was carrying the ball and Charlie tried to tackle her. To avoid him, she made a deft sidestepping motion, and he disappeared harmlessly into the billowy fabric of her dress before falling out the other side. That started us all laughing.

"Maybe you should try wearing a skirt during your games, dear," Ma chirped proudly. "It just might save you from being tackled."

"Ha ha," I said sarcastically, though I had to admit she did a good job fooling Charlie.

On the next play, I gave the ball to Pa, and Charlie grabbed him as he trotted past. Then I jumped in, and so did Ma, and we tumbled onto the grass and laughed so hard we almost cried.

By the time we went back inside, I was more than eager to continue talking about signals—I was completely engaged and needed no further prompting. Very quickly, I was explaining to them about the more complicated four-number signal Teetzel wanted us to begin using.

Under the four-number system, two numbers were dummies while two were live. The first live number named the ball carrier and the second identified the point of attack. For that reason, every player received his own number. Attack points on either side of the center and to the outside of each end position were also given numbers. The runner simply carried the ball outside of the position corresponding to the number called. Variety and a greater number of attack points were the benefits of the four-number system.

"I understand about formations, which you don't have to call out between plays unless they change," Pa said, "but what about the snap?"

"What do you mean?" I asked.

"In the yard, you just said 'hike.' In a game, you use numbers."

"Oh that's simple," I replied. "After I call the signal that tells the fellows what play to run, I call another signal that tells them the snapping number. The two signals are related." At that point I realized I was reciting very fast, which was good. It told me I was at least comfortable with one aspect of my quarterbacking duties. "If the first number of the first signal is odd," I proudly continued, "then the fellows know the snapping number is the third number of the second signal. If the first number is even, the snapping number is the second number."

"Stop!" Pa said. "I can't keep up."

"But it's easy," I teased, and then he smiled.

After lunch, my folks dragged me and Charlie outside again for another round of signal practice. Half an hour later, we had rehearsed twelve different plays over and over in rapid succession.

I appreciated my family's desire to help me—they were definitely the exception in those days. But while our little signal practices had been a useful memory exercise, I realized they did nothing to improve my ability to select plays based on what the defense was doing. That kind of knowledge would only come with experience. But the most valuable thing to have happened that day, thanks to Ma, was my decision to forego talking with Teetzel about a position change. And by evening I was actually feeling pretty enthused about taking another whack at playing quarterback.

A boy's enthusiasm has the potential to carry him a long way, and it was a good thing. Because I would need it.

Chapter 9

I went to school early Monday morning and found most of the team already gathered in the hallway outside of Professor Righter's science room. It was a team tradition, meeting like that the Monday after game day. I joined the fellows in 1902, but because of my scrub status, I was only allowed the slightest leeway to speak. To attempt any more would have exposed me to hard ribbing and, in some cases, physical retribution.

However, this time it was different—I was now one of them. But my past cautions were hard to shed, and so I participated cautiously.

No one criticized my fumble or my weak signal-calling, in fact they pretty much agreed I performed admirably in spite of having only three days of formal quarterback practice.

Emboldened by their graces, I added a few comments of my own as they replayed all the good blocks and tackles and the best of the running plays. I even managed a chuckle or two when some of them bragged about the jabs and punches they threw when the officials weren't looking.

Everyone was scraped and bruised, including me. Some of the fellows had more serious injuries, but we typically didn't discuss them unless we were sharing remedies or if the injury was especially visible. And no one could resist an injury that had the potential for spinning a good joke. That morning, it was Bridgman's turn.

"Run into a door," Butts said, getting the ball rolling. Bridgman took a savage blow to the face that by all rights should have benched him. At the end of the day, his right cheek was black and blue and the white of his eye was soaked with blood. Monday morning it looked like raw meat.

"Yep," he replied with a wide grin. "Was a door alright. You don't think any of those milquetoast Kershaws could've inflicted this do you?"

"You see Doc about it?" I asked, trying to be serious.

"No…but he found me. Gave me a watery mixture of borax and camphor to drip into my eye every two, three hours."

"Waste of time," Ossignac butted in, speaking in his slow Indian way.

"What?" Bridgman queried.

"Waste of time," he repeated. "My grandfather uses an eyewash made by boilin the dried root of golden-seal weed. Works out the redness every time."

"Come off it!" Butts bellowed.

"Don't laugh," Ossignac said with a wrinkled brow. "I've used it myself."

We all laughed again, but it wasn't just at Ossignac's recipe—we were laughing at everything due to our happy attitudes.

By the time we broke for class, I'd heard enough to know that our victory over the Kershaws was having huge repercussions around town. Through the grapevine, we heard the most serious football enthusiasts were even pleased with us, including those who thought we were doomed to a mediocre season without Hub Allen. That meant they'd been leery of me, the featherweight, and I couldn't blame them. Their turnabout lifted my spirits, but secretly I wondered if they had any idea how many of our plays were actually selected by Jacob.

It was obvious to me we won because of our veteran players. Teetzel's coaching had yet to take firm hold, and I was still so wet behind the ears I was nearly drowning in my own incompetence. But the fellows themselves were magnificent—raw with talent and spirit and a gutsy nerve that never ceased to astound me.

It was obvious Barratt O'Hara agreed.

O'Hara was about twenty-one at the time, a social reform–minded young man who had a great love for sports, football in particular. And even at his young age, everyone in

Bungtown knew he was someone to watch, that his star was on the rise. O'Hara, you see, grew up and went to school in a small town just south of Benton Harbor called Berrien Springs, at least until President Cleveland appointed his old man to a consul position in Nicaragua and the entire family moved there. The O'Haras were back in Michigan by the time the Spanish-American War broke out, which is when Barratt enlisted in the Thirty-third Michigan Volunteer Infantry. Although he was only sixteen at the time, he participated in the siege of Santiago and proved valuable because of his ability to speak Spanish.

In 1899, O'Hara was living in Bungtown, a high school senior playing on the school's first successful football team. After graduation, he worked as a reporter for the *Benton Harbor Evening News* but soon left to take a position at the *St. Louis Chronicle*, which belonged to the Scripps-McRae league of newspapers. During his first football season, he was promoted to sporting editor in response to his articles, particularly the ones where he criticized certain western colleges for paying students to play. As editor, he led the *Chronicle*'s effort to abolish prize fights. In 1903, O'Hara jumped to the *Chicago American* where he was given the sporting editorship of the noon edition.

Having an especially keen eye for football was O'Hara's gift, a rarity in 1903. That's because the game was quick, the formations were tight, and it was hard to tell who was doing what due to the numberless uniforms. Identification was twice as difficult when the players were covered head to toe with mud, which was most of the time.

O'Hara was dating a local girl named Florence Hoffmann, an arrangement that caused him to spend much time in Bungtown. Florence also liked sports, and when she prodded him into taking her to our first 1902 football game, his old Benton Harbor spirit was immediately rekindled. He followed us all the way to our game with Ishpeming and was on the sidelines that first game when we thumped the Kershaws. He didn't say much about me in his article, good or bad, but there were no doubts regarding his impressions of the backfield.

The following is a snippet from the article he wrote for the *Evening News* about the Kershaw game:

Leo Baushke, George Bridgman and Jacob Graham would have shown anywhere and under any conditions. They played mighty good football—that which would be stamped "varsity caliber" by the newspaper correspondents in college towns.

I saw Baushke on three or four occasions hurdle the line as cleverly as I have ever seen the trick done by a university player. Graham pounded the line hard enough to leave you pitying the opposing players, and Bridgman now and then broke out for a dash that bore considerable similarity to a bolt of lightning flying along the line of white chalk marks.

O'Hara's review resulted in good things all around. Of course, it heightened player morale, which was most important, but it also excited our supporters and encouraged some of Benton Harbor's stingiest businessmen to dig into their pockets. Financial support was always critical—but there was more. In his article, O'Hara predicted we would go down on record as one of the greatest football aggregations in the history of Michigan's interscholastic athletics. He even suggested the possibility of arranging a game between us and Chicago's Hyde Park. Now that was some news— the previous season, Hyde Park was recognized by most sports writers as the best high school team in the country.

O'Hara admitted it was much too early in the season to predict how the chips would fall, but just the talk of a game with Chicago's premier gridiron stars thrilled the Benton Harbor sports enthusiasts to the bone. Except for me—it doubled the pressure I already felt.

I may have been down during the previous weekend due to my performance in the Kershaw game, but I must admit that by Monday afternoon my bruised self-confidence was mending nicely. Acceptance was the medicine, administered first by my teammates and then by the enthusiasts, but it was the positive response by the student rooters that really pushed me over the top.

I hadn't realized just how popular varsity football players could be among their fellow classmates. After the Kershaw game, they showered all of us, including me, with congratulations and praise, and you could tell by the looks in their eyes they truly regarded us as damn special. Some actually viewed us as heroes. Those who thought we were crazy we usually ignored, most of them being teachers and doctors and other reform-minded individuals. The ranks of the football reformers were especially filled with those riding the prohibition and suffrage bandwagons.

I didn't agree with them on much of anything, but as I look back now, I think they were partially right about football.

The Kershaw score may have been lopsided in our favor, but that's not to say the playing was easy. It was extremely hard, and rough. Busby received a serious shoulder injury while Baushke's left arm was nearly twisted off. Lathe's knee was scraped so bad that by Monday it was already starting to boil, which meant it was blistered yellow with infection. And all of us were mapped with cuts and bruises. Even those who considered themselves unhurt had noticeable limps and hobbles, including me. But it was George Bridgman's bloody eye that took the prize.

Bridgman's eye was so noticeable that it was reported in both the *Benton Harbor Evening News* and the *St. Joseph Herald*. When O'Hara asked him about it after the game, he casually shrugged it off and talked instead about our good showing.

"Now you know we're not four-flushers," he said.

Our injuries didn't come as a surprise—each of us joined the team with the understanding that our participation would involve some pain. Just how much pain was the gamble. But we believed the odds were stacked in our favor. We also believed a combination of skill and hard conditioning, along with a dose of good luck, would prevent most injuries from being serious. And even if it worked out that one did turn serious, we still didn't complain—that would have been a sign of weakness. Being tough meant you were able to take the abuse without complaining, but it also meant playing without much protection. And that was part of the problem.

In those days, there was a belief among enthusiasts that football players didn't need protection, or very little. In fact, players who packed their uniforms with cotton or folded rags were often viewed with disgust, criticized as being soft or for looking like stuffed pillows. They believed the toughest footballers didn't need extra padding. That was the mind-set in Michigan. Fools, every one of them. Me included.

Without a doubt, the lack of adequate protection contributed to the high injury rate, but uniforms weren't even part of the argument back then. At least in the way you would think. Instead, the anti-football crusaders used the argument that players who padded their uniforms were living proof of the game's danger. They believed the rules promoted the violence, and as I look back, I can't disagree. The game was mostly played between a mass of players from one team struggling to advance the ball against a mass of players from the other team. Nearly everyone on the field was in the same place at the same time. The game's opponents complained that letting players interact in such close quarters made it convenient for them to inflict injuries without being seen. And they were right. Kicking, gouging, or disabling your opponent with heavy blows about the eyes, nose, and jaw happened all the time. So did knees to the head and gut. And the nature of the scrimmage line only added to the problem.

The neutral zone hadn't been invented yet. In 1903, the line of scrimmage was still an imaginary line passing through the ball, and as the opposing linemen assembled for the snap they held their foreheads so close together you could barely slip a piece of paper between them. That's why faces were often gashed and bruised and bathed in blood. It was the banging of foreheads together that contributed to the fighting. But this seemed normal back then—not a big deal. That's because it could get a lot worse.

As pressure from the serious enthusiasts and gamblers was put on a team to win, weapons were sometimes used to disable key players. It may seem unbelievable now, but in some regions, brass knuckles, billies, blackjacks, sharpened shoe spikes, and even knives were sometimes used. Monroe Morrow told me he once saw a game out east where a star player was struck in the head and knocked unconscious by a steel bolt flung from a slingshot. Said it was done by a player from the other team who wasn't detected because his teammates shielded him from the officials and the crowd. The deal was planned, you see. Monroe said the man sitting beside him knew it was going to happen and advised him to watch for it. But that brand of violence was pretty extreme. Most of what I witnessed was bad enough, and it was done by God's own weapons.

By that I mean hands, knees, and feet.

Many of the injuries I witnessed were caused by a stiff arm or a slug to the face, which routinely resulted in split lips, gashed tongues, and broken or knocked-out teeth. Flattened ears and smashed noses were also common. Players were cold-cocked all the time. A kick to the shin or a knee to the thigh or belly could easily leave a fellow with cracked ribs, and the twisting of limbs happened all the time. If you made it safely through those hazards, then you had to survive within the stack of bodies on the ground. Murder piles. That's what we called them. For a few seconds before and after each play was whistled dead, the pile was the scene of horrendous kicking, punching, poking, and jabbing. Jacob always said to look for an ankle and give it a hard twist, that it was a bloodless way to eliminate a player.

By the end of a hard game, our bodies were mottled with blue and green bruises and stung with a myriad of abrasions, most of them received in the bowels of the murder piles. When we were stripped down in the changing rooms, we looked like zebras from the iodine streaked across our bodies. Now that's the football I remember. We eagerly traded our health for the fun and glory.

As I think back, I'd have to say that most injuries could've been reduced if only the officials would've curbed the game's lawlessness. The rules to stop it were in place—they just weren't enforced. For instance, hitting with the closed fist was illegal, but you never would have known it. Penalties for slugging were rarely called, especially if the illegal actions of one player were offset by those of an opposing player. The officials might get serious if the fighting continued after the play was over, but only if it was severe or one-sided. Sometimes they were too late—players actually died from their injuries. And it was dead football players that caused the anti-football crusaders to begin to agitate for government intervention.

In some regions, prosecutors threatened to prosecute any player who intentionally slugged another player. State legislatures considered bills that would disqualify players who committed intentional injuries, while others pushed for legislation that would flat-out ban the game altogether. Thankfully, most of our local politicians were good rooters.

We thought about the rules back then, but we thought about them in their existing form and not in a way they could or should have been. Changing them to make football safer seemed ridiculous. Sure, the rules, the enforcement, and even our meager uniforms may have contributed to the injuries, but the fact remained that we believed it was a player's duty to disable his opponent. Being a winner meant you outlasted the other fellow. That's why most of us continued to play with our injuries, regardless of the severity, and why we tried to hide them from the coach to prevent being pulled.

In a nutshell, we willingly played until we dropped.

Chapter 10

During the final week of September, our practices were geared toward our game against the team from South Haven High. We continued to concentrate on speed and endurance and ran more conditioning routines than you could count. There was no room for fat lineman in Teetzel's style of football—we had to be lean-limbed, quick-footed, and filled with wind. For us, his determination translated into buckets of sweat.

We also worked hard on our hurry-up game plan, which meant my work continued after practice.

I went home both Monday and Tuesday evening and ate dinner and did my homework. Later, after everyone had gone to bed, I studied my playbook at the dining room table and then while lying in bed by lamplight. Both mornings I woke up still propped against my pillow with the book flat on my chest and the lamp emptied of oil. At Tuesday's practice I had many play questions for Teetzel, which he patiently answered, and then at the Pastime Club while the team was getting rubdowns, we had a serious discussion about offensive strategy.

By Tuesday night, my head was bursting with formations, plays, signals, techniques, and strategies, and with it came an appreciation for how much responsibility a quarterback really had.

The physical duties of the quarterback were specialized you see, but he also needed to have a good grip on the skills required to play every other position. For instance, it was critical for him to know how to interfere, block, open a hole, run with the ball, and use the stiff arm. He also needed the defensive skills required to fend off blockers and tackle the runner. But his most important duty was to take the ball from the center and transfer it safely to the designated runner. In those days, the ball could be passed, thrown, or batted in any direction except toward the opponent's goal. The forward pass was illegal. Sound easy? That's what I thought.

The ball couldn't be caught and advanced by the runner unless it came to him at exactly the right time and place. Poor execution was the cause of most fumbles, which is why Teetzel performed extra duty coaching me on the use of the various passes. There were five altogether. In a nutshell they were the underhand throw, the underhand spiral, the round-arm throw, the round-arm spiral throw, and the simple handoff.

The handoff was used when the ball carrier attacked the line close to the tackles—the ball was simply placed in the pit below the runner's breadbasket. The underhand or overhand passes were used when the play went wide, but when throwing against the wind or for long distances, the spiral was the undisputed champ. But the spiral required skill. Teetzel had me throwing them by the hundreds that week.

Our off-field practice continued Wednesday evening at Bird's Drug Store.

Teetzel and I were sitting at the lunch counter eating ice cream and discussing play strategies while Burger leaned on the counter half listening. That's because the other half of him was conversing with a couple of fellows sitting next to us. Teetzel and I were talking about how best to use the Iron Man in tackle-back formations when something I said caused him to steer the conversation to the subject of passing. Soon he was quizzing me about the different techniques and when best to use them. I did okay at first, but then I stumbled. That's when he grabbed my arm and pulled me off the stool for some full-body instructing—he acted as the ball carrier while I went through the motions of passing to him.

"After passing to the halfback," Teetzel said while crouching with hands on knees, "follow the runner and help him to break through."

"Yes sir," I answered as I stagger-stepped and followed him to the end of the counter.

"Watch out for the candy rack!" Burger hollered.

"And in runs outside of the tackles," Teetzel continued without so much as an acknowledgment, "the ball must leave your hands just as soon as possible, arriving ahead of the runner and thereby making him come up to it. Like this," he said, and then he stepped back and went through the motions of making an overhand throw.

"Eight ball in the left pocket," I said confidently, which meant I clearly understood. That's when he let his arms and shoulders fall limp, much like a deflating tire.

"Fletch," he said in a voice tinged with despair, "it may seem easy now, but the results can be quite different when a defensive tackle is bearing down on you. You must be able to execute your maneuvers flawlessly regardless of the pressure, which means you won't have time to think about them. Do you understand?"

"Yes sir," I replied sheepishly.

"And remember this," he added. "Nothing about playing quarterback is an easy eight ball in the left pocket."

He was talking game situations, meaning I had to know instinctively how to execute the proper moves while at the same time calling the plays based on my interpretation of what the opposing team was doing. And all of this while playing at a physically exhausting pace.

"It's all up there, Fletch," he said, pointing to my head. "Think about your plays, think about your moves, and don't stop thinking about them until you fall asleep at night."

We sat back down at the counter and continued eating our ice cream. He didn't say anything for a couple of minutes, and neither did I. Couldn't imagine what I could say after that.

"You are a smart boy," he finally said as he finished his last spoonful of ice cream. "And intelligence is the key."

"That's right, Fletch," Burger added. "Use your marbles and this team will be yours."

Teetzel and I walked home in the dark. We talked and talked, mostly about play strategies, but he also had some questions about the fellows and what types of families they came from. We split up in front of Doc's house on Columbus and I walked the remaining distance alone, thinking about all we'd gone over. It was overwhelming—particularly the strategies. By the time I reached our front door, the task before me seemed more daunting than when Teetzel first picked me to replace Winters.

It wasn't that I felt unprepared physically—it was the mental stuff that worried me.

In those days, there wasn't a platoon of assistants working with the head coach like there is today. Instead, the team captain and the quarterback worked with the coach, both to train the players and to develop overall team goals, strategies, and to formulate specific plans of attack for individual games. His role was critical. The quarterback, on the other hand, had an equally important role, but in a different way.

The quarterback was the team's strategist under fire. While a game was in progress, he was easily the most important player because of the total control he had over the operation of the team. If the coach or the team captain needed to consult with him, the rules only allowed it at the half or during a time out. And given the fast pace of the game back then, the quarterback had to make lightning decisions that were based on an array of ever-changing situations and conditions.

Through Teetzel's incessant teaching, I learned the smart quarterback knew who was good at what and when to use him, and he rotated the ball-carrying duties among all the backs to prevent the strongest of them from giving out too early in the game. It was crucial that each ball carrier be able to perform when needed and for as long as possible. The quarterback constantly gauged the team's field position, the weather conditions, and remaining time, all of which influenced his play selection—line buck, end run, tackle-over play, or kick. The alert quarterback constantly scanned the other side for tired linemen, a slight limp in a defensive back, or a watery eye in a key player from a blow to the face. That's where he would hammer his backs. He could also carry the ball himself, which was a new rule for 1903, but it was something I rarely did. Teetzel said because of my small size I might get hurt and put the team in trouble.

Playing quarterback was akin to being a military field general, and the more I learned about it, the more daunting my task seemed. But with each passing day, my confidence grew. That, combined with a good dose of horse sense, went a long way to pull me through those first practices.

As I said before, we practiced long and hard that week, and an enthusiastic crowd of men gathered each afternoon to watch. Most were gamblers. Sometimes there were as many as thirty, most of them standing in bunched-up groups, smoking cigars and talking about our progress, while others parked their rigs at the edge of the field and watched leisurely from their seats.

The South Haven game was two days away and the battlefield had yet to be selected. The 1902 game was held at Eastman Springs, which meant it was our turn to go to South Haven, but the board members wanted us to play in the safety of Benton Harbor and so permitted Burger to bribe them with good money. Of course they refused. Burger then agreed to play the game in South Haven if they would pay for our train tickets, which was customary, but the South Haven manager said the train was too expensive and offered instead to pay our way by lake steamer. Burger flat out refused. He argued the weather was much too unpredictable in late September and that rough seas could make us seasick and unfit to play.

The negotiations ended there.

Our supporters heard about the transportation stalemate and got rankled. A crowd formed Thursday evening at the Star Drug Store to converse about it. Manager Burger, Coach Teetzel, Monroe Morrow, and Walter Banyon were there, with only Butts and me representing the team. There were also a lot of older men I recognized but didn't know by name. Deputy Sheriff Irving Pearl was one I did know.

"Now men," Burger said above the clamor, as he stood with his back to the lunch counter, "you know we've always had a good relationship with South Haven."

"Then what's the problem, Bert?" Deputy Pearl growled. The deputy could really growl when he was agitated, and it was obvious he was agitated. "We need to get the thing ironed out."

"Why won't they play at Eastman Springs?" someone else questioned. "We offered them good money."

"Men," Burger said, "I think they're a little nervous about playing us...especially after what we did to the Kershaws."

"That may be," Deputy Pearl replied. "But the game has to go on."

"Yes...and I will take care of it," Burger said, trying to sound reassuring.

At that point, Walter Banyon removed his hat and shyly stepped forward. "I don't think they're nervous," he said.

"What?" Burger replied in disbelief.

"I think they're trying to intimidate us."

"How can you...?"

"I agree with Walt," Shorty Blake interrupted. Blake was the boisterous manager of St. Joe's Whitcomb Hotel.

"What makes you say that, Shorty?"

"Because I talked to a fruit buyer at the hotel yesterday who'd just come down from the South Haven market. Said he'd heard some things."

"All right then," Burger said as he glanced at the granite faced men staring at him. "Let's air it out."

Blake cleared his throat before continuing. "He said the South Haven boys are pretty sure of themselves, that they're going to whip us. He said they're working hard, that they're even playing on the beach under moonlight to extend their practice time. A victory beach party with a bonfire and corn roast has already been planned. Says they've already dug the pit. Saw it with his own eyes."

Deputy Pearl grumbled, "They can't beat us if they don't play us!" He was answered with a vigorous outburst of agreement from the crowd.

"Quiet, men!" Burger shouted.

"And there's something else," Shorty added. "The buyer told me South Haven is borrowing two players from the Allegan team to use against us."

"That's flat out cheating!" someone shouted.

"And what's worse," Shorty continued over the rising din, "I heard one of the fellows they're borrowing is the one they call the Gill!"

"That's all right with me!" a man yelled. "Jacob Graham will take care of the bastard!"

"But that's still cheating!" someone else hollered.

"Come on, Bert!" a voice rang out. "You've got to do something!"

"I will…I will!" Burger said as he held both hands in the air to quiet the crowd. "Tomorrow I'm supposed to be in touch with their team manager again, and I give you my word I will take care of it."

The meeting ended with the full load in Burger's lap, which Butts and I talked about as we walked home. We decided he would handle it just fine. We didn't know how, just that he would—always did. We were more worried about having a full team on the field and were concerned about Baushke and Busby. Both practiced all week with the team, but neither were in the best shape.

We also wondered what Jacob would say when he discovered the Gill would be playing for South Haven, and if their recent fight would affect his game.

All my worrying about these possibilities came to naught, however, because something happened the next day at practice that was worse than ten Gills. Jacob got injured. He wrenched his right shoulder during practice and was in so much pain Doc had to put it in a sling. A reporter from the *Evening News* asked Jacob about it as he was sitting on the grass watching us practice. He shrugged it off with his usual confidence and said it wouldn't be a problem. "I'll be in the game or bust," he promised.

After practice, Teetzel argued with Burger that Jacob shouldn't play Saturday, that he should rest up for the more important games. Burger said he sympathized, but that the board members would leave it up to Jacob. Of course, there was never any question about it. Jacob said he was playing.

In spite of Jacob's injury, which worried the hell out of me, everything else came together Friday just fine. At the end of the afternoon's practice, Busby and Baushke announced they were feeling well enough to be in the lineup, which really was good news. The Iron Man's knee was still oozing puss, but Doc was treating it and said he also could play. Then Manager Burger told us he'd worked out the money problems with South Haven. Said we were taking the train and that we'd be reimbursed thirty-five dollars for traveling expenses, meals, and the hotel rooms where we'd change into our uniforms and wash up after the game. He also asked about the two Allegan players and was assured it was a rumor.

Doc negotiated with Agent Wolfenden of the Pere Marquette Railroad Company for a charter and was guaranteed a train if we could bring out at least 150 passengers. The cost was seventy cents a head, round trip. Doc assured him we could easily get that many and took the tickets. Principal McClelland held a small pep rally Friday morning, and another Al Clark cartoon appeared in the Friday edition of the *News*.

Friday evening, all 150 train tickets were sold. Early Saturday morning, the rooters beat a path to the depot for more, while dozens of excited men gathered in Bird's and Bell's drug stores to place bets. Some were as close as five-to-twelve in our favor while others were as high as twelve to twenty-six. Showing his confidence, Teetzel made high wagers at both stores.

Everything was ready to go and my mind was still drowning in the details of a thousand plays, signals, and passes. At least that's how it seemed—which is why I was so damned nervous all over again.

Chapter 11

A t 9:30 sharp, the conductor opened the doors and we crowded aboard the four railroad coaches that comprised our charter. The students dubbed it the Rooter Special Number One. Ten minutes later, the engine steamed and revved and finally lurched us into motion, its funnel spewing huge thunderheads of black smoke and cinders. The sky was overcast and it looked like rain, but we had a strong crowd, and that's what mattered most.

There were well over two hundred of us on board, which meant the most rooters ever were traveling with us if you didn't count the 1902 game against Ishpeming. One half of the contingent was players and serious football enthusiasts, which included the board members and gamblers and other hangers on, scrubs too. Family members and local businessmen were also among that number. And I remember seeing such local notables as Judge Elsworth, Editor Harkrider, and Postmaster Owen.

The other half traveling with us were students. And for the first time, there were more Sisters of Football than team members.

The Sisters were a group of high school girls who helped to raise money for the team, a thankless job if you ask me, but they were dedicated. Their fundraising schemes, whether selling cookies or cigars, were always successful. And they also formed an admirable cheering section. Overall they were a great asset, and their efforts did not go unnoticed. Officials representing other high school teams often commented on the large number of girls that showed up at our games. Some folks thought that was unusual—in those days, I suppose it was.

Butts and I sat together in coach three, the team coach. The board members and their wives were there with us, along with Doc and Mrs. Bastar, Principal McClelland, and Bob Busby's six-year-old nephew, Willie, our team mascot. Willie was a coffee-colored little boy, bashful to the core, but if you were lucky enough to get him talking, you'd be rewarded with a funny little story or at least a couple of warm, toothy grins. His uniform was a natty black tuxedo and top hat.

He wasn't the only one in costume that day.

Board member Monroe Morrow was wearing a black-and-white checked vest and a pair of twenty-two-inch shoes. For nearly the entire ride, he bantered back and forth with a couple of gamblers, peppering the conversation with jokes and stories that sometimes got them laughing so hard it seemed they'd never stop. I heard him say he placed a bet where he'd get kicked if we lost, but that he'd do the kicking if we won. A good joke it was, but I didn't believe him about that—Monroe never bet anything but money.

Most everyone in the car was talking and having a good time, but because of my nervousness, I didn't feel much like joining them. And I was apprehensive as hell over the thought that Jacob might not be able to play because of his injured shoulder. To ease my mind, I looked out the window and stared at the passing corn-fields and marshes and stumped hillsides. We also passed tracts of good timberland edged with clumps of wild huckleberry canes and sumac whose leaves were already fevered with the crimsons of autumn. Looking at the cut-over areas made me think of axe-wielding lumberjacks. The thought of axes brought to mind the sport of axe throwing, which reminded me of Jacob. Damn how I prayed his shoulder would hold up.

"Did you hear that?" Butts said with a howl as he elbowed me.

"What?" His jab startled me.

"Monroe."

"Oh yes, Monroe." I turned back to the window just in time to see a small, white clapboard farmhouse and barn disappear behind a sprawling orchard. "What about him?" I added.

"You're not listening, are you?"

"Nope."

"Why not? Those fellows up there are raising the roof."

"I'm reviewing the plays so when we get on the field I can keep you cretins pushing in the right direction."

"You're no damn fun at all," he muttered and then turned back to enjoy the conversation.

I continued to look out the window, and then I dozed. When I awoke I saw another farm, and then another, and soon the little farmsteads were everywhere. That's when I figured we were getting close to South Haven. Sure enough. Soon the train slowed as we passed a rail spur that serviced a clapboard-sided warehouse with a platform stacked with hooped barrels waiting to be loaded. There were a few more such buildings and then some houses. A minute later, we eased into the South Haven depot.

It was a few minutes after eleven when we stepped off the train. Gear was unloaded, and we players searched for our individual bags while everyone else formed into small groups and stood quietly, which was out of character for a crowd of Benton Harbor rooters at a football game. But I knew why—I felt it too. Except for two fellows manning the depot—a ticket agent and a baggage handler—there was no one around. Something was out of place. The air was wet and still, and the thunder growling in the distance only added to the feeling of discontent. Seemed a bad omen.

"There's nothing to worry about!" a lone voice suddenly rang out above the crowd. "It's just Monroe and his big feet making all the noise!"

It was Bridgman.

In an instant, a flood of laughter rolled through the crowd and everyone came back to life. For the next few minutes, folks talked and chuckled about his wisecrack, which then led to stories about other funny things he'd said in the past. Bridgman was always coming up with the damnedest sayings, and usually at the most unexpected moments. The hearty laugh we had served to ease me some, but not enough to stop my churning stomach.

Folks were engaged in a lively banter when the call was made to form a parade line behind Professor Null and the band for the march through town. We lined up, and a sharp drum roll started us walking to a spirited march that set our hearts on fire. We strode down the middle of Kalamazoo Street and into the heart of South Haven waving our ribbons and banners and singing fight songs. When we got to the end of town we turned around and marched back again, finally stopping in front of the Hotel El Arding as the band played a couple more numbers. The El Arding is where Burger secured rooms for us to change into our playing togs.

The gamblers went looking for South Haven money, while the rest of the folks fanned out to see the sights or find a suitable place to buy lunch. I heard later they rented every livery rig and hack in town. In the meantime, Teetzel gathered the team together in the lobby of the El Arding and ran us through a quick signal practice. Must have been quite a sight for the bellhop and the handful of guests loitering in the lobby. But it didn't last long, and it was worth the effort. We did pretty well. And it calmed my jitters.

We ate lunch in the hotel restaurant, and then we went outside and broke into small groups for a quick stroll to settle our stomachs.

I was walking with Jacob, Heck, and Joe Ossignac when we came upon a couple of football players from Kalamazoo sitting on a bench outside a small dry goods store. They were Gerry Whitney and Milo Bennet. We recognized them from our game with them the previous year.

"Well, well, well," Heck said in a voice loud enough for the Kalamazoo players to hear. "They say the Kazoo coach is usin molly-coddles this year."

"Cap it, Heck," Jacob said quietly. He was standing between Heck and Ossignac. I was off to the side with an eye toward avoiding trouble.

Ignoring Jacob, Heck continued, "And they have a coach who sends his players out to spy on other teams. Seems cheating's the only way they can win a game."

"Hey, you little ape," Whitney said as he stood up. He was big as a bear, strong, and I knew he had a terrible temper. "We can watch any football game we want…and there's nothin you can do about it."

"How'd you like a mouth full of knuckles," Heck said as he balled his fists. That's when Jacob placed his right arm against

Heck's chest and held him back.

"You'd better get him out of here," Bennet said, "or Gerry'll wipe up the street with him."

"And take that cigar store Injun with you," Whitney added.

Ossignac balled his fists and I thought he was going to start slugging. Probably would have if Jacob hadn't put up his left arm. Suddenly he was holding both of them back.

"Whitney," Ossignac said. "You just wait…"

"What's going on here?" Teetzel interrupted as he walked across the street toward us. I don't know where he came from—it was like he smelled trouble.

"Nothin, coach," Jacob said. "We're just goin back to the hotel to change."

"Let's go then," he ordered. "We don't have much time."

"Thunderin jackasses," Heck mumbled under his breath just loud enough for the two Kalamazoo players to hear.

"You two get along now," Teetzel said to Bennett and Whitney. "And Graham, save it for the game."

"You betcha, coach," Heck said in a half grumble as we turned and started walking back to the hotel.

"See ya later, chief," Whitney called out sarcastically.

Ossignac kept walking, but under his breath I heard him mutter, "You can count on it."

At a few minutes past two o'clock, the entire team crowded aboard a horse bus for the ride to the playing grounds. The driver hupped the team into motion and we rode quietly, each one of us immersed in our own thoughts. Mine were about the game. I busied myself with quizzes, trying to organize and retrieve a seemingly endless stream of details and numbers. Formations, play signals, offensive strategies—it seemed a daunting task—but I felt confident my performance would be adequate and was actually anxious to prove myself. But I was just as anxious in a nagging way over the possibility I might have to do it without Jacob. I was barely aware of the surroundings until we made the Black River crossing. The thundering sounds of the horses' hooves and the grinding of the iron-rimmed wagon wheels over the plank bridge brought me to my senses. I looked up as seagulls exploded into the

air from their perches on wood pilings and from the rigging of a
moored scow schooner to hover squawking above us. Just beyond
the bridge, the teamster steered the bus onto the grounds of the
city park.

The field was located at the edge of a wooded copse, between
the river and the base of a steep hillside. Our rooters were already
in place, most of them crammed into the one small grandstand
where they had tied orange and black ribbons along the entire
length of the top rail. The South Haven rooters were still trickling
in as we climbed down from the bus.

While a couple of scrubs were unloading blankets, water buckets, footballs, and other gear, Teetzel gathered us around him for a
quick inspection. Then he turned, and together we ran to the field
with little Willie Busby in close tow. When we sprung over the
gridiron side wires, our rooters swarmed out of the bleachers and
bunched up, cheering along the sideline. The South Haven team
arrived a few minutes later, but their entrance was not as dramatic.
Neither was their crowd. It was obvious they were put off because
of the way our supporters claimed their bleachers.

We started our conditioning routines and so did South Haven,
which is when I spotted the Gill. Jacob apparently noticed him too
but said nothing. After the warm-ups, we gathered around the bench
and Teetzel told Jacob to protest the Gill and the other Allegan player
when he met with the officials for the toss of the coin.

The South Haven captain wanted to play halves of fifteen and
twenty minutes, but Jacob would have none of it. He insisted we
play two regulation thirty-minute halves. The South Haven captain
finally agreed, and they also agreed that the scoring team would
kick to the defending team after each touchdown. The Spalding
rule book said the scoring team had the option to kick or receive,
but in Michigan that rule was always negotiated prior to the game.
Sometimes it was agreed that one team should kick the first half
and the other team should kick the second, regardless of who
scored. Sometimes it was agreed that the team scored against
would kick.

We won the toss and Jacob chose to receive—he never mentioned the Gill.

Just before the kickoff, Teetzel gathered us around him in a semicircle. He told us some things about the South Haven team, its strong and weak points. Then he pulled a piece of paper from his pocket and commenced reading down a list of our worst mistakes from the week's practice.

"Pay attention to them," he cautioned us. "And remember the entire population of Benton Harbor is awaiting the final results of the game. Don't let them down."

We took to the field excited and ready to play, and lined up to receive the kick.

A South Haven player put his toe to the pigskin shortly before 2:30 and made a high kick, which Jacob caught at the thirty-yard line and advanced fifteen yards. I immediately went to work and ran a series of line bucks using Jacob, Baushke, and the Iron Man, but the yardage came hard.

I could tell from the first snap that we were in for one whale of a fight. South Haven played a different game than the Kershaws—they fought harder, like hungry wolves. But so did we and I know why. It was the stakes. The game counted for the state championship. That meant the loser would be out of the running, but it also meant they'd spend the remainder of the season playing against second-rate high schools, two-bit football clubs, and any group of thugs who wanted to call themselves a team.

Jacob was letting me call the plays, and we made two quick first downs. My performance was already much better than during the Kershaw game, but I wasn't executing according to Teetzel's idea of a proper hurry-up offense, I knew that. I should have been sending the fellows down the field on wings.

Another reason for the hard playing was the Gill. He was playing a bruising right tackle opposite Lee, who was tough enough in his own right, but the Gill managed to break away and make some good tackles. He and Jacob were already going at it, pushing and shoving at every turn, and our rooters were eating it up. Every rooter was glued to the sideline cheering as hard as they were physically able.

We continued to move the ball until we stalled at the South Haven forty-five and lost it on downs. I cursed myself.

South Haven took possession and made some pretty good gains, usually with the Gill carrying the ball on tackle-over plays. He was a demon of a runner, fast and strong, and he piston-pumped his knees while using his left fist and forearm to bash would-be tacklers out of the way. He growled and snarled and spit in a way that made me hesitate to get near him, which was good for my well-being. Using the closed fist was illegal, but the officials refused to penalize him.

Less then ten minutes into the first half, the Gill carried the ball thru the line behind two teammates smashing interference. Jacob cuffed the first one out of the way with his right hand and kneed the second in the gut before slamming into the Gill and knocking him hard to the ground. Blew the wind clean out of him. Jacob stood up and spit on him and our crowd went crazy while the South Haven rooters booed—the referee called a penalty and sent us to our bench.

Teetzel grabbed Jacob by the sleeve and told him in no uncertain terms that he was out of line. Said he should also stop pushing and shoving after the whistle and concentrate on getting ready for the next play.

"But Jacob didn't start it," Bridgman protested.

"I don't care who started it," Teetzel replied. "When you engage your adversary on his terms you lose. You are not playing football…you are brawling."

He was madder than I'd ever seen him.

The game started again and South Haven ran a few plays but lost the ball on downs at about our fifty, which is when I ran a series of end runs and line smashes using Jacob, Bridgman, and Baushke. I was struggling some with the plays, but every time I began to slow down, Jacob would advise me enough to keep our speed respectable. Thanks to him we finally planted the ball on the five-yard line.

"Last down, two yards to gain!" sang the referee. We needed two yards for a first down and five for a touchdown.

Jacob whispered for me to give him the ball and I called out an appropriate mass play—the fellows took their positions and crouched. A hush fell as I took the snap and faked a handoff to

Bridgman before giving it to Jacob. He shot into the line with me and Baushke, but then the Gill busted Baushke, grabbed Jacob by his right arm, and gave it a violent twist. Folded like a jackknife.

The whistle sounded and the officials began to untangle the heap of bodies until there was one player left. It was Jacob. He'd made the first down, but the look of pain on his face told me he was done. I could hear the Gill laughing from somewhere off to the side and I got a sick feeling in my stomach. Heck and I lifted Jacob to his feet and helped him from the field.

"Don't you worry, Jacob," Heck said. "I'll take care of the bastard."

"Don't be stupid," he sputtered painfully. "We've...got to win this game." Jacob's face was twisted into such a hard grimace that he could barely speak. "Nothin else matters...you hear? Nothin!"

"He's right, Heck." I said nervously. "First things first. We'll get back at him later."

"Thunderin jackass!" Heck shouted as he looked over his shoulder toward the South Haven players, ignoring us completely. "You bleedin, thunderin jackass!" he said again so the Gill could hear.

I heard the Gill laugh again, and I was afraid Heck would go after him right then and there, and was relieved when he didn't.

Jacob's shoulder was dislocated. You could see it by the bulge where his loosened arm bone pushed out against the skin. Doc said it was one of the most painful injuries you could have and I believed him. As Teetzel was telling us which play to run next, I heard Jacob moan loudly and I knew Doc was trying to work the bone back into place—I couldn't look.

The official blew his whistle, and we ran onto the field with Cunningham in for Jacob.

The rooters were screaming like crazy as the line formed and I called the signals and took the snap. I faked a handoff to Baushke as he and Cunningham flew past me to the left. When the defense was solidly committed I tossed it to Bridgman, who hesitated for a split second longer before snapping the ball under his arm and tearing wide around the right end for the touchdown.

In an instant, orange and black was everywhere. The rooters howled with delight while waving their hats and ribbons and shaking hands with one another. Baushke kicked the pigskin through the goal to make the score 6 to 0.

We kicked to South Haven and they came at us hard. But we were determined to rub their faces in the dirt for what they did to Jacob and we stopped them cold. The ball went over to us and I called for a series of short line bucks that got us nowhere. That's when I began to get worried, but then I spotted a weakness in the South Haven line—their left tackle was beginning to line up wide, probably in anticipation of a Bridgman end run. I sent Cunningham to the fellow's inside and he punched through for a magnificent twenty-yard run. Then Baushke ran for six more and Busby made eight on an end-around play. That's when I put the fellows into a tackle-back formation and gave the ball to the Iron Man.

The Iron Man was a slow runner, but I decided to try him out for short yardage, and it worked. He lumbered three or four yards on each of the next two downs, and on the third, he dragged a couple of South Haven players for a touchdown, my first without Jacob. I was so thrilled I leaped three or four times while throwing both fists into the air. The rooters were still clapping as we lined up to attempt the point-after goal.

Baushke kicked the ball through the goalposts and then Handy heaved. The crowd cheered them both.

Unfortunately, our second touchdown put new energy into the South Haven players. They held us for downs, but then we held them and they held us. The game seesawed back and forth like that for a long time. We should have been doing better, but I simply wasn't calling the plays that would keep us moving the ball forward. Frustration was becoming my enemy. I missed Jacob's play selections along with his ability to carry the ball out of danger whenever things got especially tough. Bridgman tried to fill the gap, but it wasn't the same.

To make matters worse, the game was getting rougher by the minute. Players on both sides were pushing and shoving longer after the whistle was blown. Heck used every opportunity to attack the Gill, which also caused our playing to suffer. Finally, when both of them were tangled up in the pile, the Gill kicked

him in the face with the flat of his shoe. Saw it myself. I also saw
Heck's eyes roll into the back of his head until there was nothing
but white. The officials pulled us off the pile and there he was, his
limp body so scraped and smeared with mud that he looked like a
warrior's corpse. But then Doc came out and brought him around
with the smelling salts. After sitting up for a minute, Owens and
Clyne, both scrubs, came out and helped him off the field. Jones
came in to play left guard and Lee shifted to center.

We got nowhere on our next two plays. They stopped us on the
third play too, but the South Haven fullback took a gut hit from
Ossignac and had the wind knocked out of him. The referee called
time.

We walked to the bench sweating and breathing hard without
the normal applause from the supporters. They were worried—I
was too. A two-touchdown lead was nothing to be confident
about, especially with the Grahams sitting on the bench. Teetzel
was just getting ready to scold us for fighting when the band began
to play a rousing rendition of "A Hot Time in the Old Town
Tonight." Without hesitation, Bridgman grabbed hold of Baushke
and pulled him onto the field where the two of them began waltz-
ing in wide, sweeping circles. First the rooters laughed and then
they cheered. So did we. Teetzel finally yelled for them to stop,
which they finally did, but even he couldn't resist laughing. It was
one of the funniest damn things I'd ever seen.

After Teetzel scolded us for fighting, we took the field and
made the first down, which inspired me to step up the pace.
Behind the running of Bridgman and Cunningham, we finally
planted the ball on the seven-yard line. Using the guards-back formation, Baushke carried it across for the third touchdown of the
day, but then he missed the goal attempt. The half was called
shortly after with the score at 17 to 0.

We were sweating and breathing hard from the fast playing,
and it felt wonderful to wash the cotton from our mouths with
cold dippers of water. At that point, I decided to risk the bellyache and swallowed two or three mouthfuls. Then we walked to
a grassy spot away from the field where some of us sat while others laid down. Doc began cleaning dirt from our worst cuts and

scrapes with cheap whiskey, which he used in place of rubbing alcohol—allowed him the convenience to drink while working. He stopped the bleeding with silver nitrate or with cat-gut stitches. Heck was fairly alert and Jacob's shoulder was set, but they were a sad-looking pair sitting together on the grass wrapped in blankets. Heck looked especially bad.

The Gill's cleats had left a waffle-iron pattern of black and blue smudges on the side of his face, some of them deep enough to be trickling blood. He was definitely done for the day. And even if he'd been fit to play, which neither he nor Jacob were, the rules wouldn't allow it.

We continued to sip water as Doc patched us and Teetzel talked about the mistakes of the first half and formulated strategies for the second. He was mad as hell about our pushing and shoving and fighting—said it gave the game a bad name. Called it "hooligan football." When he finished berating us, we walked back to the field and ran through some light conditioning routines while the band played "We Won't Go Home Till Morning."

It still looked like rain, but all we'd had till then was sprinkles.

The second half started with a bang and immediately got rougher, if you can believe that. The South Haven boys played the slugging game for all it was worth, and though we tried to avoid hitting back, they finally got us riled to the point that bare-knuckles fighting began to break out after each play. I resisted for awhile, but I finally got so damn mad that even I started throwing punches. Eventually we could barely get a play off without being penalized for slugging. Some of the rooters made it worse by egging us on, and more than once the game almost turned into a brawl. But to their credit, the officials aggressively kept us pushed apart and eventually settled us down to where we could play out the clock.

Baushke and Bridgman each scored one more touchdown, making the final score 29 to 0.

We left the field without congratulating the South Haven players, and for good reason. It probably would've turned into a fight. Instead, we climbed into the bus and followed behind the band as they marched back to town, drumming and playing "The Dutch

Companie," with our supporters walking in a herd behind and on either side. They were loud and praising, and some of them were calling us the "Half-a-Point-a-Minute" team. Most of us leaned out the windows, which had no glass back then, and talked with friends and family members—a couple of the Football Sisters doted on me, the star quarterback.

The bus carried us to the hotel where we washed and tended to our cuts and scrapes. Then we changed into our street clothes and met the rooters at the depot where more congratulations were heaped upon us, especially from the gamblers. Shorty Blake was one of the more vociferous. He won seventeen dollars and was so pleased that he pledged three dollars to Miss Fitzgerald's high school basketball team.

Gambling money tainted with blood from her students would rub Miss Fitzgerald the wrong way, Shorty knew that. We all did. But money was needed, and Principal McClelland would see that it was duly accepted.

By the time we rolled into Benton Harbor it was dinnertime and the rain was falling in sheets. We scrambled from the train and crowded beneath the depot overhang while the carriages and rigs assembled to take us home. By then, our bruises and black eyes were well formed and colorful, sure signs that we'd be a rough-looking bunch at school Monday morning. But we didn't care. We were happy, and we accepted our injuries without complaint.

Personally, I was riding the clouds.

My playing had not been great, and the game was anything but clean, but I played much better than I did a week earlier. And I was especially excited because I played most of the game without Jacob. I actually thanked him for getting injured. But then I quickly told him he had my permission to heal up and rejoin the team. That's because our next challenger was Grand Rapids High, and I couldn't imagine going against them without Jacob.

Chapter 12

G rand Rapids was already a big city in 1903, and in our minds
that meant their high school football team was big too. We
were scheduled to play them the Saturday following our trip to
South Haven, and in spite of our two blistering victories, I was
anything but confident we could win. Teetzel was in Chicago on
Monday taking care of some business related to his law practice,
and Jacob was in charge of the afternoon's practice. His shoulder
was bound up in a sling, but it didn't soften his determination to
get us ready for Saturday's game.

In fact, he worked us like dogs.

I may have been apprehensive about playing Grand Rapids, but
most of the fellows couldn't wait to get at them. They talked about
it constantly at school, each one of them bragging and boasting
about how they would pound their opponent into the mud. By
the end of practice their enthusiasm had rubbed off on me and I
actually found myself feeling cocksure right along with them.
That's why it was such a letdown when Burger met us later at the
Pastime Club to give us the bad news. Said Grand Rapids had
backed out.

We didn't know what happened until later that evening when
Monroe got hold of an article from Sunday's edition of the *Grand
Rapids Press*. It reported that the high school football team
wouldn't be playing any hard games before their annual
Thanksgiving Day game against Detroit Central High, their big
rival. We had to read between the lines a bit, but it was still pretty
damn clear—they'd chickened out.

The following day, we read another article with a quote from their team manager, a fellow named Markoff, that proved us right:

Benton Harbor has one of the strongest teams in Michigan. They have already beaten the Kershaw Club 40 to 0, and the big Purdue varsity team only beat the Kershaws 36 to 0. In addition, Benton Harbor defeated South Haven's heavy eleven 29 to 0. They are distinctly out of our class just now.

Cancellation aside, that was one hell of a compliment. And it was good to hear an opposing team manager talk about us in such a glowing manner. But it also meant we'd be without a game that Saturday, and that was bad. We needed to play.

Burger immediately went to work and managed to get us a match with the high school team from Elkhart, Indiana. We played them in 1902 and had an easy 10 to 0 win, but their manager argued they were much improved since then and would give us a good run. We reasoned there might be something to that claim because of their recent 6 to 0 win over South Bend.

Our game with Elkhart would be an exhibition game, which meant the playing would be easier and less dangerous—good practice for me. There were other advantages, too. We could lose and not hurt our chances for winning the state championship, and because Elkhart was located just across the state line, we wouldn't have to pay a lot of money in train fees to get them here. We'd also save money by not having to pay for a referee sanctioned by the State Athletic Committee—all formal interscholastic games required the participation of one such official. They came from the University of Michigan Athletic Department and were expensive. Bill Machesney, our former coach, was visiting Benton Harbor that weekend and agreed to act as referee.

Just because Grand Rapids canceled didn't mean we got a break in our training. Teetzel was back on Tuesday and worked us hard, mostly with an eye toward improving our wind, but he also had us play two twenty-minute halves against the scrubs. Afterwards at the Pastime Club, he required each of us to present two written criticisms of our performance against South Haven. Individual mistakes, overall team mistakes, and the spirit in which the contest was played were all fair game.

Teetzel read through our comments while we were getting our rubdowns and afterwards commented on their merits. He added helpful suggestions where he saw fit, and of course he harangued us for what he called "ungentlemanly" conduct. That's when Caully, who was in the locker room picking up towels, felt the need to intervene.

"Come on, Coach!" he said in his gravelly voice. Teetzel stopped talking and politely let him speak. "I was present at Saturday's game, and by the looks a things, your boys need *more* trainin with their fists, not *less!*"

"Now Mr. Bourke," Teetzel said politely. "You know well enough that fisticuffs are not part of football."

"Yes sir, I certainly do. But ya can't be lettin the other fellows box your men right outta the game."

"Thank you for your opinion, Mr. Bourke," Teetzel added. By then Lee, Heck, and a few others were nodding their heads in approval. "But I have commanded them to walk away from any player who tries to pick a fight."

"That's ridiculous," Caully continued. "With your permission, I'd be willin to have a talk with Bert Burger bout a trainin program for the team."

"Boxing is great sport." Teetzel replied. "But it has no role in football."

Caully skulked out of the room defeated, and we all had a good chuckle. Teetzel too. But then he resumed his lecture and told us in no uncertain terms that fighting must be eliminated from our strategy. He demanded we put our energy into playing the game according to the rules.

Wednesday night we concentrated on signal practice while the scrubs lined up against St. Joe. The scrubs were scheduled to play the farm boys from Twelve Corners on Saturday before our game with Elkhart, and I suspected Spud Wadsworth would be in the lineup.

In the end, I think it worked out just fine that Grand Rapids canceled like they did—we needed the breathing room. Jacob especially needed time to heal. Suddenly, we had a week without an interscholastic game, which meant we could start preparing that much sooner for the Kalamazoo game scheduled for the following Saturday. They were expected to be very tough.

The only real fun we had that week was Thursday night at a party thrown for us by the Graham sisters. But before I tell you about that, I should mention the debate Teetzel had with Miss Fitzgerald.

After our first two victories, Teetzel had become a popular man around Bungtown. He was in demand for luncheons and dinner parties and other such meetings, either as a guest or a speaker. The tangle he got into with Miss Fitzgerald happened at a meeting of the Delphi Society, which was an oratorical club for high school girls. Emily Fitzgerald was their advisor.

The meeting was held on Wednesday morning the week of the Elkhart game, and the featured speakers were Principal McClelland, Professor Righter, and Coach Teetzel. The girls told me later that McClelland's speech was a humorous collection of anecdotes from his own high school life while Righter's concerned the world's latest engineering triumphs. Teetzel gave a chalk talk. And that's where it got interesting.

Teetzel started his speech by reviewing the history of football. He explained how the game was played in old England where entire villages sometimes engaged in competitions that often lasted for days. Back then, they used an inflated pig bladder for a ball. Then he outlined the game's evolution from rugby to American football, which was fine, at least until he criticized the people who opposed the game for being wrong about the brutality. That wasn't fine with Miss Fitzgerald.

"Mr. Teetzel," she interrupted. "I presume you have read the most recent edition of the *North American Review?*"

"Are you referring to President Merrill's article?" Teetzel asked. Merrill was the president of Colgate University.

"Yes...the one in which he makes seven objections to the argument that football is good sport."

"I have read it, Miss Fitzgerald, but..."

"Then you wouldn't mind if we discuss the article now...in front of the girls? It might be informative for them."

"As you wish," he said, nodding his head in deference.

Miss Fitzgerald walked to the front of the room and stood about ten feet to Teetzel's left. "Dr. Merrill's first objection concerns player safety. He makes the point that twenty-five boys were killed last year while playing football and more than eighty were seriously injured. How, Mr. Teetzel, could you call a game with that fatality rate good sport?"

"There are injuries associated with all sports," Teetzel said. "In fact, I can name other games that are rougher and more brutal than football. Boxing is one example, and rugby another. Watching football players pile on top of one another may appear unduly harsh, but the boys are seldom injured to any great extent. When you see a player writhing on the ground in apparent agony, he is probably buying wind for his teammates. The players are all protected, and aside from a few sprains and bruises, which usually work themselves out with exercise, they seldom bear any marks or injuries a week later."

"But deaths are occurring, Mr. Teetzel."

"Yes, they are. But they also occur in professions like fire protection, life-saving, seafaring...railroading."

"But Mr. Teetzel, those are occupations that typically do not employ children and are dedicated to the good of society, which justify the risks. But such risks should not be part of good sport."

"The fatalities associated with football occur for three reasons," Teetzel replied, unwilling to concede to her argument. "They occur because of poorly prepared players, poorly equipped players, and the refusal of some officials to penalize unnecessary roughness."

"But can any game that requires such extraordinary attention for the mere preservation of life be good sport?" Miss Fitzgerald said, her eyes meeting his.

"Yes," Teetzel said. "If the rules are enforced."

"But the rules are precisely what we are talking about."

"Excuse me?"

"The very nature of the game, Mr. Teetzel."

"Please make your point, Miss Fitzgerald."

"Thank you," she said before pausing to collect her thoughts. "President Merrill argues that skill has very little chance against brawn and that the team with the largest players will always win the game."

"I am aware that your point is the opinion among the anti-football critics at large, and were it not for strategy, the point would be well taken. But strategy can and does have a great influence on the outcome of the game, and so does the speed of the players."

"But how fair is a game that stops strategy by opposition and interference?"

"Do you mean blocking and tackling, Miss Fitzgerald?"

"Yes. In other words, what other sport denies the participant a fair chance to complete his task? The baseball batter does not have his bat lassoed by the other team just before swinging at the ball, and the pole vaulter is not shoved as he prepares to jump."

"Let me…"

"In other words, Mr. Teetzel," she continued. "Is it good sport when an athlete's skill is not allowed to attain its highest possible result?

"Miss Fitzgerald, are you not the coach for the girl's basketball team?"

"I am."

"Is it not interference when one of your girls has the ball blocked while she is shooting? And is there not a time clock that effectively ends the play for the team that is in sight of scoring?"

Miss Fitzgerald had been so determined to advance President Merrill's arguments that she failed to see the hole she was digging for herself, at least until she fell in. And then she recovered.

"Why yes…there is," she said. "But in basketball there is not as much effort put into each individual point. Why, for instance, is the time clock used to stop the team that is in sight of a touchdown, which makes their effort up to that point worthless? Why not permit the second half to begin where the first half ends? Or why not use a system of credit where the advantages won in the first half are applied to the final result of the game?"

"Miss Fitzgerald," Teetzel said. "Both teams have equal opportunities to possess the ball at the half. It depends upon the skill of the players."

"Skill, Mr. Teetzel? To what result? How fair is it for a player who has fought nearly to the end of the game to be removed? For reasons of good sport, would it not be better to let the exhausted man die on the field, or collapse from weakness, than to introduce fresh players? Could it not be argued that the team using the most substitutes will win?"

"All team sports use substitutes, Miss Fitzgerald. It can be no other way. And in football, they are used sparingly, usually when a player is exhausted to the point where he can no longer continue."

"But who makes that determination? Correct me if I am wrong, but I believe there is no rule against the number of players a team can use."

"Yes, you are correct, but..."

"Again, I go back to my point about brawn. It seems that the team with the largest players along with the best substitutes will win the game."

"Size is important, but so is training, strategy, and the overall speed of the players."

To end their discussion, both of them made a final statement. Miss Fitzgerald argued that football was not a sport at all, but a lesson in war that relied on unfair tactics and advantages. In her opinion, the violence should be an awakening call for all parents who are concerned about the mental and physical health of their children. She believed they should not allow their boys to play football nor should they let their daughters watch it. And she supported her view with the argument that any game requiring the presence of surgeons was not good sport. Teetzel, on the other hand, maintained that football was the best American sport of all. He believed it was near perfect. In his mind, the only necessary changes had nothing to do with altering the rules, just enforcing them.

Some of the girls told me later they thought Teetzel was magnificent. They said he was handsome, calm, and polite, and he made the stronger argument. They said Miss Fitzgerald was more emotional, but they conceded she also made some good points.

Another reason Miss Fitzgerald was against football, other than the injuries to the players, concerned the effect it had on the student body in general. Our classmates were almost as crazy about it as us players, which worried most teachers back then. They'd never seen anything like it. During football season, the students were consumed with following their team and hardly talked about anything else—including their studies.

Imagine that.

Chapter 13

W ithout a doubt, we liked parties. And one of the best that season was thrown by Jacob's sisters, Eva and Lila. It was held at
Lila's small two-story clapboard house on the corner of Niles and
Monroe the Thursday before the Elkhart game. The girls spent the
day cooking and decorating the inside of the home with orange
and black pennants, streamers, and little footballs. By six o'clock,
the downstairs was bulging with people, mostly players, but also a
number of schoolmates and Football Sisters. Teetzel arrived with Al
Clark of the *Evening News*.

The sun was dipping into the tree line when a group of girls
dragged us outside to play some running games. We humored
them and actually had a pretty good time. Afterwards, we went
back inside and found the dining room table groaning with food.
There was an oyster casserole, a peppercorn ham and a special roast
turkey with hickory-nut dressing. The air was especially thick with
the scent of ham. There were also side dishes of mashed potatoes,
baked acorn squash, cinnamon apples, baked beans in molasses, and
cat-head biscuits. We sat wherever we could find a space, which
meant the floor for some of us.

Lila said there were four courses. I suppose that meant they
brought the food out four different times, but truth be known, I
didn't know where one course ended and the next one began, and
I didn't really care. The food was good and that's all that mattered.
For dessert, we had our choice of apple, pumpkin, or steaming hot
mince pie.

Then the fun really began.

Carrie Krieger, who was one of the Football Sisters, announced that Clyde Miller would give a temperance speech. Clyde was a classmate of ours and a do-gooder. He'd jumped on the prohibition bandwagon at the urging of his mother, who was active in the movement. He wasn't much of a football enthusiast, which made me wonder from the beginning why he was even there, and when I asked Jacob about it, he just shrugged his shoulders and said he didn't know. After Carrie made her announcement, we knew she must have invited him. She was a prohibition do-gooder too, but at least she had a reason. Her father was a drunk, and I felt sorry for her about that. But I also felt that our party was not the place to give a speech about the evils of alcohol.

Nevertheless, we went into the parlor and sat down, most of us on the floor while others stood in both doorways. Jacob's sisters seemed uneasy, probably because of us, on account of how boisterous we could be without warning. I guess they were afraid Clyde's speech would set us off.

Clyde stood in the middle of the room and talked about statistics and battered wives and about children who went hungry because their fathers drank up their paychecks. Good points, all of them, but his delivery stunk. He was preachy and arrogant, and he obviously felt he was surrounded by a flock of boys teetering on the very edge of depravity. After a few minutes of listening, I disliked him—even his looks. He was tall and thin as a twig and wearing a suit, which was okay, we were all wearing suits. But instead of a regular necktie like the rest of us, he had on one of those old-fashioned flowing bows that we considered effeminate.

I feel safe in declaring the rest of the fellows were in agreement with me. Personally, I'd have welcomed a tornado to make him stop, but then something even better happened.

Bridgman.

Clyde was in mid-sentence when Bridgman rose out of his chair and stood in front of him with one eye closed. Then he opened the other one real wide, like he was possessed. He reminded me of one of those lathered-up camp meeting preachers we sometimes watched for fun when they sermoned in their big tents at the fairgrounds. That stopped Clyde altogether. Then his eyes got big as saucers and his face flushed—he had no idea how to recover. Meanwhile, I couldn't contain myself and began to snicker along with the rest of the fellows.

Al Clark took out a small notepad and began scribbling as Bridgman started to orate. This is how it played out in the next day's paper:

> "Brothers," said he, with a glarified gaze in his lamp. "Brothers. This is the happiest moment of my life. For years—fifteen I think—I have longed for this moment to arrive. Brothers, I do not wish to preach to you but merely to caution you to be temperate in all things. Fellow members, it has wrung my heart to witness your errors and shortcomings. How many times have I told Biffy Lee not to slug when the referee wasn't looking! How many times have I told Dice Baushke to let a sweater alone when its owner has it marked for himself! How often have I implored Butts Lester to stop talking in a game so we can hear the signals!
>
> "Brothers, this is an age of degeneracy and you're a lot of apes. I did not begin my modest effort with the intention of telling the truth, gentleman. No temperance orator does.
>
> "But I find that I am not sufficiently hardened, murder must out, and I repeat my former statement, you're a lot of apes and if..."

Bridgman never finished that last sentence because Butts jumped him and the rest of us followed. Guests scrambled out of the way as our whirling mass of legs and arms tumbled from the parlor to the dining room and back again. Bridgman fought hard, but we finally wrestled him to the floor and piled on, leaving the room in shambles with a toppled coal stove and a broken window.

Everyone was laughing uproariously except for Carrie and Clyde. They were so put off that they got their things together and left. But we didn't care. I couldn't remember when I'd had a better laugh. I also couldn't believe Clyde had the guts to speak about abstinence to a boisterous bunch of football players. I thought he deserved the trouble he got from Bridgman.

After making our apologies to the Graham sisters, we put the coal stove back into place and pasted a piece of newspaper over the broken window. Then we took turns giving speeches of our own. Teetzel gave one too, but none were as good as Bridgman's. His was ace high. Finally, a group of students from the school band played some music, marches mostly.

The guests were gone by 8:30 except for me, Bridgman, and the Iron Man. Jacob's sisters were working on the dishes, along with Heck, who they bribed with another piece of apple pie. The rest of us sat on the back steps and talked. It was a clear, cold night. Autumn was in the air, and the stars were brighter than I'd ever seen them.

"Too bad you won't be playing Saturday," I said to Jacob. I was feeling better about my quarterbacking skills but still would have been more confident with him there.

"Yeah," he replied while chewing a smoke-hole in the end of a five-cent Creamo cigar. "The coach thinks I need to put in some more time letting my shoulder heal. But I'd be there, Fletch, if I thought you needed me."

Of course I need you, I said to myself—I never would have said it out loud.

Bridgman was also smoking a cigar, and the smell was strong in the cool night air. "Besides," Jacob said, "those Hoosiers aren't much at football anyway."

"Yeah," Lathe added, "won't be nothin to it."

"Just keep your head cool at all times," Jacob said. "And don't get hurt. There's no one else who knows the plays like you do."

"Yeah," Bridgman said, "you get hurt...and we have to get Wadsworth to come out." Jacob shot him a hard look.

"Something you're not telling me?" I asked. There was a long silence.

"Tell him, Jacob," Bridgman finally said. "Hell, he practically runs this team. He ought to know."

"Yeah...maybe you're right."

"What are you thunderin jackasses talkin about?" Heck said as he came out the back door. "Feels like a wake or somethin."

"Cap it, Heck," Jacob said. He puffed on the Creamo and then began to talk. "Some of the board members are afraid we'd be in big trouble if you got hurt...being there's no backup quarterback."

Jacob knew about the thinking of the board members because he went to all their meetings. The team captain was part of the team management back then.

"What about Ludwig?" I said.

"Mit's alright," Bridgman said. "But he's more a lineman than a quarter."

I felt my heart drop into my stomach. Spud Wadsworth had suddenly become the potential grim reaper of my football career, the one who would steal my coveted place on the team. I was immediately flushed with anger for having been so unsure of myself. But I didn't know what to say.

Then Jacob spoke again. "Billy, Monroe, and Ben Curry are pushing for Teetzel to talk with Wadsworth. But the coach is dead set against it...says Wadsworth isn't eligible since he's not in school. They had one hell of a fight over the deal."

"Yeah," Bridgman said, "but they say they'll get him to enroll."

"But that's still against the rules," I said, seeing a glimmer of hope.

"It is," Jacob said. "But they know the State Athletic Committee'd likely overlook it if they ever found out."

"Hell, Fletch," Lathe said, "you're fussin over nothin anyway. Wadsworth's never been on the field with the likes of us before. Once we give him a good goin over, he probably won't stay around."

"That may be," Jacob said. "But Teetzel and the board members are plannin' to be at Eastman Springs Saturday to watch him play with Twelve Corners against the scrubs."

"True," Lathe conceded. "But I'll betcha Teetzel ain't done with this fight. You know how honest he is."

"Whatever it takes to win," I finally said, remembering the oath we made about beating Ishpeming. "I'm part of this machine and I'm here to do whatever it takes to win. Even if that means having Wadsworth on the team."

"That's right, Fletch." Jacob said. "We're a team...and we have to let things take their natural course."

I was acting like the good team player, but on the inside I was sick. Teetzel was against having Wadsworth on the team on the grounds that it was illegal for a player to start school that late in the season, but I also knew the board members would put a lot of pressure on him. That was the way things were done, especially with Billy.

"Hey, Jacob," Bridgman said, after blowing a smoke ring toward the stars. "Heard anything from your old man?"

"Naw. Don't expect to, either."

"You talk to anyone out there about him?"

"Yeah, I talked with Ben Purnell himself. But he won't say much, just that he's travelin in the south somewhere preachin the Israelite gospel."

"Hell's bells," Heck said. "You know damn well Purnell's a flim-flam man. You won't get much out of that lyin, thievin son of a whore. And you know I'm right, Bridget."

"Maybe so," said Bridgman. "But don't you think your old man should have told your ma where he was going?"

"They don't talk anymore," Jacob said.

"Shouldn't he have told you then?"

"Yeah...he should have...and that does bother me," Jacob continued, but then he stopped and took a long draw on his cigar before completing his thought. "We're on good speakin terms and it seems he would've said somethin."

"It's most likely," Heck said, "that Purnell told Pa not to say anything because of all the secrets he's supposed to have."

"Maybe so," Jacob said. "But I still don't like it. It's just not like the old man to do somethin like that."

"What about your ma?" I asked.

"She's sellin the farm," Heck said. "Be movin in here with Lila and her husband."

"She'll be better off for it," Jacob added. "She never liked the country much anyhow."

That was the first I'd heard about Hutcheon Graham leaving town to preach for the House of David. But it didn't surprise me. He was from Northern Ireland, and he brought some serious religion with him to America. One of the first things he did when he got to Benton Harbor was to build a small Episcopal church on Pipestone Road. But I also think it was Hutcheon Graham's passion for the Lord that made Jacob and Heck see it the other way. They weren't religious at all and never went to church. Claimed they had no use for it.

While the Grahams distanced themselves from the Lord, I was considering a better relationship. In fact, with Wadsworth breathing down my neck, I planned to pray extra hard in church Sunday.

Game day finally arrived and we slaughtered Elkhart 41 to 0. The Indiana boys fought hard and held us for downs a few times, but they never really had a chance. If it hadn't been for two of their players, Wilkinson and Darling, the crowd would have lost interest before the end of the first half. Wilkinson played fullback and was a great punter, while Darling was the quarterback. His interference on offense was first-rate, and on defense he sometimes broke our blocking and nailed the runner so well our own rooters cheered him.

For us, it was Bridgman and Dice Baushke who carried the day, with Bridgman gaining the most ground and putting on the best show. When interference started around the right end, the crowd knew he was the probable ball carrier and immediately went up on their tiptoes and howled like Indians. He seldom disappointed them. He made at least fifteen brilliant hurdles and scored four touchdowns.

Baushke played faster than he'd ever played before and kicked four goals, all with an injury he received early in the game when he single-handedly tried to stop an Elkhart ball carrier being pushed by three of his teammates. The play was a textbook mass play. He grabbed the fellow but was overpowered and went down. But even then he refused to let go and was dragged, stomped, and kicked to a bloody pulp before we were able to make the tackle. The referee called for a time-out and Dice got up and stumbled with a bruised hip to the sideline where Doc wiped the blood from his face and arms. Then he quickly cauterized the worst gashes with a stick of silver nitrate and slapped on a few pieces of black tape before the game restarted.

By the fourth quarter Dice could barely walk. Teetzel finally called for him to come out of the game, but he refused, and Teetzel called again. Dice begged to stay in, which is when some of the fellows tried to help him from the field, but he broke away and limped back to take his place behind the line and the rooters went wild. Machesney, who was the referee, finally said he wouldn't start the game until Baushke left the field, which is when he finally walked over to the bench and sat down mad as hell. The crowd cheered him one final time.

Ossignac, at left tackle, also did well that afternoon. His blocking was great, and he made some good gains running from the line. Lee played well at guard until he was injured and had to be pulled from the game. He pleaded with tears in his eyes to stay in, but Teetzel again held his ground and put Jones in his place. Jones ran well with the ball but was weak on defense.

The lineman of the day was the Iron Man. He carried the ball numerous times around Lester's end for five- and ten-yard gains and scored twice. His first touchdown was a five-yard, tackle-through-tackle play where he dragged a half-dozen Elkhart players over the line with him. His strength was astonishing. With a little more speed, he'd have been impossible to stop.

Cunningham, Butts, and Busby also played flawless games. Cunningham took Jacob's place at fullback and made some spectacular line hurdles and always gained yardage when called upon. He scored one touchdown. Butts smashed his usual interference and made some great runs, and when Dice was taken out, he was moved to halfback where he played so well that Bridgman had to hustle to keep from being overshadowed. Busby kicked two goals and played great on defense. Not once did Elkhart sweep his end.

Handy played his finest game ever. Elkhart ran a play where they made a successful double pass and it was Handy who nailed the runner after chasing the fellow halfway across the field. Because of that play and a few others, we decided to stop calling him "big, fat, lumbering Handy" and to quit saying he was too slow to make a player. I should also add that it was the first game he didn't heave.

Heck also showed his hard bark. His work at center was brilliant, overshadowing the work of Bell, the famous center of the 1902 team. He also blocked one of Wilkinson's punts and roughed him up pretty good in the process. Penalties for roughing the kicker weren't even a thought back then—the mere suggestion would have been laughable. After all, the object of the game was to rough up your opponents as much as possible.

Jacob didn't play because of his lame shoulder, and he wasn't happy about that. But he shouted and cheered with the rest of the rooters and helped Teetzel with the coaching. I knew it bothered him to be on the bench, but that was the price we sometimes had to pay. The risk of getting injured was part of the deal, which reminds me of something Machesney said.

Machesney told us he had a great time that afternoon and that we were already faster than the 1902 team—all around damn impressive. He praised Teetzel for doing a good job, but said he was concerned about our high injury rate. He knew, as we all did, that we'd have to be in healthy shape to beat Kalamazoo the following Saturday and Ishpeming at the end of the season. Our injuries would heal, that was not the question. But would they heal in time?

And I didn't know if I'd be leading the team.

It's not a pleasant subject for me, but I need to mention one more thing about the Elkhart game. The best player that day didn't play for Benton Harbor or Elkhart. He played for Twelve Corners in the game against the Little Athletics, which was our name for the scrub team. He was Spud Wadsworth. His team lost 24 to 18, but he put on a brilliant show. He coached and quarterbacked his team, ran with the ball, tackled, blocked, scored all their touchdowns, and kicked the extra points. The rooters loved him. The only one who had a problem with Wadsworth was me. And it affected my playing.

Truth be told, I was the weak link in the Elkhart game.

Although it was said I ran the team faster than any Benton Harbor team in history and that I used good judgment and was cool at all times, it was anything but a flawless performance. That's because I made two fumbles, mistakes that caused more than a few critical comments from the serious enthusiasts and board members. And I couldn't blame them. Fumbles were bad news and potentially fatal. One fumble could make the difference between a win or a loss, and one interscholastic loss would mean no state championship. In the words of one old-time coach, "It was better to have died a young boy than to have fumbled this ball."

No one could figure out what happened to me but I knew— it was my apprehension over Wadsworth. I couldn't deal with the possibility he might steal my position. But that was a piss-poor excuse, you see, because all the fellows had to compete constantly with scrubs scratching tooth and nail to steal their positions. That's just the way it was. My fears about Wadsworth should have been easy to overcome—after all, I was riding the inside track. But it tied me up in knots nonetheless.

Because of my fumbles and our need for a backup quarterback, I got ready for the big push. I knew the board members would try harder than ever to get Wadsworth to come out for the team.

Chapter 14

"They wouldn't listen," Teetzel said.

We were at my folk's house sitting on the front porch after he'd attended an early evening board meeting at Burger's house. "Didn't expect they would," I replied.

A dray rumbled along the street and the shod hooves of the two Belgians made sharp, snapping sounds that split the neighborhood quiet like gunshots. It was suppertime in Bungtown, the time of day when most everyone was inside, and the only sound to be heard once the horses passed were some kids yelling in the distance.

"I told them it was against the rules to let a new player on the team this late in the season, at least when that player was not enrolled in school by October 1. But they said they didn't care about that."

I decided to cut through the bullcrap. "Wadsworth?" I asked.

"Yes...they want him on the team. Manager Burger talked to him and he's agreed to play...and to start taking classes."

"What did they say about the rules?"

"They don't care about the rules, Fletch. They pick and choose when to obey them."

I didn't know what to say. I sure as hell didn't want Wadsworth on the team, but I decided to play devil's advocate as a way to gather information.

"But it's always been done that way," I went on.

"That still doesn't mean it's right." The tone of his voice hinted frustration.

"But they want to win," I continued, "just like everyone else in this town."

"I argued that we could win with you at quarter and with Ludwig as backup. And I meant it."

"Thanks," I said, "but they don't want to take chances. They're afraid I'll get injured and the team will be left without any hope of beating Ishpeming."

"Yes, that is a possibility," he said as he juggled a stone from hand to hand. "But things have to change if football is to survive. And it's the small things, like Wadsworth, that add up to become big problems."

He was beginning to sound like Miss Fitzgerald, which I dared not say, but I felt some obligation to stand up for the local traditions.

"It's been okay every other season," I argued.

"It smells, Fletch," he said. "Pray that I'm wrong, but this decision will come back to haunt us."

"If it does, you won't be to blame."

"Yes I will," he said as he tossed the stone, "and for good reason, I'll have been responsible for letting it happen."

"No you won't," I said as the stone skittered over the sidewalk and into the street. "The board will."

"It really won't matter in the end, Fletch. What matters is who suffers, and that will be you and the rest of the team."

"I just don't see how it could happen, Coach."

"I hope you're right."

"Me too. But even though we don't exactly agree," I continued, "I want you to know that I appreciate your stopping by to tell me about Wadsworth."

"It's the least I could do. I didn't want you to hear it from someone else, but I also wanted to encourage you to keep up the good work and not give up."

"I've worked too hard to give up," I replied. I wasn't about to loose my position to some hayseed from Twelve Corners.

Teetzel stood up, brushed a smudge of dirt from his pants, and said good night. I watched as he walked the length of the sidewalk and turned north toward his uncle's house. I continued to sit on the steps and think about our conversation until I couldn't think anymore, and then I went inside, lit and adjusted the gas lamp in the parlor, and fell into my Pa's stuffed chair to stew. It wasn't ten minutes later I answered another knock at the door.

"Come outside for a minute?" Jacob said. "Got something I need to say."

The rig from Young's Dry Goods store was parked in the street out front. Jacob was working for Mr. Young part time making deliveries and had stopped by on his way back to the store after making his final run. He was wearing a white pin-striped shirt rolled up to his elbows, suspenders, and a wool newsboys cap. And he had a half-smoked cigar wedged into the corner of his mouth.

"I already heard," I said quietly. "The coach just left."

"Did he tell you the whole story?"

"I only know what he told me."

"He put up one whale of a fight, Fletch." Then he mussed my hair with his big hand, which I tried to knock away, and then he said, "I'll bet he didn't tell you that."

"He made it sound one-sided," I answered while running my fingers through my hair to force it back into place.

"It wasn't," he said as he blew a cloud of blue smoke out into the yard. "Billy acted as spokesman for the board, and he argued that only a fool wouldn't take advantage of the opportunities presented. But Teetzel stood his ground, and by meeting's end, Billy was raging harder than the devil's own blacksmith. They almost came to blows over the deal."

Billy was a short man, but he was steady and strong and not afraid to use his fists if that's what it took to get his way. Born of hard work and toil, he trusted no man to tell him how to run his business or his family. And he believed it was his sworn duty to succeed at both, regardless of the measures employed. He brought that same gut-fighter attitude to his duties as a board member.

"Harper got into one of his fits?" I asked.

"Yeah. You should a seen him. His face glowed redder than the ovens of hell, and he got so riled, I half expected to see his hair bristle up like it does on the back of a mad hog. He started bangin his iron fist on the table and threatened to send the coach back to Chicago without his money. His rage would have ground up a lesser man."

"Is that why Coach gave in?"

"Course not. He gave in because of principle. Said he was against lettin Wadsworth on the team, but that he'd promised to do his utmost to take us to the state championship. He agreed to take him if he could cut it. There was nothin I could do about it, Fletch. That's why I came by. Didn't want you hearin it from someone else."

"Wadsworth may be good," I said, "but he doesn't have the job yet."

Jacob broke into a wide grin. "Make him work for it, kid."

"You can count on it."

"Oh, and there's something else. Did the coach tell ya Arthur Baushke's comin out?"

"What?" I said in disbelief.

"Yeah. Leo's in pretty bad shape you know, because of his lame hip, so the board asked Arthur to play out the season."

"Isn't he twenty-one?" I said.

"He swore to the fact that he was still twenty, in fact he signed an affidavit to that effect. But the coach still got fightin mad on account that Baushke would also be late startin school. First Wadsworth and then Baushke...both illegal...but there was nothin he could do but let it happen."

"Baushke's a great player," I said. "It'll be good to have him back on the team."

"Amen to that."

With a quick wave of his hand, Jacob was off, bounding down the sidewalk to his rig. And there I was, left to wrestle alone with the uncertainties posed by my newest challenge.

Wadsworth and Arthur Baushke practiced with us the following Monday and Baushke fit right in. He'd already been playing organized football for a couple years, but Wadsworth was another matter. He seemed a little confused about the rules, and he also had trouble with our precision strategies.

In contrast to my small size, Wadsworth was tall—nearly six feet. He was tanned and freckled and had hair the color of tarnished copper. As an athlete, he was fearless, the kind of kid who'd bang his head against a brick wall if he thought it was the right thing to do. He was a 150-pound bundle of raw bone and muscle, but what made him most dangerous to me was his quick mind. The bastard was smart. He may have been confused in the beginning, but my gut feeling told me he'd soon be well into our plays.

We had a twenty-minute scrimmage on Wednesday, and for the final ten minutes Wadsworth played quarterback for the scrubs. I was praying for Lee or Ossignac or Lathe, anyone, to break his arm, but no one did. And it wasn't for a lack of not trying—they hammered him every chance they got. Lathe hit him so hard once I thought he'd killed him, but he staggered to his feet, brushed the dirt from his jersey, and called for the next play. "Don't you be workin too hard, Iron Man," he said sarcastically under his breath as he prepared to call the signals. "Sweat too much and your dangler might rust off."

From his three-point stance, Lathe put a finger to his nose and blew a plug of snot onto the ground. A couple of plays later, Lathe drilled Wadsworth again—and a number of times after that—but he always managed to get back on his feet. The scrubs may not have scored that day, but Wadsworth put up one hell of a fight. Without a doubt, he was tough—I felt it firsthand. He blasted me once when I was carrying the ball and I went down very hard. His attitude was cocky, but at the time I credited his cockiness to self-assurance.

Already I hated his guts.

The fellows were fair to reasonable in their confidence we could take Kalamazoo, but by mid-week I detected some undercurrents of concern among them. Jacob was expected to rejoin the team, but that was still in doubt, and Dice Baushke was definitely out because of his lame hip. Neither of them were positive developments, and the fellows were worried about it, especially about Jacob. It was probably me, still starting at quarterback, who had the most to lose if the team was hung out there without Jacob. I was already on shaky ground—thanks to my poor performance against Elkhart.

Thursday after practice, we were at the Pastime Club when Teetzel announced Butts would be taking Dice's place at right halfback while Mit Ludwig would play end. Jacob also announced that he planned to be in the lineup and I rejoiced, literally. I didn't holler out, but the fellows surely must have heard it when I made a deep sigh of relief. From that moment on, my confidence soared, and it showed during the question-and-answer period in which Teetzel quizzed us on the rules. But it showed even more when we talked strategy.

Teetzel presented a number of defensive scenarios and then asked Jacob and me to discuss how we would move the ball against them. We had to give him our proposals and then explain why they were chosen, but we also had to tell him who would carry the ball and why. Since no two players were exactly alike, he wanted us to match the talents of each individual with specific situations, whether it be for short yardage, long yardage, or for runs into the line or wide around the end. I got hard into it. In fact, Jacob and I sometimes debated at length before coming to an agreement, and sometimes we agreed only after Teetzel asked us questions that got us thinking in another direction. A few of the fellows joined in, but mostly they sat and listened. I was so engaged that I completely forgot about Wadsworth, at least until the end when Teetzel spoke to him.

"Wadsworth," he said, "I hope you listened well to this discussion."

"I did just that," he answered

"It's easy, Waddie," Bridgman interrupted, "just remember to let me carry the ball whenever there's a question."

"Remember, Mr. Bridgman," Teetzel said. Then he crossed his arms across his chest, paused, and with a reprimanding look in his eye added "You are but a cog in this machine…"

"Yes sir," Bridgman interrupted with a smile that was calculated to convey bashfulness. "That I am."

"…one who happens to be blessed," Teetzel continued, "with a strong pair of legs…I might add."

"Good for dancing!" Butts blurted out and we began to chuckle among ourselves.

"However," Teetzel went on, his voice rising above the noise. "It is fortunate for us that you are a cog that also need not worry about decisions of strategy."

That's when we really busted up. We howled and whistled and said all kinds of chiding things to Bridgman, but through it all, no one laughed harder than he did. Once Teetzel got us to calm down, he said there was one more thing he wanted to talk about. It was the Kalamazoo team—he wanted to tell us what he knew about them, which wasn't much. He said they were big and strong and very experienced, that they were fast but not quite as fast as us. He said our best hope would be to outlast them.

The meeting broke up and I went home, ate dinner with the family, and then went up to my room to study my playbook. Quizzing myself on the plays eased me considerably, and I continued to study them until I fell asleep. Don't know the time, but it was late. I vaguely remember Pa coming in to blow out the lamp.

By Friday we were solidly on track. Jacob practiced with us and everything went well, which meant the team was at near full strength again, and it was a good thing. The *Evening News* touted Saturday's game as the hardest we would play that season, and rightly so. Kalamazoo was a powerhouse with the history to back it up.

The Kalamazoo team of 1901 was led by a bear of a fellow named Shorty Longman, who was playing for the University of Michigan in 1903. Kalamazoo faced Ishpeming for the 1901 state title, and the match seesawed back and forth to make it by far the hardest of Ishpeming's three championship victories. They won 27 to 21. In 1902, we beat Kalamazoo 6 to 0 in another hard game, and they'd only lost one player since then.

They were definitely gunning for us.

At the recent South Haven game, we spotted their coach furiously writing down our play signals, which was crap, and it made some of our rooters pretty hot. Friday afternoon at the Red Cross Drug Store, Burger told a group of gamblers that one, maybe two, Kalamazoo players were illegal, and the men got hotter still. Using unauthorized players always made the opposing rooters furious, but I don't know why. Most teams broke the rules that way. We did it with the addition of Wadsworth and Arthur Baushke, and no one except Teetzel said a word about it. The board obviously felt they were operating within the acceptable limits of cheating.

Our game with Kalamazoo High School was pivotal in deciding the high school champions of Western Michigan. The state's sportswriters had picked both of us to be contenders for the lower Michigan title, and most agreed it was anyone's call who would emerge on top. The victor would play the survivor of the Manistee–Traverse City–Muskegon mauling, and that winner would meet the champions of eastern Michigan.

In those days, high school football was like a game of high-stakes poker. Every move counted, whether it was negotiating for home field advantage, hustling for positive newspaper reporting, or conducting psychological warfare against your opponents. One blink and you could be in serious trouble. With Kalamazoo, we blinked first. During the negotiations, Kalamazoo's team manager was adamant about playing the game there. Burger fought hard and offered good money, but finally had to give. We would not have home field advantage.

A rally was held Friday evening. Walter Banyon called the meeting to order with a short speech in which he praised us for our determination to win the state title, and then he thanked the local businessmen for their support, which he said was the best ever. He commended Mayor Gillette for donating twenty-five dollars and said we needed more such help from the citizens. Next, Jacob gave a short speech and was followed by Principal McClelland leading the students in a series of new yells.

Cards with the words printed on them were passed out and McClelland went through them one at a time. He'd recite the lines by himself and then lead the students, who were timid and unsure on the first go-around, but by the second or third time were shaking the Armory to its foundations. Each yell was handled in like fashion until they'd gone through them all. Then they went through the Benton Harbor standards, including the famous "Locomotive Yell," which didn't need to be practiced but was included anyway because it was fun.

Rah! Rah! Rah! Rah! Ben-ton Har-bor
Rah! Rah! Rah! Rah! Ben-ton Har-bor
Rah! Rah! Rah! Rah! Ben-ton Har-bor

R-a-a-a-h!
Konachee! Konachee! Konachee!
Konachee!
Konachee! Konachee! Konachee!
Heigh O! Heigh O!
Boom-ta-lack
High School! High School!
Orange and Black!

The "rah rah rah rah" portion of the cheer started out slowly and then got faster with each succeeding line. By the third series of rah's the chant was supposed to sound like a locomotive, which it did when performed with sufficient vigor.

Our cheers were short back then, but they were pretty impressive when hundreds of rooters yelled them at the top of their lungs. Unison was the key. Early in the season, some of the board members said the students should practice their yells each night after school to become more proficient, and it was even suggested the girls try yelling at a lower pitch to blend with the boys. They didn't, and it didn't matter. In the end, the raw desire was more than enough to get the job done. I think I speak for all of us, and by that I mean the other players, when I say rooter enthusiasm was at its all-time strongest that night.

An hour later, the rally was over and the rooters took their cheering cards with them, which they were expected to bring to the game and yell their hearts out. Few, if any, would forget. Hard chastising would be heaped upon those who did.

It was Saturday morning, October 17, and a little before nine o'clock when I arrived at the depot with my family. We joined a small group of students and other rooters standing on the wood-planked platform, which was wet and shiny from an early downpour, but I very quickly slipped away and went to a spot about twenty feet away where the team was assembling. The boarding had yet to begin, so we all stood and talked. Standing between the two groups was Deputy Sheriff Pearl, a likeable take-charge sort of fellow who was one of the county's hardest-working lawmen. He was wearing a wide-brimmed hat, a patterned vest, and a dark gray frock coat. I couldn't see his pistol, but I knew it was probably there somewhere.

Standing tall with one hand on his hip and the other gesturing, the deputy was alternately talking to the waiting passengers and bellowing orders to the baggage handlers. He was telling the passengers about his ordeal securing a ticket.

Deputy Pearl said he'd been at the depot since three o'clock that morning waiting for the ticket window to open, which seemed hard to believe. But tickets were limited and I suppose he wanted to be damn sure he got one. Then again, he might have told that to the missus as an excuse to keep from going home after working the night shift, probably to have a nip or two with some night-owls over a friendly hand of poker. I noticed he had a ticket safely in hand, but my suspicions seemed confirmed, first when I detected a slur in his speech and second when I caught the incriminating glint of a silver whiskey flask protruding from his hip pocket.

It was a little past 9:30 when the Rooter Special Number Two steamed out of Benton Harbor. Over four hundred of us were on board, including the team members, the band, and mascot Willie Busby. Mounds of gray clouds hovered just above the treetops while the fields and valleys were infused with a thin, rolling blanket of mist, but nothing could dampen our spirits. We were determined to have a good time regardless of the weather, and we did, at least until we hit the uneven stretch of rail bed running between Hartford and Lawton.

The big ten-wheeler and its six wooden coaches constantly banged and rattled and swayed from side to side, even at the level places. It got so bad, some of the passengers opened the windows and hung their heads out to keep from getting sick. The smell of cigars was bothersome, but so were the burnt oil fumes that filtered into the air from the lamps swinging on their chains. After Lawton, the tracks mercifully became smoother, and we eased into Kalamazoo a little before noon.

We disembarked from the cars and were met by some Benton Harbor girls who were attending the local seminary. I didn't recognized a one of them. Others obviously did by they way they hugged and talked and carried on. Folks were standing around in small clumps rearranging coats, umbrellas, and satchels when the call went out for us to form a parade line behind Billy Harper and the band. A wagon and a team of draft horses carrying our gear brought up the rear.

Professor Null struck up the band and we marched loud and happy through downtown Kalamazoo. We did a lot of chanting, and at each block the locals swarmed to doors and windows to see what the hell was going on. When we passed the Kalamazoo House, which was the headquarters for the local representatives, the occupants rushed to the front porch to have a look at us. A man standing out front on the sidewalk turned to his wife and said, "What do you think of a town that will turn out a crowd like that on a rainy day to see a football game!"

"I'd say they were crazy," she replied.

She was right about that. We were crazy.

While we checked into our hotel to change, the rooters ducked into the nearest restaurants for lunch. Then they regrouped and walked to Recreation Park where the playing grounds were located and found the Kalamazoo rooters already in place in the north bleachers. A bank of girls, each one holding a red and white banner, was positioned in front of them. Our rooters were impressed.

Our rooters climbed into the south bleachers and ambled around until they were settled comfortably among friends. Senator and Mrs. Burrows were at the park and surprised everyone when they drove their carriage to our side of the field and parked. There was a rumor the senator was promised the Benton Harbor vote if he'd root for us. I can't say if any such promise was made or not, but it wouldn't have surprised me.

The Benton Harbor gamblers were also busy.

From the moment we struck town, the gamesmen were looking for Kalamazoo money. Many of them quickly disappeared into the seedier districts looking for gaming houses, pool parlors, and such, and most didn't reappear until just before the kickoff. But apparently Kalamazoo was not much of a gambling town. The gamblers said they had to fight for what little money they could find, and even then there were few willing to place an even bet. Kalamazoo was asking odds of 2 to 1 on the final outcome, but those odds were eventually doubled. Immediately before the game, there were offers of 10 to 3 that Kalamazoo would not score.

It was a quarter to three when the Kalamazoo team ran on the field, and their rooters cheered them long and hard. Then we trotted into view from the southeast, and our bleachers exploded into a mass of orange and black. The band struck up the tune "Ain't It a Shame," and our rooters chanted:

Oh! ain't it great, just simply great,
To wipe Kalamazoo right off the slate!
Roll up the score, we want some more
To make Kalamazoo go way back and,
Sit down!

The last clause of the cheer was hurled like rotten tomatoes at the Kalamazoo crowd. And it didn't stop there. Our rooters continued chanting, and then the Kalamazoo rooters, getting madder by the minute, yelled back even harder. The vocal showdown went back and forth like that and the atmosphere became charged, the confrontation between the rooters every bit as vicious as the one about to take place on the gridiron. You had to be there to believe it.

On the field, while we were running through our conditioning routines, I tried to gauge the fellows' nerves. They seemed jittery, except for Jacob. Don't know how he did it—I was shaking like a wet puppy. Then I noticed Ossignac paying particular attention to Whitney, the fellow who tried to pick a fight with him in South Haven.

"Easy, Joe," I said. "We need you to have a clear head."

"Whitney's been starin at me," he said as he adjusted the strap on his head harness.

"He's just trying to get at you."

"And it's workin," he growled.

"Don't start slugging with him. You might get thrown out of the game."

"He's already started it." Then he turned, and I heard him make a strange grunting noise as he walked away.

I was worried about him. We were about to play the game of our lives and I was in charge—the game plan was my responsibility. I also had to set and maintain the pace and call the plays that would get us into the end zone—and I had to do it on a muddy field with Wadsworth breathing down the back of my neck. The last thing I needed was for Ossignac to start slugging with Whitney.

Shortly after my talk with Ossignac, the officials walked Jacob and Milo Bennett, who was the Kalamazoo team captain, to the center of the field. The coin was tossed and we won. Jacob chose to receive from the west end of the field because of a strong wind that was blowing diagonally from the southwest. And as we were about to discover, every advantage, no matter how small, would be crucial.

Chapter 15

It was almost three o'clock when we walked onto the wet field and were greeted by an explosive round of cheering from our rooters. The Kalamazoo team walked out a few seconds later, and the noise doubled, causing such a din that Jacob was forced to cup his hands around his mouth as he called for the Iron Man to adjust his position. The referee sounded his whistle and Jacob paced backwards, paused, and started the game with a soaring kick.

The ball dropped into the arms of Kalamazoo's left tackle and he advanced ten yards before Lee and Busby wrestled him to the ground. The Kalamazoo team immediately took the ball into play and stunned us with a series of fast line plunges to plant the ball near the fifty-five-yard line. Whitney was playing right guard opposite Handy, while Ossignac was positioned across from Kalamazoo's other guard. It was a good thing. He and Whitney probably would have started slugging before the first snap.

On the next play, Jacob blasted one of Kalamazoo's halfbacks causing him to fumble the ball, and Butts made a great recovery.

I called out my first play, barked the signals, and we got nowhere. My second play was also a flop, but at least we got another chance when Kalamazoo was penalized for being offside. But it didn't matter—we failed miserably. Busby punted the third down, but the ball sailed against the wind and traveled a miserly fifteen yards before a Kalamazoo man fell on it. We immediately went into a defensive formation, which called for me to play deep, or defensive, quarterback.

Kalamazoo ran a series of plays, made a first down, and then

Whitney took the ball on a guard-over play that developed so damn fast I was caught flat-footed. It was my fault—I'd made the defensive quarterback's cardinal mistake of being drawn in too close. Whitney broke through the line and shot past, leaving me faked out of my moleskins in front of a thousand witnesses. I made a redemptive attempt to catch him, but he covered ten, twenty, and then thirty yards as each stride of his powerful legs increased the distance between us. Butts, on the other hand, had read the play perfectly from his right end position and was actually closing the gap from the other direction. Still, Whitney covered forty, then fifty yards before Butts finally nailed him with beautiful flying tackle. They both went down, but the forward momentum carried them into the end zone.

The Kalamazoo rooters cheered and stomped and shook their ribboned sticks above their heads, turning their bleachers into a blaze of red and white. The roar of their celebration came across the field so strong it sent chills down my spine.

The goal attempt was successful and the score became 6 to 0.

Kalamazoo kicked to us and Busby took the ball and ran thirteen yards before he was tackled. It was a good run and the fellows seemed anxious to get back into the fight. On the first play, I gave the ball to Bridgman, but before he reached the line of scrimmage he was buried by a tide of Kalamazoo players. He stood up and staggered, and I grabbed his head with both of my hands and looked into his glazed eyes.

"You okay?" I asked as my guts flared with apprehension.

"Yeah," he mumbled. Then he shook his head a couple of times and said, "Call the damn play!"

I called out the next play and Bridgman took his place in the backfield. I scanned the line as I walked up for the snap and couldn't believe the beating the fellows were already taking. Most were smeared with mud and gasping hard for breath. Through clenched teeth, a few of them still managed to growl obscenities at their Kalamazoo counterparts, while the Kalamazoo players continued to jabber senseless numbers to trip me up. I ignored the bastards, took the snap, and handed off to Ossignac, who got nowhere. On the third down, I called for Busby to punt.

The ball soared to the Kalamazoo thirty-five-yard line, and we brought the runner down at about the forty. On the next play, we jumped the signals and were penalized five yards for being offside, but then we held them. For the third down, Bennett broke through and made a six-yard gain to tag the first down. On the next play, the runner went through the line again, this time for four more. On the next snap, they made another five-yard gain to plant the ball on the thirteen-yard line.

The bastards were tough, don't get me wrong. But I also felt we weren't playing our best, either. I blamed myself for the poor performance on offense, but defense was another matter. I think we were trying too hard—our rhythm was off. We were getting out-blocked, overrun, and we were being drawn in by their deceptions. Our chances were looking pretty bleak when our rooters began shouting for us to hold them, and then someone started the locomotive yell. It was slow and loose at first, then it got louder and tighter until every member of the crowd was yelling in unison.

"First down, five yards to gain!" sang the referee.

A hush fell over the crowd, and the Kalamazoo quarterback took the snap and handed it to Whitney. I remember that play like it was yesterday. He plunged at our line like a wild steer, but Ossignac outfoxed his man, got free, and nailed him for a loss.

Our rooters went crazy as the referee cried out, "Second down, seven yards to gain!" Kalamazoo attempted to take it up the middle, but we plugged them up again.

"Third down, five to go!" the referee yelled as the mass of bodies untangled, everyone breathing hard for air. Our rooters broke loose once more, chanting and pleading for us to hold them. We tightened our muscles, crouched, and when the Kalamazoo backs hit the line they might as well have hit a wall of stone. They got nothing—the ball was ours.

I called out the formation I wanted while the fellows were still getting off the ground, and then I called the play. They obediently went to the line and crouched. Kalamazoo must have expected our usual hair-trigger start because I easily bluffed them offside to the tune of a five-yard penalty. Breathing room. Next I called for a mass play with Butts as the ball carrier, and we advanced two yards. Then I called for Bridgman to carry the ball around our right end, thinking that his going wide would string out the defense enough to let him perform. I was right. He took the ball and hurdled the first would-be tackler. Then he jogged and broke tackles and kept running until a Kalamazoo back brought him down fifty yards later. Our rooters were wild with excitement, yelling and stomping their feet until I thought the bleachers would come down. That play was our first offensive windfall.

I ran the next series with renewed vigor, but the result was disappointing. Kalamazoo held us and we lost the ball on downs.

I was so furious I could've spit. I felt it was my fault for not calling the plays that would keep us moving the ball forward. Too predictable—that was my problem. I couldn't think of any other reason. It was almost as if the Kalamazoo players knew before the snap who would be carrying the ball and where.

Kalamazoo took possession near the twenty-five-yard line and ran a series of plays, but made little progress. We took our turn at it and also failed, then Kalamazoo tried again but got nothing. The game turned into a bruising battle in the mud. There was an increase in foul banter between players, more frustration, more aggravation, and finally it turned damn ugly.

That's when the game ceased to be sport.

With each succeeding play, the hostility between players increased. First there was more pushing after the whistle, and then it escalated into open shoving. Soon the players were covertly jabbing and throwing elbows while in the piles. Blood started flowing on a few players' faces, and pretty soon those who weren't cut had someone else's blood splattered on them, mixed with mud and grass stains. The officials worked hard to secure the ball quickly after it was downed, first to keep the ball carrier from eking more distance, but also to minimize the battling within the pile. They were actually grabbing players by the back of their jerseys or sweaters and jerking them from the heap. It was a valiant attempt, but it didn't stop the most determined players. Whitney and Ossignac were openly attacking each other, and a Kalamazoo player had to be helped from the field when Jacob put a bear hug on him that broke some of his ribs. I actually heard them snap. Murder pile.

It was we who finally ended the stalemate by advancing thirty yards into Kalamazoo territory. At last I was calling the right plays, but then I gave the ball to Lathe and he fumbled. I couldn't believe it, after all the hard work. Kalamazoo recovered the ball but decided to kick because they were afraid of losing it too close to their own goal. Jacob caught it and advanced ten hard-fought yards, leaving a string of Kalamazoo players sprawling in his wake.

For the first play, I called Jacob's number, and he punched through the Kalamazoo line for another good gain. Again I called his number and our crowd was on its feet howling as he battered his way down to the five-yard line. Next I called for an end-around play and the fellows scrambled into position. Both crowds were cheering as I dashed through the signals, took the snap, and handed the ball to Busby, who was already in motion. He plowed through the line behind Jacob and Butts, with me pushing from behind to make the touchdown.

Immediately after the score, I saw little mascot Willie take his top hat off and throw it spinning into the air. An instant later, nearly every man and boy in our stands threw their own hats and then they danced like maniacs—shrieking and yelling and pounding each other's backs. Pa told me later that a few men accidentally broke their walking canes banging them against the bleachers.

Busby kicked the goal from a difficult angle and the score was tied 6 to 6.

I'll never forget what happened next. The crowd was still cheering when the clouds parted for the first time that day and a rainbow appeared. Red, green, and yellow streaked across the northern sky, reflecting through the mist and the layers of gray clouds. Everyone at the field stopped cheering and looked up, and then I heard someone in our stands cry out that it was a sign from God. There was a smattering of cheers. Then someone else yelled that the colors were orange and black, which brought even more cheering. I'll have to admit it was one of the strangest damn things I'd ever seen, the timing of that rainbow.

The game started up again, but we had less then a minute of playing time before the clock ran out the half with the score locked up tight at 6 to 6. It was anybody's game, and we were already beat up to hell and back.

We walked off the field to a grassy spot beneath a big oak tree—a couple of scrubs had already moved the water buckets there. We were gasping for breath while trying to drink water at the same time.

"Don't swallow!" Teetzel commanded. "Rinse and spit." Some listened, some didn't. I didn't swallow to protect myself against a bellyache.

One by one, the fellows sat or laid down on towels or blankets while Doc began patching and stitching the worst cut among us. Teetzel stepped into the middle of our circle with his pad of paper.

"Before I go through my list of mistakes," he said with a look of concern pressed across his face, "I want to tell you I don't like what I'm seeing. You're wasting time and energy with all the pushing and shoving."

"But coach," Bridgman said, "it's just eye for an eye."

"Turn the other cheek, Mr. Bridgman," he shot back.

Bridgman hesitated, then forced a sarcastic smile and said, "I did and it's black and blue." He turned his cheek as would a demure girl for all of us to see, and some of the fellows chuckled. I didn't see a bruise, but then again he was so smeared with mud it would have been impossible to detect anyway.

"The meek may not win a football game," Teetzel continued without hesitation and without smiling, "but neither will those who slug. The player who fights is desperate. He is either tired or outplayed and is as good as beaten. Know that and you will win this game."

"But how can I let some hardcase get away with slugging me?" Lee protested. Some of the fellows grumbled something or another to relay their agreement with the question.

"Simply walk away. Know that you will benefit by putting the energy you save into the game. And do not forget that you cannot play to the best of your ability when injured, and to be injured from fighting is a terrible injustice to yourself and your teammates."

No one said anything, but I wasn't sure if their deference was due to consent or exhaustion. I agreed with Teetzel—always had—

but I suspected some of the non-response was more of an effort to save energy for the second half. We sat quietly while Doc drank whiskey and wrapped Handy's ankle.

Teetzel casually reached in under his coat and retrieved his pencil. Then he reviewed his notes for another half minute before starting in on us.

No one would escape his analytical criticism.

Teetzel went down the list of mistakes made by each individual player, things like missing blocks, being out-maneuvered, or not getting into the plays fast enough. Then he talked about overall strategy and play selections. That's where my own blood-letting occurred. I expected to get hammered and did. He nailed me for not properly reading the defense and for not calling the plays that would best match the various situations. I couldn't argue with that—I was fully aware. The entire first half had been like playing in a fog and trying to guess where all the trees were. Just when I could almost see them, they'd disappear again. Was frustrating as hell.

"And you must start every play less than twelve seconds after the previous play is whistled dead," he went on. "That means getting off the ground, selecting your play, and moving back into position."

We sat and listened as he lectured us on the benefits of speed, his favorite subject. He made great sense, but his expectations were hard ones. For me, they seemed all but impossible.

While Teetzel was roasting us, Professor Null and the band played and marched around the field. Soon, most of our rooters left the stands to walk behind them singing and chanting fight songs while shaking their orange and black–ribboned sticks. It was obvious the Kalamazoo folks were galled that a visiting crowd would have the guts to show such disrespect on a home team's playing grounds. They didn't do anything at first, but their anger festered until they could stand it no longer. In a rush, hundreds of them spilled out of the bleachers and onto the field to face our rooters. That was a challenge our toughs couldn't refuse. They immediately sifted to the head of the crowd to confront their Kalamazoo counterparts.

At first, there was a lot of yelling and swearing, then it degenerated into shoving and finally a flurry of slugging ensued. Deputy Pearl got into the middle of the fray, along with a couple of Kalamazoo officials, but it was the deputy who got the thing settled down when he pulled a blackjack from his back pocket and bashed two fellows in the head. Knocked them out cold, both of them, one on each side. Said he did it that way so no one could accuse him of being partial. The Kalamazoo High School principal told Professor Null it would be best if the band stayed on their side of the field and he agreed. Our rooters went back to the bleachers grumbling about the bad sportsmanship shown by the Kalamazoo rooters.

Our lineup in the second half was the same as in the first, except for the addition of Cunningham for Busby. Teetzel pulled him from the game because his injured shoulder was bothering him. The initial injury occurred during the Kershaw game, and he'd been nursing it ever since.

The referee whistled for the second half to begin, and the playing was unbelievably fierce. I worked hard to run our offense faster, but Kalamazoo stood tough and kept us out of the end zone. The next few possessions seesawed back and forth with neither side able to gain much until I noticed a Kalamazoo lineman who was dazed, probably from one too many blows to the head. I selected a play that would exploit that. Bridgman took the ball and busted through the lineman's position behind Jacob and the Iron Man and then shot out of the pack with no one but Bennett anywhere near him. Bennett ran hard but Bridgman was able to maintain an arm's length between them, at least until it was clear he wouldn't be caught. That's when Bennett lunged and snagged Bridgman by the ankle, which caused him to stumble for a few steps and finally go down. Almost as one, our crowd rushed to their feet crying foul. A couple hundred of our men and boys swarmed over the sideline onto the field, but Teetzel helped the officials hold them back.

In those days, tackling below the knees was against the rules. So was intentional tripping. It was considered cowardly and unsportsmanlike and almost always brought the most composed spectator screaming to his feet, at least in Bungtown. The referee penalized Kalamazoo fifteen yards, but some of our rooters were shaking their fists and yelling that it should have been at least fifty.

The ball went back and forth again as we pounded each other into the cold mud. The playing was so intense that all player talk and cross-team cackling had ceased in an effort to conserve energy. Just when I felt we were getting the upper hand, Lathe twisted his knee in one of the piles and had to be helped from the field. I couldn't believe it. The Iron Man was out. I was afraid his loss would give Kalamazoo just enough of an advantage to overtake us, so I had no choice but to ratchet up the pace. I knew the fellows were already playing at the very edge of their physical limits, but I didn't know what else to do.

As I began calling plays at a faster pace, not a soul on that field—player or official—misunderstood my intentions. No one under my command pleaded for more time and no one expected any. The crowd even quieted somewhat as most of them watched with intense interest.

It was during that part of the game, while we had the ball and were playing the fastest we had all season, that the strap on my head harness broke. Within seconds, I had it off and was tossing it on the grass near our bench as I called out the next play. I refused to call a time-out and give the Kalamazoo players the opportunity to catch wind.

We were able to move the ball without Lathe, but Kalamazoo put up a stubborn defense. There were only two minutes of game time left and Whitney was doing a hellish job keeping us out of the end zone. That's when Ossignac went to work on him.

"What's matter, little sister," he chided sarcastically after a play was whistled dead and Whitney was gulping hard for air. "You feelin a little stretched?" Whitney shoved the big Indian but Ossignac simply walked away.

Ossignac continued his taunting after each play until Whitney got so mad he began pushing and shoving the Indian, even after the play was whistled dead. But Ossignac stayed cool. He simply laughed and walked away, which made Whitney madder and more angry until he couldn't stand it and attacked him with balled fists.

Ossignac put up his hands to deflect the blows, but Whitney landed a couple of solid ones before the officials pulled him off and ejected him from the game. As Whitney walked from the field, Ossignac smiled and waved.

"Good-bye, little sister," he growled in his deep Indian voice. The Kalamazoo coach exploded, arguing that Ossignac should have been tossed as well, but the referee stood his ground.

The Kalamazoo crowd booed raucously.

While the officials were dealing with Whitney, I dashed over to our bench and ripped off a strip of towel and tied it around my head to cover my ears. We had no spare harnesses and no one had an extra to lend me. The towel would at least hold my ears tight to my head and prevent them from being bashed and stung or worse. Sometimes players grabbed an opponents ear and ripped it, and I knew of at least one player who had an ear kicked off.

I ran a series of plays using line bucks and hurdles with Jacob, Bridgman, and Cunningham alternating as ball carriers. Without Whitney, the yardage came easier, and we made a first down. After that, the Kalamazoo players began losing steam and had to take a time-out—some of them were so exhausted they actually laid down on the sodden field to catch wind. That was my cue to step up the pace again. I may not have had the experience to call the best plays, but at least I was learning to call them fast.

There would be no mercy from me.

The fellows took their places and we were off. The next play was unfolding two seconds after the referee put the ball down, and it was the same for the play after that, which got us a first down. Still I didn't let up. I was gasping for air myself, and sweat was running into my eyes, burning and clouding my vision, seeping into the cuts and scrapes that covered my face and hands. Stung like hell. Once I nearly gagged on the pungent smell of mildewed grass and mud in my nose. But there wasn't time to worry about that either—we were at war. I wiped my face with a muddy hand and called out the next play.

We got another first down, and then Jacob planted the ball on the Kalamazoo ten-yard line. Two plays later, Bridgman ran wide, clipping the corner of the end zone for the touchdown. Busby attempted to kick the goal, but it was from a difficult angle and he missed. I should have called for a punt-out attempt but didn't. The rooters didn't even care. They were out of their minds with excitement. The game ended shortly after that with the score 11 to 6.

We limped victoriously off the field while Professor Null struck up the band and played "Ain't It a Shame," which was his way of taunting the Kalamazoo rooters. Kalamazoo's Coach Mitchell offered his congratulations to Teetzel and bid him luck in our fight to win the state championship. Teetzel accepted the compliment graciously, but with a forced smile and a handshake.

It was obvious even he was unnerved by our condition.

My folks told me later they barely recognized us players after the game because of the grime and the mud caked into our hair. And they were right. We were a mess. Jerseys were ripped, sweaters shredded, straps were hanging from broken shin guards, vest lacing was stretched and pulled apart, and just about everything was smudged with dirt and grass stains and blood. The game was by far the hardest playing we'd done that season, and some said it went far beyond what was considered normal. One of the game officials said it was the roughest high school football game he'd ever seen.

I can't argue with that. We were scraped, bruised, and completely exhausted.

But the rooters loved it. While some of them truly felt sorry for us, others wanted it to be rough—the bloodier the better—which convinced me they regarded us with no more compassion than fighting pit dogs.

We showered and rubbed our bodies with a mixture of alcohol and raw quinine, something we always did after playing in a cold rain, and Doc treated the worst of our injuries. It was 8:30 when the Rooter Special Number Two finally eased us into Benton Harbor. The night was wet and cold and black as ink, but a fair crowd had assembled to welcome home the victors. They knew we'd won because the score was wired ahead.

We waited for the rooters to get off the train before we painfully eased into our coats and hats and gathered up our bags. As we limped off, some young boys shot roman candles while the crowd cheered. It was pretty damn emotional. I'd never been part of anything like it. Teetzel and Jacob gave short speeches and the crowd cheered again before we broke up and climbed into the carriages that would carry our weary bodies home.

I couldn't get to sleep that night. My cuts and scrapes stung, my bruises throbbed, and my shoulder and thigh muscles couldn't have ached more if someone had pounded me with a baseball bat. But that's not what really kept me from sleeping. I was awake because my mind was reeling with the thrill of a hard-fought victory, and specifically since my work at quarterback was partly responsible. Everyone congratulated me, even those I suspected had trouble believing a little guy like me could lead such a big team. Wadsworth complimented me too, in his own sarcastic way.

"Must have been giving your hands a daily soak in the manure pile," he said.

That comment was a direct reference to my small hands and the two fumbles I made during the Elkhart game. He was implying that I must have fertilized them, and I almost slugged him for it. That's how invincible I felt.

I was pleased with myself, but if I'd been a more seasoned player, I would have been concerned. I would have seen the high cost of our victory. We were scabbed and stiff, and some of the fellows had sprained wrists and ankles that were nearly incapacitating. The swelling was pitiful. Of the more serious injuries was Lathe's twisted knee and Busby's reinjured arm. Add to that Dice Baushke's hip, which was still critical, and Jacob's unhealed shoulder, and I would've understood just how tenuous the situation was.

Whether we players understood it or not, any rational physician would have agreed the health of the team was in doubt. And while Teetzel seemed concerned, the board members acted like it was nothing. That's because they saw it from the outside. They believed injuries always healed, which was an accurate belief if the injury was given the proper time to heal. But we only had fifteen players and couldn't afford to lose even one, especially since our next game was against the college boys from Notre Dame.

Teetzel's Machine

Chapter 16

"Damnation," Jacob said, wrinkling his nose in disgust. We were gathered at the practice field Monday afternoon preparing to begin our routines. "You smell that, Butts?"

"Yes sir. And I'd say it's onions."

"It is onions," Busby admitted, and we all looked at him. "For my sore feet."

"Jesus, Bus," Mit said. "How the hell do you use onions?"

"You roast em, peel off the outside, and then mash em up like sweet potatoes. After they cool, you smear on the paste and let your socks hold it in place. My Aunt Sadie swears by it." Aunt Sadie was from the southern hill country, and when she came north, she brought a bag full of old slave remedies with her.

"Would it work for sore leg and shoulder muscles?" Lee asked seriously, which started the rest of us snickering. "You fellas laugh," he argued in his defense, "but I got some places that are damn near killin me."

"Me too," Heck said, "but I ain't rubbin food into them."

"Well," Busby replied, "I suspect if it works for feet it'll work everywhere else. Flesh and muscle is the same no matter what bone it's connected to."

No longer able to restrain himself, Ossignac said "I know somethin else you might try."

"I suppose your grandaddy's got something for sore muscles?" Mit asked.

"Fact he does. Says a leaf from the burdock weed'll do the trick. But you have to take out the hard fibers and then soften em up on a hot skillet. After that you fold it up and fasten it to the sore spot with a cloth bandage."

"At least that wouldn't smell so bad," Butts said.

"But wouldn't be easier to just buy something like Mustang Liniment?" Bridgman asked. "I read an ad in the *Evening News* that claims it soaks right through to cure all hurts and pains."

"We use that stuff on the farm for the horses," Handy said.

"That's right." Bridgman added. "The ad claims it's good for man or beast."

"Don't be fallin for that crap," Lathe replied. "Damn stuff kilt my Uncle Hank."

"How old was he?" Butts asked.

"Eighty-four, but…"

"Alright men!" Teetzel interrupted. He'd arrived while we were jabbering, and I hadn't noticed. Apparently he was standing nearby talking to a group of men who were there to watch us practice. The coach walked over and asked us to sit down. Said he had something to say.

"I couldn't help but overhear your conversation regarding family remedies," he began. "If they help you, then by all means use them…I will not stand in the way. But I believe there are some things I too can do to help your situation. First, I've told Caully to have his rubbers continue their standard five-minute rubdowns, but to follow up with two more minutes of rubbing with ice."

"Brrr!" Butts said while wrapping his arms around his chest and shaking the imagined cold from his shoulders. Brought a bevy of smiles from us all.

"The only time Bridgman uses ice," Heck added, "is to cool down his beer." Most of us began to snicker.

"The ice will ease the swelling," Teetzel answered after waiting patiently for us to quiet down, "and help to recirculate your blood."

"What's the deal, coach?" Mit asked

"He's feelin guilty for workin us so hard," Lee quipped.

"Truth be known," Teetzel replied after we stopped laughing again. "I am feeling guilty. You men should not be in such poor physical condition, and regrettably it's my fault. For that I must apologize."

"Means your giving us shorter practices, coach?" It was Bridgman.

Teetzel took a couple steps toward him and said, "Mr. Bridgman, I think you misunderstand me. As you well know, the success of my theory that the team should operate as a well-oiled machine depends in a large part upon the health of the players. Am I right?"

"Yes sir," he answered. "That means we should be allowed to skip the first hour of school for the extra sleep time." A number of the fellows seconded that motion, but it was hard to hear them because the rest of us were laughing so damn hard.

"Therefore," Teetzel went on undeterred, "the more conditioned player will be healthier and less susceptible to injury than one who is less so. Am I right?"

There was a long pause until Mit moaned, "Oh no!" Then one by one, we followed suit as the implications of his statement sunk into our thick skulls.

"With that being said," he went on, "I am stepping up the intensity of our training. We will not practice any longer nor will we do anything different. But we will do everything faster. And I do mean everything."

"But coach," Cunningham said. "What's that got to do with preventing injuries?"

"I'm glad you asked that, Mr. Cunningham, because it is a very simple principle. Experience has proven that any player with strong muscles will be more resistant to twists and sprains. I'm not so naïve as to believe all injuries can be prevented, especially those caused by illegal kicking or slugging, but be assured there are ways to diminish their frequency."

"Aw come on, coach." Butts argued. "Everyone knows that all the training in the world won't do any good against a knee to the breadbasket."

"Then let me ask you this, Mr. Lester. When does most of the rough playing take place?"

"Second half."

"Correct. And why?"

"Because the players are fighting mad."

"Correct again. They are fighting mad because the game is going against them, probably because their opponents are better conditioned. That's why I don't want you expending energy fighting back. Use their anger against them. When they try to fight you, disengage and get the ball back into play and drive them to the point of exhaustion. Make them too tired to fight."

Within ten minutes after his talk, Teetzel's new war cry unfolded before our very eyes. It was a simple "speed, speed, speed!" He hammered those three words at us throughout Monday's practice as though he were coaching a bunch of Chinamen who'd never even seen a football before. And he refused to let up, even when we ran to the woods for a piss. He pushed and shoved and then told us constantly we had to work harder, which we did.

But the drill only intensified.

Throughout Tuesday's practice, Teetzel continued his merciless regimen, with no detail being too minor to ignore. He followed us like a hawk, correcting our mistakes and driving us hard toward perfection. During signal practice, we ran our plays at a phenomenal ten second gait, but even that didn't dampen his criticism. At times, my body and mind were so exhausted I didn't know if I could continue.

By Wednesday, I felt like paste. My physical existence had become a continuous blur of sleeping, eating, going to school, and playing football, which left me almost no time for chores or studies. In fact, most of my dedicated homework time was used up learning new offensive strategies and Teetzel's four-number signal system. Each night in bed, I studied my play book by lamplight until Ma called for me to blow out the flame.

My muscles were so sore that simple maneuvers like pumping water for washing clothes or cleaning Mattie's stall had become huge ordeals. And the pain in my legs never went away. At practice, it took a good fifteen minutes of brisk exercise before I was limber enough to run without a noticeable hobble. Thursday morning, I actually considered going to the root cellar for onions. But I didn't—the hazing at school would have been unbearable.

Now don't get me wrong, in a strange way I loved every bloody minute of Teetzel's training. All of us fellows did. We just never realized it could be such a hard business.

That being said, we arrived at the practice field Thursday afternoon physically and mentally ravaged. We dreaded going another round with Teetzel, and it wasn't because he was mistreating us. His gentlemanly coaching philosophy remained the underpinning of his personality, but suddenly he had more conviction and a stronger determination to mold us into his ideal of the perfect team. There was a snap in his voice that demanded our complete attention and dedication to the art he was teaching us. And we tried to please him, even as he delivered a steady stream of curt commentary regarding our errors and how we should correct them, remedies that usually involved more mental and physical torture. After winning the Kalamazoo game, we mistakenly believed we were near perfect, but now we were beginning to think we weren't even cut out to be scrubs.

We understood Teetzel intended for his new regimen to protect us from further injury, but after a while his criticisms seemed to grind us down further. And those who observed our practices knew exactly how we felt—I suppose they read it in our faces. Before Teetzel arrived to start Thursday's practice, a pair of gamblers came over to where we were gathered together fretting over what Teetzel might have in store for us that afternoon.

"How you fellows feelin today?" one of them said. He was wearing a derby bowler while the other was carrying a rolled-up newspaper under his arm. Both were wearing well-worn wool suits.

"Jus dandy," Heck growled sarcastically as we all turned to face them. Some of the other fellows grumbled similar comments.

"Now I know the coach has been putting you through some tough training," derby man continued. "Jess and I have been here everyday this week and seen it with our own eyes."

"Been a fun week," Bridgman said sarcastically. "But the truly hard work takes place in the morning when we're trying to get out of bed."

"Or when we're trying to walk up the stairs at the high school," Butts interjected and we chuckled.

"I just wanted you to know," derby man went on, "that you are improving just fine. In fact, I'd have to say you boys are the fastest team Bungtown ever produced. That right, Jess?"

"Yes sir. Fastest I've ever seen."

"Hell," Bridgman said, "we know that."

"Yeah," Heck added, "it's jus Teetzel who don't."

Derby man tipped his hat back and scratched his forehead. "Yes he does," he finally said. "He does, but he thinks you can do even better."

The fellows half laughed and half grumbled at that comment, and it was Jacob who spoke next. "We got work to do, fellas."

"One more thing," derby man added. "Show them, Jess."

Jess took the newspaper he'd been carrying, opened it, and said, "Here it is boys, right here."

It was an article about us, and we crowded around to have a look, but couldn't see the small print. "Read it to us Cunny," Jacob finally said, and Cunningham took the paper from Jess and began to read. The best part went as follows:

> The boys have been taught to eat the sod when they hit the line and to run with a shifty dodging step when a play is shot around the ends. The halfbacks have learned to pick a hole and go through like a charging steer, and when Captain Jacob hits the line he rears up on his hind legs like a billy goat and goes into the line so close he bites buckles off of shin guards.

Teetzel arrived to the field about ten minutes later, and when Bridgman asked him if he'd seen the article, he said no, which we suspected was a lie. We didn't press the issue, but we were still feeling pretty good about ourselves until the last half of practice when we started running play formations. That's when we noticed Teetzel shaking his head back and forth and saying, "Slow, miserably slow."

I guess it didn't matter that we were Benton Harbor's fastest team ever—we had to be faster.

Our next interscholastic game was scheduled for October 31, which was two weeks after Kalamazoo High. The college boys from Notre Dame were sandwiched in between, which meant we wouldn't have a free weekend, but at the last minute the Catholics canceled when the bishop of the diocese made a surprise visit. I was damn happy about that. I had no desire to bang heads with that bunch anytime, let alone on the heels of the Kalamazoo game. But that meant we had two full weeks without any game at all, and that wasn't good either. So we scrimmaged.

Saturday, October 18, we went to Eastman Springs and played a formal game against the scrubs. The event was advertised by word of mouth, and a fair crowd showed up. The halves were short and we won 23 to 0, even with Teetzel and Bridgman playing in the scrub backfield and Wadsworth at the helm. Dice was still out, and Lathe didn't play because of the injury he received in the Kalamazoo game. Overall, it was a damn good time.

The scrimmage was given one paragraph in Monday's edition of the *Evening News*, while the remainder of the article focused on the state's other important high school games, including Muskegon's victory over Traverse City.

The Muskegon game was for the bragging rights of Western Michigan, which meant the winner would play the survivor of the Ann Arbor–Lansing game for the lower peninsula title. The big city sports editors were already predicting we would slug it out with Lansing for the lower Michigan title, which meant the newspapermen were looking past our game with Muskegon.

Unfortunately, that was a luxury we couldn't afford.

Muskegon was a lumber boomtown located sixty miles north of Benton Harbor along the Lake Michigan shoreline. Some folks called it the "Lumber Queen of the North." There were more than forty sawmills there, and it also served as the center of local industry and government, a place where lumberjacks, Indians, and immigrants of all stripes walked the same streets with wealthy industrialists and timber barons. We called it the "Sawdust City," and I describe it here only because of the potential effect it had on us as a football team. Muskegon was a sporting town with a lot of money and muscle.

Fortunately for us, Burger was able to negotiate with the Muskegon team manager to play the game at Eastman Springs, which meant we would benefit from having the full power of our rooters behind us.

During the days leading up to the game, our rooter's interest in football waxed considerably. We were so talked about that anyone who tried to change the subject was usually squelched or ignored altogether. Bear stories about the strength of the Muskegon team flew everywhere, along with a rumor that they had a spy lurking in Benton Harbor, which bothered the hell out of everyone who had anything to do with the team. It particularly angered the toughs, who said the spy had better remain anonymous if he was at all concerned about his health.

Some of the student rooters volunteered to sell admission tickets to help pay for Muskegon's expenses, and on the first day, three hundred were sold at fifty cents apiece, which encouraged Manager Burger to predict a gate surpassing a thousand rooters.

Friday was Halloween, except there was no Halloween back then. At least none that we players celebrated. Back then, it was mostly a nighttime romp for troublemakers who roamed the alleys pushing over outhouses. Halloween for us was an afternoon at the Old Athletic Field. Our treat—a no-contact signal practice, which pleased us just fine. Teetzel said he was easing up so we could rest for Saturday's game. Later, at the Pastime Club, he gave us an inspiring talk about winning and then told us what he'd gleaned about the Muskegon team. Al Clark was on hand and took a statement from Jacob. It appeared in the *News* as follows:

> I am confident of winning. The boys are all in good condition, each one going into the game with the determination of winning. Every man will play a square game and will play it to the best of his ability. If they beat us, they will have the better team.

But that's not how I remember it being said. Clark cleaned it up and I know why. First of all, Jacob's command of the English language was not overly polished. Sure, he could put a sentence together, but he often trimmed off the beginnings or endings of words, and he used lots of slang. To the best of my recollection, what Jacob said was, "I feel we can beat those fellas from the

Sawdust City. Every man on our team is fit as a mule, and each and every one of em will fight till they can no longer stand up. Now I'm not sayin it won't be rough, cause it likely will, but everyone should know we can fight fair and square with the best of em. If they beat us, it's because they'll have the best horses."

Now that's how he really spoke. I suppose Clark was trying to make Jacob's statement fit the image of a student athlete, and I can't blame him, but it wasn't accurate and I just wanted to clear that up for posterity's sake.

After Clark finished with his questions, we showered, took our rubdowns, which included the ice treatment, and went home for dinner. But the day's activities weren't quite over. Teetzel requested we meet him later at the depot to welcome the Muskegon team—they were scheduled to arrive on the 8:15 from Grand Rapids. When Butts and I strolled up a little after eight, Teetzel and Burger and most of the fellows were already there, along with a strong contingent of rooters. Most were students, but the most active among the crowd were the gamblers.

Chapter 17

The Muskegon players stepped from the coach decked in their Sunday best. We welcomed them with a shout of nine rahs before the gamblers muscled their way to the front and began to examine them the way they inspected horses at the fairgrounds racetrack. They sized up their height and weight and skin color, and some of the men even tried to get a look at the quality of their teeth and the brightness of their eyes. I'd seen them do that before and it stunk. But I guess I couldn't blame them—they were about to wager a lot of money on us.

Manager Burger introduced himself to Muskegon's Coach Walker and then requested he make a short statement, and he obliged.

"We are honored to be in Benton Harbor," he began, while his team gathered behind him. We clapped and whistled, and then a lone voice rang out from the back of the crowd.

"We'll be damn honored to send you back defeated!"

"Please excuse that man," Burger said to Coach Walker as the clapping tapered off.

"No apologies needed." The coach then continued with his statement. "We will play hard football from the first blowing of the whistle until the end of the game."

"Your boys best be fast!" another voice rang out.

"Yes," the coach answered. "And the fastest team will win."

Coach Walker thanked us for the welcome and we cheered again. Then the Muskegon boys grabbed their bags and climbed into a couple of wagons for the ride to the Hotel Benton.

Before leaving, Teetzel gathered us players around him and suggested we go home and get a good night's sleep. He said Saturday would be one of the most important days of our lives, one that would test us to the limits of our physical endurance. And I believed him.

"How do they look?" Pa asked as I walked through the parlor on the way to the kitchen.

"They're a healthy looking bunch, about the same size as us, maybe a midge lighter."

"Good for them! They'll need every ounce they can muster if they hope to have a chance against Mr. Teetzel's machine."

"I don't know, Pa. We're undermanned because of injuries, and all of us are so sore we can barely walk a straight line until lunch time."

"Yes, yes, I know," he went on. "But I've heard the reports...the men are talking about you all over town. They say that once you fellows get on the practice field, you limber up quick and operate with the speed of a college team."

"Yes sir," I replied respectfully. "I hope so."

I went into the kitchen and cut myself a piece of pie and sat down. Ma came in and adjusted up the flame in the wall lamp and sat down.

"How are you feeling, dear?" she said.

"Fine, Ma. And I wish you wouldn't call me dear."

"It's because I worry about you...I can't help it." She paused while I took a bite of pie. "Are you ready for tomorrow?"

"Ready as I'll ever be."

"I want you to be careful. You know it bothered me greatly how bruised you were after the Kalamazoo game."

I didn't tell her it had also bothered Teetzel, and me too, for that matter. And neither did I tell her I'd have traded almost anything for a day without aches and pains. I smiled as convincingly as I was able and said, "I know, Ma. I'll be careful."

"Please do."

I climbed into bed shortly after finishing my pie and studied my playbook for a good half hour before blowing out the lamp. Then I couldn't fall asleep. Charlie was already breathing slow and easy in his bed next to mine, but I laid there for a long time with a busy mind. I went over and over the plays and signals I would use the following day, trying to remember everything Teetzel taught me about matching the skills of my ball carriers with various game situations. Then I thought about Coach Walker's speech at the depot, particularly the part about the faster team winning.

For some reason, the way he said "faster" continued spinning around in my head until his voice sounded suspiciously like Teetzel's. Suddenly he was Teetzel, standing alone in the middle of a wide field covered with cropped weeds and grass. And he was pointing his finger at me. Suddenly, I was running hard conditioning routines and speed drills followed by dozens of signal practices. I ran until I fell down exhausted. Then we sat on the grass together and he quizzed me about rules and strategies, then we were at the Pastime Club talking about defensive formations. Finally, he lectured me on the virtues of playing smart and not fighting.

I don't know when I fell asleep, but in the morning I awoke feeling unrefreshed. It had been a rough night. But I decided not to worry about it because it no longer mattered. I was a disciple, you see, an apprentice pledged to sacrifice every fiber of his being to his master. And my master was Clayton Teetzel.

I climbed out of bed and prepared to do my job.

Beginning at first light, a group of our student supporters swarmed through the business district draping everything in orange and black. By the time I got there, which was just after ten o'clock, crepe paper hung from store fronts and power poles. Ribbons were pinned to horse harnesses, women's hats, and tied through the buttonholes of men walking the streets. Buggy whips were wrapped up like candy canes.

At two o'clock we stepped from the trolleys at Eastman Springs and found the place jammed up with livery rigs, hacks, carriages, and bicycles. We expected a good crowd, but nothing like the huge mob that greeted us. Nearly sixteen hundred tickets had already been sold by the time we arrived. Burger said over two hundred young boys, along with a few men who claimed they were broke, had been admitted without paying. He let the boys in because they were great rooters.

People were everywhere. Some were watching the game between the scrubs and St. Joe, which was almost over, while others strolled through the park. Groups of people sat on the grass warming in the sun, some of them eating picnic lunches, while others were lined up at the vendor stands buying snacks. Colonel Eastman had a tent set up at the north end of the field where he was hawking water. A number of jugs were lined up on a table made of planks laid across two sawhorses.

"Silver Queen water!" he shouted. "With certified medicinal qualities…good for catarrh, diaretis, dyspepsia, hay fever, and ague! It also combats diseases of the kidneys, liver, urinary organs, and cases of debility from whatever cause! One dollar a jug!"

I always liked it when he said his water cured ailments from whatever the cause. Covered all his bases with that one, and apparently with good results. Business was brisk. He set a couple of jugs next to our bench and we all took a swig of water for good luck.

By the time we trotted onto the field to warm up, the people were three deep on the east side of the field and two deep everywhere else, even in the end zones. The number of Muskegon rooters present was small. I spotted Al Clark talking to a couple of reporters I didn't know, but I suspected they were from the *Muskegon Chronicle*.

The Muskegon team took to the field shortly after us and went through their formations in a clumsy manner, which made us suspicious. Teams sometimes did that for the purpose of making their adversary feel overconfident.

The Muskegon captain was a fellow named Jiroch and the referee was Dr. May, a professor from the University of Michigan— all interscholastic games had to be worked by a representative of the university's athletic department. Dr. May met with the captains at the center of the field where they agreed the game would consist of two twenty-five-minute halves. They also agreed we would kick off after each score during the first half and Muskegon would kick during the second half.

The coin was tossed and Muskegon won. Jiroch chose to defend the north goal.

"Okay, men," Teetzel said as we stood in a semicircle around him.

"The footing is bad for fifteen yards north and south of the fifty-five-yard line. Be careful there. And remember your speed. I've told Fletch to run you hard and fast…so trust your memories regarding the plays. All of you know them. There will be no time to ask your teammates about your patterns should you forget them."

"He's right," I said to Jacob and Bridgman as we were walked onto the field to take our positions.

"He's always right," Bridgman replied.

"I mean about running the team," I added. "I'll be running you fellows faster than the wind."

"See to it that ya do," Jacob grunted as he tightened the strap on his head harness. "Show them no mercy…us either."

Dr. May blew the whistle at three o'clock sharp and Jacob booted the pigskin to Muskegon's ten-yard line. Jiroch caught it and advanced fifteen yards before being tackled. They ran two plays and had to punt. The crowd was pressed against the sidelines, cheering and howling and screaming so hard for Muskegon blood that I could almost feel their hot breath.

Butts caught the ball on our fifty-yard line and was brought down after advancing twelve yards. With Teetzel's "speed, speed, speed!" war cry looping through my mind, I took the fellows into play and repeatedly hammered the backs at the Muskegon line until we got the first down. Then I gave it to Bridgman, who ran wide and made a spectacular forty-yard romp to the Muskegon ten-yard line. After that, Jacob ripped through for five more. Bridgman gained two yards on a cross-buck and then Arthur Baushke, who was playing in place of Dice, plunged into the end zone behind Jacob and Bridgman for the touchdown.

Instead of kicking the goal, which would have been from a very wide angle, I used the punt-out option to try moving the ball closer to the middle of the field. During a punt-out play, the player who received the snap was required to immediately kick the ball to one of his teammates. He could not run with the ball. While the defensive team was not allowed to interfere with the punter—they could line up no closer than fifteen yards on either side of the snapping point—they could legally attack the receiver. We lined up and Busby took the snap. He made a quick lateral kick to

Bridgman running straight away. It was a good, clean shot but Bridgman bobbled it and the crowd groaned. The missed catch meant we forfeited our try at goal.

The score stood at 5 to 0.

Jacob made a long kick from midfield. Nevison, the Muskegon fullback, caught it and advanced to the twenty-yard line. On the next play, they attempted an end run, but Arthur Baushke hit the runner so hard he knocked him back five yards. They ran two more plays and were forced to punt.

I ran a series of plays, line bucks mostly, and we muscled the ball to the thirty-yard line. Then I called for Busby to try a drop kick, which went wide, and Muskegon took possession and immediately punted to Cunningham, who caught it and made a fine run to the Muskegon thirty-five-yard line. After two plays for short gains, I signaled Busby to try another kick, but a Muskegon player blocked and then fell on it at the fifty-five.

"Come on, Bus!" I snarled. "I'm giving you the chance you wanted."

"I know," he sputtered angrily between gasps for breath.

I called out the defensive formation I wanted and then hollered, "Okay fellas, let's give em hell!"

With the crowd pressed against the sidelines screaming like savages, we lined up for Muskegon's first down. Jiroch took the pigskin and ran behind interference around the right end and broke free. I was deep man back, unfortunately blocked out of the play, and it looked like a sure touchdown. But Bridgman pulled my butt from the fire with a magnificent chase and tackle.

After that, we stopped them and they punted.

I called for the fellows to shift into the left-tackle-back formation, which meant Ossignac positioned himself a few steps behind the line. On the first play, I faked a handoff to him while on the next play he carried the ball for a good five-yard gain. For the next two series, I put the fellows back to our regular formation and then to the tackle-back-square formation, which is where Ossignac moved to the other side of the center and stood behind Handy. Then we ran a number of plays where Ossignac and the Iron Man blocked together. The results were splendid. We pounded the ball down the field until Baushke carried it over for the touchdown. Busby kicked the goal.

I was feeling good about my play selections, and with each succeeding series I decreased the time lapse between plays. The fellows seemed fresh and not the least bit intimidated by my pacing, in spite of the physical beating they took during the Kalamazoo game. It was obvious Teetzel's torturous week of training had paid off.

The game went on for another two minutes before the half ended. The score was 11 to 0 in our favor.

We sat on the ground in front of our bench and rested while Teetzel went through his list of mistakes. When the fellows trotted back onto the field, Teetzel pulled me aside and complimented me for my work.

"Good job, Van Horne," he said. "I see you've been studying your playbook."

"I have," I replied with a straight face. Inside I was prideful that he noticed.

"But don't rely too much on line bucks—Muskegon is expecting it. Send the ball wide the minute you suspect they're bunching up to stop a drive close to center. And don't telegraph."

I knew the compliment was too good to last. In rapid succession, Teetzel walked me through a half dozen other play scenarios before he said, "Keep the fellows moving and don't let up. Make them work."

"I plan to," I said as I wiped the grime from around my eyes and joined the fellows on the field.

The second half began with Muskegon kicking to us. Brimming with confidence, we made repeated gains of five and ten yards with Jacob pounding the line and Bridgman and Baushke running wide. The playing was hard and fast, and soon I was smeared with sweat. But the world was mine. We were playing good, clean football, and I felt confident the game was ours. In my mind, the only remaining question was the size of the score.

Soon the Muskegon players began shoving harder and longer during the plays, and for a few seconds after the whistle. In theory that was a good sign—meant they were getting demoralized.

"It's time to finish this thing," I said to the fellows when we were walking back on the field after a Muskegon time out.

"Amen," Jacob said. The rest of the fellows nodded their heads in agreement. They knew exactly what I meant.

The game started up again and we tore into the Muskegon players like wild dogs. It didn't matter if we were on offense or defense, we shredded them, and that's when they got angry and started to play rough. It wasn't blatant. A quick jab or a punch in the murder pile was all. But Heck and some of the others felt obliged to return the favor, and soon enough faces on both sides began to speckle up with fresh blood. That angered the Muskegon players even more. They may not have been great at football, but they played the slugging game for all it was worth.

I felt Muskegon's frustration firsthand while running interference at Bridgman's left hip and some bastard elbowed me in the face. Dropped me like a lead weight. The blow caused fireworks to pop in my head, but thank God I didn't black out and was up again within seconds trying to get my bearings. I recovered quickly, but my right eye-tooth was loose and I wiggled it with my tongue until it dropped. Most of the fellows had lost teeth playing football, but that was my first and it made me mad as hell. That's when I decided to make Muskegon pay. Our line was already reforming, so I held the tooth in my cheek, and with the taste of warm blood in my mouth called out the next play.

We ran a series of plays where I hammered the fellows forward so fast and furious that the Muskegon players couldn't even get lined up properly before we were off again. Finally, Jacob carried the ball across the goal line for our third touchdown and Busby kicked the goal. I ran over to the bench, tossed my tooth on the grass where I could find it later, and grabbed a wad of gauze from Mit and clamped it between my teeth.

Muskegon kicked, and the ball went to me, which I caught and should've shoveled back to Jacob or Baushke or the Iron Man but didn't. I was still angry about losing my tooth and decided to keep it and show the bastards they couldn't push me around. I started running behind interference and made about fifteen yards before a Muskegon player came at me full bore from the side and I made a sudden jog to the left. It didn't help. The fellow blasted me and I went down. Like dominos, a dozen or more bodies crashed on top of us.

The players untangled themselves from the pile, but when I tried to move my leg, a searing pain shot through my right thigh. I could hear a gasp from the crowd when they saw me writhing on the ground. Tears welled up in the corner of my eyes, burning like fire, but I thanked the Lord when they didn't run down my cheek. Jones and Handy pulled me to my feet, and the crowd applauded as I limped off the field between them. The referee called time and both teams trotted to their respective benches.

I sat down on the bench and Doc gave me a quick going over. He looked concerned but said not to worry—the pain was probably caused by a bruised muscle. I wasn't fooled by his nonchalance, in fact I was worried as hell. While he was wrapping a rubber bag filled with ice to the back of my leg, Wadsworth ran out onto the field and took his place at the helm of my machine.

My worst nightmare had just come true.

Chapter 18

M onday after lunch Pa and I rode the trolley in together and got off at the downtown area called Four Corners. He strolled to his office while I went to the Graham Building at the corner of Main and Water. Walking on the flat wasn't bad—I was using one of Pa's walking canes—but negotiating the stair climb up to Doc's office was a struggle.

"Have a seat, Fletch," Doc said from the examination room doorway where he had appeared at the sound of my entering. There was no receptionist.

"Old John Krieger came in this morning with a broken arm," he whispered. "Fell off a ladder while picking apples. Got to get to him first, you know."

"Yes sir," I said. "I've got time." He closed the door behind him and then I was alone.

The waiting room was shadowy. The walls were painted a forest green, and the maple wood floor was covered everywhere but at the edges with a maroon patterned Turkish rug. Furnishings included six dark oak wood chairs with brown leather seats, a coat tree, and a wall-mounted gas lamp. I sat back, leaned my head against the wall, and tried to doze, but sleeping was not possible. My mind churned with the memory of the Muskegon game....

I remembered sitting on the bench furious at myself for getting injured, doubly so because it was caused by my own damn stupidity. I was also in pain, but my dedication to the team kept me focused on the game and I watched with high hopes.

Wadsworth carried the ball himself on the first play and did a fine job advancing ten yards for the first down. He handed off on the next two attempts, got nowhere, and the possession went to Muskegon. They ran a series of plays, made a couple of first downs, and I felt sure they'd score, but the fellows rallied and stopped them. Wadsworth then ran three plays and failed to make a first down. Our rooters groaned while Teetzel simply looked at the ground and shook his head.

But then things started to improve.

Muskegon took the ball into play and the Iron Man single-handedly stopped a mass play off-tackle. On the next down, Jacob grabbed Muskegon's Torrent behind the line of scrimmage and threw him for a three-yard loss. Torrent then tried to gain around our left end, but Butts stopped him and the ball was ours.

On our next series, Wadsworth's confidence improved and he picked up the rhythm. We made a first down and the pace of the game got hotter. I remember hearing someone yell into a huge megaphone, "Watch Wadsworth!" Then I heard other rooters repeat that message down the sideline. He didn't disappoint them. Wadsworth repeatedly hammered the backs at the Muskegon line with Jacob carrying the ball, followed by Bridgman, Baushke, then Jacob again, and finally the Iron Man. All were unstoppable. Time was called when Ossignac injured a Muskegon player, and shortly thereafter Bridgman went over for the fourth touchdown of the day, and Busby kicked the goal.

The punishing pace of our offense was too much for Muskegon, and they couldn't recover even after the Iron Man reinjured his knee and had to leave the game. Midway through the second half, they'd used their last time-out to catch wind and even the rooters began to lose interest.

Baushke scored the next touchdown. I didn't even see it—I was sitting on the bench with my head in my hands. My thigh hurt, my jaw throbbed, and I was mad and miserable and worried that Wadsworth's performance might mean the end of my quarterbacking career....

"It's your turn, Fletch!" Doc said from the examination door. I snapped out of my dreaming just as Mr. Krieger came out with his arm in a sling.

"Now John, remember to keep that arm elevated for a few days. And don't do any work with it."

"You say so, Doc," he grumbled as he picked his floppy brimmed hat from the coat tree and put it on. Then he turned and faced me as I struggled to my feet.

"Damn fine game, kid," the old man said.

"You were there?" I asked, annoyed that he called me kid but proud that he knew who I was.

"Yes sir. I hitched the wagon to Jane and Sarah, the finest pair of Morgans in the township, and brought the missus in with me. I like your style."

"Thanks," I said, pleased by the compliment. Then he stuck out a calloused hand and I shook it.

"Although it pained me to see you get yourself hurt. But it's a good thing Wadsworth was there to back you up—he did a damn fine job himself."

"I want to see you in two weeks," Doc interrupted. Good thing. It saved me from saying something about Wadsworth I might have regretted.

"I'll be here," he answered as he opened the door. Then he winked at me and slammed the door behind him.

"Come in here, Fletch, and let's have a look at that leg. And by the way, John was right. You certainly showed admirably Saturday." I thanked him as we entered the examination room.

Doc instructed me to take off my britches, which I did, and then he had me sit up on the wooden table and lay down. He went to work moving my leg up and down and sideways while asking me questions. His words were muffled because of the cigar in his mouth, but I understood and answered truthfully. It felt uncomfortable. Then he began prodding his stubby fingers into the muscle at the back of my thigh and finally hit paydirt.

"That's it," I replied calmly. Actually, it hurt like hell but I didn't want him to know.

He prodded a few more times and again I signaled the painful areas. "Just as I thought," he said. "You have a posterior femoral muscle strain."

"A female what?" I asked. It puzzled me that a man would have such a muscle.

"Fe-mor-al," he said, slowly emphasizing each syllable. "In common parlance, that would be a hamstring tear. Probably happened when you made that sudden change in direction to avoid being tackled. There's even a nice bruise forming."

"Will I be able to play Saturday?"

"Are you keeping up with the hot compresses?"

"Yes," I lied.

"How does this feel?" Doc continued to press into the muscle and again it hurt like hell.

"Fine," I said. By then he must have known I was lying because of the twisted look on my face every time his fingers pried at the tender spots. But then maybe he didn't. The grind of everyday practice and the games I'd already played left me hurting practically everywhere. My muscles ached and my skin was like a sack, bruised and scraped raw, holding a collection of loose, rattling bones that ground together every time I moved. My joints felt like they were filled with sand. And that was before I injured my leg.

"How often are you applying the hot compresses?"

"I kept ice on it Saturday evening," I said truthfully.

"Good. But how about Sunday?

"I put on a hot compress after breakfast." My desire to get back on the playing field was dogged, but I just couldn't see how hot compresses were going to get me there. Of course, it was a reasoning based on impatience and stupidity.

"How about Sunday afternoon?"

"No."

"Well, Fletch," he said as he struck a match and relit his cigar. "You'll need to do better."

"It doesn't hurt that bad, Doc." I couldn't stop myself from lying. "I must get back on the field."

"I hope so too, son," he said. "But it doesn't look good. You have to realize that a damaged hamstring muscle can take a long time to heal if it's bad…and you must keep up with the hot compresses."

"Feels better today than it did Saturday."

"That's a good sign," he replied. "You'd better keep it up if you want any hope at all of returning to the team. And say, how about that run Bridgman made at the end of the game?"

"What?" I said, momentarily confused by the abrupt change in subject. I was still reeling from his prognosis that I might not play again that season.

"Bridgman's run."

"Yeah...was first-rate," I mumbled.

Doc was referring to something that happened during the last minute of the game when I was sitting on the ground with my back against the bench and my knees up—my head was hanging between them like a beaten dog. A sudden, raucous explosion from the crowd made me look up just in time to see Bridgman, framed against a sea of waving orange and black ribbons, break through the line with the ball in one hand and the other hand holding onto the leather strap attached to the back of Jacob's belt. Heck was supporting Bridgman's left side. Over the cheering of the crowd, I could hear the sounds of thrashing knees, elbows, and forearms, along with the grunts and groans made by players being blocked or jabbed. Whenever the Muskegon players swarmed around Bridgman, our players knocked them away. I watched in disbelief as Bridgman, supported by the Grahams, dragged the remaining mass of players fifty-seven yards for a touchdown. Busby missed the goal, but the rooters barely noticed they were so busy jumping up and down and dancing like maniacs.

Time was called shortly after Bridgman's run with the score at 33 to 0. And it was a good thing it ended when it did—the Muskegon players might have begun dying from exhaustion. Thinking about the game again, along with Doc's dire prediction regarding my leg, made me want to get back on the team more than ever.

Using my best let's-cut-through-the-crap voice, I said, "But Doc, there must be something you can do to make it heal faster."

"Don't think so, Fletch. I'm afraid time is your best friend now."

"You're sure there isn't something else you can do?"

"Well..." he said as he wrinkled his brow and stared out the window. He took a long draw on his cigar and then said, "Yes, by

God, there is. Sit tight and I'll be right back."

At that moment, my spirits soared to heights unknown since I was a kid going with Pa to the drug store lunch counter for ice cream. I was so excited I actually began whistling a ditty under my breath, and I didn't stop until Doc came back into the room and I saw what he had in mind. And then I stopped mid note. He held a jar of leeches—big, black squirmy devils so ugly the mere sight of them made the hair on my neck bristle.

"Jesus, Doc!" I said as I felt the blood drain from my face.

"Roll over, Fletch, and let me put some of these where it hurts most."

"But Doc!"

"Easy, Fletch," he said as if he were speaking to a spooked horse. "If I bleed you enough, it just might help you to get through this problem."

I knew about leeches from my folks. When they were kids, most doctors still believed in bleeding the sickness out of their patients. I knew some doctors who still did it, old Doc Davis being one of them, which is why no one went to him except for the old timers. But not my Doc for Christ's sake.

"I'm fine," I said calmly after I'd gathered my composure.

"But you're not fine. That's why I think we should try the leeches."

"Believe me, Doc…I'm feeling just fine."

"You sure?"

"Yes. I'm as sure as the sun will rise tomorrow."

"Because if you're not," he said as he held the jar in front of my face, "a little leech treatment just might be the ticket."

"There's nothing wrong with my blood," I said with a shudder.

"All right, Fletch. But if your leg doesn't heal soon, you might want to reconsider. You do want to get back playing again don't you?"

"Yes sir," I said. "More than anything in the world."

"Then you'd better keep heat on that leg. You can't be letting that Wadsworth kid steal your thunder, especially after all the work you've been through. By the way, he showed pretty well, didn't he?"

"Yeah…just great."

I'm sure he detected the sarcasm in my voice. He didn't say it, but I know he did—probably what he wanted. I don't think he cared one way or the other who played quarterback, me or Wadsworth. He was more interested in having the best man lead the team, which is why he tickled my competitive spirit by mentioning Wadsworth's name. And he used more than Wadsworth.

"Have you seen the *News* yet?" he went on.

"No."

"Here, have a look while I put a wrap on that thigh."

I began reading the article while Doc worked on my leg. It was all there, including my injury, followed by statements taken from both coaches. Coach Walker's was as follows:

We were outclassed and could not have won against Benton Harbor under any condition. Benton Harbor plays a hard and systematic game and it will require a good team to defeat it. I doubt if the teams of the small colleges in the state could play successfully against Benton Harbor.

As usual, Teetzel's statement was short and to the point, but this time he actually offered some analysis:

Muskegon played as good a game as Kalamazoo. Our team was fifty percent faster than at the Kalamazoo game and Muskegon could not get its interference into place to do effective work. However, in order to win the state championship our team must be faster.

The article concluded by reporting the Muskegon team left on the 7:15 train for home and that Teetzel and the fellows were there for the send-off.

That's right, I said to myself bitterly, *all of them but me.* I was home nursing my leg and a bad attitude.

"Pretty good press don't you think?" Doc said.

"Yeah," I replied. By then I felt so helpless I could've cried. "I just wish I could've seen it through to the end," I said in all seriousness.

"You might get your chance yet," he said. "Keep up with the hot compresses and continue to use the walking cane if it eases the pressure. Later today I'll mix up an ointment of Cantharides blister for you to apply, and in a few days we'll start in with some light stretching exercises."

I left the office feeling pretty damn down because of my bum leg. The way I figured it, I had less then a fifty-fifty chance of healing in time to play again that season.

I went to the playing grounds that afternoon to watch the fellows practice. My leg was stiff and sore and useless, and my gut feeling told me nothing short of a miracle would get me back on the playing field that season. And the cane made me feel like a cripple in front of the fellows. I wished I'd left it home.

"How's the leg, Fletch?" Teetzel asked.

"Fine, coach. I should be back on the field in a week or two."

"That right?" he said suspiciously.

"Yep," I said with all the confidence I could muster.

"What did Doc say about it?"

"Said it was a hamstring." I wanted to lie about that, tell him it was just a bruised muscle, but I knew he'd eventually hear the truth from Doc.

"That can be a very serious injury, a long-time healer. Are you aware of that?" He was staring into my eyes, searching me.

"Yes, I am. But it's not that bad."

"Well," he said cautiously. "If it doesn't heal and you can't play again for the rest of the season, you will be missed. Your playing in the Muskegon game was first-rate."

"Thanks, coach." I was trying my damnedest to plug my leaking eyes.

"In the meantime, why don't you plan on helping me coach the fellows? And maybe you can help Waddie with the plays and signals."

I wanted to help with the coaching, but I wasn't so sure I wanted anything to do with helping Wadsworth. In fact, I would have prayed for his complete failure if it wasn't for my dedication to the team. I was already wishing he'd lose teeth, get boils on his legs, and maybe break an arm or leg for good measure. My other option was to simply say no—that would have been the easy way out.

"Be glad to," I replied.

I stood with Teetzel and watched the fellows run through their routines and yelled out advice when I had something to say. Wadsworth never asked for my help and I never offered. Was just as well.

During a break in the practice, I told Jacob about my visit to Doc's office and about the leeches, which started him laughing. And the more I talked about it the harder he laughed. He called some of the other fellows over to hear my story and they laughed too. I couldn't see what was so damn funny and said so.

"Tell him, Jacob," Bridgman finally said, grinning like a fox who'd just found the chicken coop door unlatched.

"No...you tell him. You fell for that trick once."

"Alright. He was playing with you, Fletch. He was trying to scare you into following his advice...to get you to keep heat on it."

"Yep," Jacob said. "He drags that jar of leeches out whenever he can. Makes for guffaws at the card games and such."

Well, the fellows had a good guffaw at my expense. I could handle that, but Wadsworth was there and he guffawed the hardest. Made me want to bust him in the mouth.

During supper that evening, I wasn't hungry and mostly used my fork to nudge the food around. I didn't speak much either and my folks knew why—they'd already pried it out of me what Doc said about my leg. But they made a valiant attempt to cheer me up. Pa said most of the serious enthusiasts agreed I played a flawless game and was mostly responsible for breaking the school record for the most points scored in an interscholastic contest.

He was right. I ran the team at a lightning-fast pace. In fact, by the time Wadsworth took the helm we'd already run Muskegon into the ground—they were fagged and frequently disoriented before the ball was even snapped. Dice Baushke told me he heard Teetzel mutter "we must be faster" several times during the first half, and I heard him say it myself during the second half when I was on the bench. Maybe he was right, but no one from Bungtown could deny we were the fastest and hardest-hitting team ever to trod the turf of a Bungtown gridiron. And I, the featherweight, had led them.

And that's what made it all so damn hard on me. I couldn't believe I might not see it through to the end.

Next Pa tried to bribe me. He promised to buy me a new tooth for Christmas, which should have made me feel better since most of the fellows on the team couldn't afford them and had to live with gaping holes in their mouths. But I didn't care about a new tooth. I was worried about my position, and they finally realized there was nothing they could say that would make me feel any better.

"Keep your chin up, Fletch," Pa finally said. "Think positive and it'll all work out just fine."

That was easy for him to say. In my mind, all that was left for me was the glory I'd already earned.

After dinner my brother trudged upstairs to bed and Pa went to his study to work on a case while I went to the parlor to read the paper. I could barely hear Ma in the kitchen washing dishes, which left the tick-tock of the mantle clock as my only companion. I settled into Pa's stuffed chair and tried to get comfortable but couldn't because of the throbbing pain in my thigh. But even without the pain, I quickly discovered my mind was racing much too fast to read. All I could think about was getting healed and back on the field. I wanted to be back because I loved the game, but also because of my pride and my growing resentment toward Wadsworth.

I went to practice again on Tuesday for the reassurance. I couldn't play, but being there at least reminded me I was part of the team. It made me feel better when the fellows talked about the games, past as well as future, especially when they talked as though I were still one of them. That's because I understood their worries, confidences too. I almost forgot about my injury when we began reminiscing about the season's greatest plays and victories. Our win over Muskegon left us feeling pretty damn invincible, but I can tell you here and now it was an illusion at best. The season hadn't even begun to get rough. And the roughness wasn't the only demon we would face.

The fellows were focused on the Notre Dame game rescheduled for that Thursday, November 5, when something unexpected happened that threatened to put us out of the running entirely for the state championship.

Chapter 19

Wednesday after school we met at the Old Athletic Field for our regular practice and found Teetzel having a serious discussion with Manager Burger.

"Come over here, fellows!" Teetzel hollered when he noticed we'd all arrived. "Have a seat."

We sat on the grass in a loose semi-circle and listened while Burger told us about a controversy that had developed with the Muskegon team. He said it came to light that morning when a wire arrived from the editor of the *Grand Rapids Press* saying the Muskegon team management had accused us of cheating.

The editor said there were three violations stated. The first was Wadsworth. They claimed he wasn't enrolled in school until after October 1, that he was a former quarterback at Northwestern University, and we were paying him to play. The second and third violations involved two players who were clerks in a local dry goods store and not taking classes. Names weren't given. The editor wanted Teetzel's side of the story—particularly in relation to Wadsworth's identity and hometown.

Seemed like a damn joke.

"Anyone know anything about this?" Burger said. He was answered with an immediate outburst of boos and unkind phrases about the gender of the Muskegon players.

Burger quieted us and then said the rumor regarding Muskegon's spy in Benton Harbor was apparently true—he or she must have tipped them off on the afternoon of the game. He said if any of the charges were proven to be true, the result of the game would be revised and Muskegon declared the winner. The entire thing seemed ludicrous, but it was obvious Burger wasn't about to leave anything to chance.

Teetzel told us he wired back and assured the editor Wadsworth had never played anything but high school football. Said he was a nineteen-year-old farm kid from Twelve Corners and that he started school on September 29, which of course, was the true lie. The two players accused of working in a dry goods store were Jacob and Arthur Baushke. Teetzel answered those charges by telling the editor Jacob was going to school during the day and working evenings as a clerk at Young's Dry Goods store. No falsehoods there—he needed to work to help support his ma. Baushke had a similar arrangement with Kidd, Dater, and Price.

The truth of the matter regarding Jacob and Baushke was that they would quit school the minute football season was over, and that truly was illegal. The State Athletic Committee regulations demanded all high school athletes attend classes for the full nine months. But almost everyone, the state officials included, ignored that rule. Strict adherence for many high school teams would've made it impossible to field a team, period. There simply would not have been enough players.

After practice, the team began their regular jog over to the Pastime Club for rubdowns while Teetzel and I rode with Doc— Teetzel sitting on the bench next to Doc while I perched myself on the buggy's back bed with my legs dangling free. When we arrived, we found Burger in the club room with Tuesday's edition of the *Muskegon Chronicle* that included an editorial written by Muskegon's Coach Walker. While waiting for the fellows, Burger laid it out on the counter while Teetzel and I read it. Caully too. It began:

So long as the interscholastic agreement between the high schools of Michigan, by which the high school football championship of Michigan has been decided each year, served as a protection and safeguarded athletics in those schools it was a good thing. But I am satisfied that not only has it failed to assure this purity in Michigan high school athletics, which would be a failure bad enough, but that it has also proven an actual protection to fraud.

Coach Walker was right. Fraud was a part of the game, which led to some of the state's largest schools not signing the inter-scholastic agreement. Not one Detroit school was still in the pro-gram and even Grand Rapids was considering to pull out. But there was more to the letter than fraud. Lurking between the lines was the great hypocrisy:

> I do not believe that Muskegon High School will next year enter the interscholastic agreements. I have felt reluctant to say anything because anything I might say would be apt to be mis-interpreted and attributed to the fact that we have been recently defeated. But I feel that no school that enters the interscholas-tic agreement can keep its own skirts clean without being put to a disadvantage. This has been impressed upon me by our Benton Harbor experience. I not only believe that the inter-scholastic agreement fails to protect the schools that are inclined to abide by its rules, but that it serves as a cloak to positive fraud.

On the surface, Walker's arguments may have been good ones, but beneath the skim they were actually sour milk. Sure, football was a rough business, and maybe the State Athletic Committee wasn't as vigilant with the rules as they should have been. In fact, they were downright criminal during our 1902 fight with Ishpeming. But the fact remained that we humiliated Muskegon, which is why their charges against Jacob, Wadsworth, and Baushke were two-faced. And I'll tell you why.

I'm convinced Muskegon wouldn't have said a word about ille-gal players if they'd won. But they lost. Even then, their complaints might have had a ring of legitimacy if they truly believed in the ethical standards laid out in the interscholastic agreement. I say that because their skirts were anything but clean. They used at least one illegal player in their game against Grand Rapids High, and he was a paid professional—a ringer. We read about him in the *Grand Rapids Press* a couple days after the game.

Grand Rapids complained about the ringer before the game started, but Muskegon refused to remove him. And that wasn't the end of it. After Muskegon scored the first touchdown, which was called back because of a penalty, they rushed the Grand Rapids team and threatened them with balled fists. The officials managed to restore order, but poor sportsmanship characterized their conduct for the remainder of the game.

After we finished reading Coach Walker's letter, Burger said, "I should have seen it coming."

"How so?" Doc asked.

"While they were here in Benton Harbor, some of the Muskegon players complained to me about the wretched treatment they got in Traverse City the week before."

"Didn't they win that game?"

"Yes sir."

"Ungrateful whelps," Caully interjected.

"It appears that way," Burger said while shaking his head in bewilderment. "But tomorrow morning I'll be sending the Muskegon team manager a telegram offering my support in any investigation they deem necessary, but I will also request they keep their part of the agreement and pay half of Doctor May's officiating expenses."

It was then the fellows poured in the front door huffing and sweating. "Come in, boys!" Caully said with a wave of his hand. "Hot showers and rubdowns are waitin for each and ev'ry one a ya."

"A drink for the team," a patron shouted from one of the tables. The handful of men sitting with him lifted their glasses in salute.

"Jacob!" Caully hollered. "Have you come to a decision about me offer?"

"No I haven't, Caully," he answered between deep breaths as he trudged past the counter. "Haven't had the time to give it much thought."

"What offer?" Teetzel asked.

"My offer ta take him boxin on the armory circuit. The laddiebuck's a natural." When he saw the look of disgust forming on Teetzel's face he quickly added, "Of course that wouldn't be takin place till the season's over."

"Of course," Teetzel said as he turned and followed the team into the locker room shaking his head.

In the locker room, Teetzel was quiet. He talked for a few minutes about some new plays, but then he let us go without so much as another word about Muskegon's charges. Defending us the way he did must have been hard on him, especially when he lied about the date Wadsworth started school. Surprised me, his lying. But then it surprised me even more when he went on the offensive.

The following day, an editorial written by Teetzel appeared in the the *Evening News*—he said it was aimed at the Muskegon team management and that he was confident they would read it by way of their spy in Benton Harbor. In the editorial, he related all of Muskegon's charges and refuted each one. Then he criticized them for being sore losers. But the greatest slap was his claim that we could've beat them without the three players in question, that our scrubs could've beat them.

And he was right.

Burger, the board, the rooters, and all us team members viewed Teetzel as a hero for standing up like he did. But I continued to suspect the entire episode made him uncomfortable. I'm certain he lied to protect us—perhaps his good name too—but I believe he lied mostly because he felt it was his obligation. He realized the people of Benton Harbor expected him to do everything within his power to take us to the state championship game. Anything less would be viewed as a betrayal.

From that day until the end of the season, not another word was said about Jacob, Wadsworth, or Baushke, and no hard evidence was found that could be used to convict us of cheating. The fellows forgot about it and started to worry about other matters, like our remaining games, none of which were expected to be easy.

Wednesday evening after supper, I was sitting in our parlor reading the newspaper when I thought about a comment made by Doctor May following the Muskegon game. At the time, I wasn't paying much attention because of my sour attitude, but with all the reemerging talk about the state championship, the comment came back clearer than ever. While talking to a reporter from the *St. Joseph Herald*, the doctor praised us—said we were disciplined and fast—but then he said we had to be faster if we wanted to beat Ishpeming.

Ishpeming. How could I have forgotten them?

Over the previous weeks, I'd been so consumed with my quarterbacking duties, and after that my injury, that the fire I originally had for defeating Ishpeming had become a smoldering ember. Suddenly I felt the urge to fan the flames again. I put the newspaper down, closed my eyes, and laid my head against the back of the chair to think about our impending rematch.

Ishpeming football was a tale of hard work and determination, I won't deny that. Even before the Wizard took control of their program, they were a powerhouse, losing only a small handful of games since they started playing football in 1895. I'll never forget the way they used their phenomenal speed and revolving mass and fake plays against us. And I didn't even play in that game.

The defeat of Ishpeming was still the great obsession in Bungtown because of the way they humiliated us. I don't believe I've ever seen a community so consumed with getting revenge as Benton Harbor. During those final weeks of the season, that's all the rooters talked about, and that's why they were so interested in Teetzel's strategy. Most were expecting a grand scheme of trickery or an ever-changing collection of complex strategies. None were correct. He was planning to defeat Ishpeming at their own game, which was speed. We'd simply run them into the ground. We players knew—had known all along because of Teetzel's unrelenting speed work—but when it finally began to appear in newspaper articles, everyone from the gamblers and businessmen to the students knew it too.

Some of the students made up a saying. It started out as a mimic of a phrase Teetzel used on us, but ended up as a rallying cry for our rooters as well. The saying was: "Faster, boys, faster, we must beat Ishpeming!" And they said it over and over until it rolled like a fog through our streets and into the neighborhoods and homes. The great rematch with Ishpeming seemed inevitable. It was only a tick away and we were almost ready.

Immediately after our victory over Muskegon, we put our ears to the wind for any information about the Ishpeming team, which proved hard to come by. But we finally got our hands on a Marquette newspaper that reported the upper peninsula stars were preparing for the championship game by "recalling their old players in from the mines and the tall timber," which led us to believe Ishpeming would be made up of men not boys. When reporters asked Jacob about it during the Muskegon controversy he replied, "We don't care if they're giants."

And that's how I felt about it.

Some of the rooters around town talked about Ishpeming as though they were invincible, direct descendants of the Vikings or some such nonsense. But I wasn't afraid. I didn't care if they'd won three state championships or if their football players had a reputation larger than life. I'd be ready. That's what kept me going. And I'll say it again—I was confident my leg would be healed in time for the Thanksgiving Day game for the state championship. The alternative was unthinkable.

Meanwhile, looming in the team's immediate future was the grudge match with Notre Dame. That's right—the game with the Catholics had been rescheduled at the last minute—and if we hated anyone as much as Ishpeming it was Notre Dame.

Chapter 20

M iss Fitzgerald instructed us to pass our assignments to the front of the room. Accompanied by the sounds of shuffling paper, we quickly completed that task and she collected them from the person sitting at the front desk in each row.

"You are excused," she said after reseating herself.

The kids who sat near the front exited immediately while us football players took our time, and not by any choice of our own mind you—I was using Pa's cane while Iron Man Lathe was walking on crutches again because of his knee. He reinjured it during the Muskegon game. Bridgman, who also sat in that class, was nursing a freshly twisted knee himself from that week's practice. But he was walking without aid and waited while we stood up and prepared ourselves to walk the gauntlet. By that I mean Miss Fitzgerald.

As we began moving toward the door, Miss Fitzgerald fixed us with a steely gaze. She'd begun her staring routine on Monday, the first day Lathe showed up with his crutches, and it was now Thursday. She had yet to say anything to us, but the expression on her face wasn't hard to read. It was stamped with pure disgust. If even a thin coating of pity resided within the folds of her heart, it wasn't obvious. Made us uneasy. Therefore no one said anything, even Bridgman. As the three of us walked in a tight group up the middle isle toward her, I felt like we were walking into the muzzle of a loaded cannon, the tap-tapping of cane and crutch on the maple wood floor only directing her sights tighter and tighter upon us. It was excruciating.

We reached the front of the room without incident and were in the process of negotiating the right-hand turn in front of her desk. We were almost home free, but then Lathe caught one of his crutches on the leg of the front desk and faltered. In an instant, Miss Fitzgerald stood up and rushed to his side.

"Boys!" she said while clutching his huge left arm to steady him, the crutch and part of his leg completely disappearing into the folds of her dress. "Just look at yourselves!"

"Ma'am?" Lathe replied with eyes stunned wide as plums. I think he was embarrassed to have such a beautiful woman clutching him that way.

"I cannot believe how terrible you look. I don't know how you even get out of bed each morning for all the pain."

"I do whatever it takes," Lathe said seriously.

There was a long pause before someone spoke. It was Bridgman. "I'm alright too, Miss Fitz," he said politely. Then he flashed that mischievous Bridgman grin and tried to prove himself by performing a jig, which was wobbly at best.

"Yes, Mr. Bridgman, I see you are. And I hope your eyesight is better than your knee." She let go of Lathe's arm and immediately straightened the cameo pinned to the high collar of her white blouse.

"Pardon me?"

"I seem to recollect a few weeks ago when your eye looked like a piece of raw meat."

"It was nothing," he replied. "Happens all the time in football. It's all part of the fun."

"It may be fun you're having, but it's also extremely dangerous and not at all conducive to learning."

"Ma'am?" I said, puzzled at her reference to learning. She turned her green eyes on me, and at that moment I wished I'd kept my mouth shut.

"It's not conducive to learning because you're so exhausted you often fall asleep in class. How many times this week alone have I scolded you to stop nodding and sit up straight?" Then she turned to Bridgman and said, "And you too, Mr. Bridgman."

"Me?" Bridgman said with a false look of incredulity.

"You know quite well I am referring to you."

I don't know how Bridgman felt about it, but I was guilty. That didn't mean I planned to express agreement with her any more than I was willing to maintain my side of the argument. Attempts at bravery would have been useless, so I decided it would be best to remain quiet.

"But it's only a three-month stint, Miss Fitzgerald," Lathe said, taking up the countercharge. "Then it's back to normal."

"Yes, Mr. Lathe, it is a mere three months. But it only takes three seconds of play to become permanently maimed or paralyzed. Three short seconds and a life can be ruined. And you, Mr. Van Horne. How does a sophomore the size of a mere eighth grader suppose he can survive physical contact with men the size of Mr. Lathe?"

An eighth grader! I screamed to myself. *Who the hell do you think you are, comparing me to an eighth grader?* I was mad and offended and embarrassed by her comment. I wanted to puff up my chest and tell her about all the things I'd accomplished playing quarterback for Teetzel's machine. "I can take it just fine," I finally replied.

"You cannot," she shot back, getting more emotional by the second. "Just look at yourself for proof. And for the life of me I will never understand how an educated man like Mr. Teetzel can allow himself to be associated with such barbarism."

When she brought Teetzel into it I finally found my pluck. "Excuse me, Miss Fitzgerald," I said. "It's because of Coach Teetzel that we aren't in worse shape."

There was a moment of silence as she crossed her arms over her chest and took a deep breath. "Against my better judgment, I will allow you to explain yourself, Mr. Van Horne."

"He cares about us."

"That's right," Bridgman piped up. "In fact, it's his rule that we don't slug during the games, and that's something we're not exactly happy about. I'd gladly welcome a few skinned knuckles…"

"And he also argues," I quickly interrupted, "for better enforcement of the rules by the game officials."

"Amen," Lathe added, "and he's always harpin on us bout eating regular and gettin enough sleep. It's not his fault if we don't listen to him."

I could tell our standing up for Teetzel caught her off guard, dulled the edges of her tirade. She apparently didn't know how to respond and simply stood there thinking about it, which is when Lathe and I clutched our wooden walking implements and began edging toward the door. Bridgman too. But as we were filing into the corridor, she caught her second wind and threw one more jab at Bridgman, who was the last man out.

"You may have a right to play football, Mr. Bridgman," she said. "But no one says you have to risk your health by playing against college teams. I read the paper—I know you're scheduled to play against Notre Dame this afternoon."

"We appreciate your concern," Bridgman replied after he turned to face her. "But truth be told, we welcome the opportunity."

He was lying. The fellows were very apprehensive about playing against Notre Dame. None of them would ever admit it, but I could see it written all over their faces.

Our series with Notre Dame was one of our bloodiest grudge matches. A Benton Harbor club team played them in 1900, and before the game was ended, six players from each side were carried off the field. The high school met them for the first time in 1901 and lost 5 to 0. We played again the following year but forfeited before the game was over. And I would argue it wasn't our fault. We forfeited because the Notre Dame team played a hard-knuckled, brawling type of football that was beyond anything we'd ever seen even in those days. In fact, they played the dirtiest football I'd ever seen.

From the first few minutes of play in the 1902 game, the Notre Dame players blatantly broke the holding rules, which was bad enough, but they also kicked, tripped, and slugged. They and their rooters kept up a steady stream of swearing, and whenever we threatened to score they made so much noise the fellows couldn't hear the signals. It was arranged ahead of time that a Notre Dame official would referee the first half and one of our officials would take command during the second. The first half was such a mess because the Notre Dame official refused to penalize his team or the crowd.

Tom Logan officiated during the second half and attempted to tame the playing, but the Notre Dame folks pelted him with oaths and promises of punches. He issued penalties but they did little good. Finally, the slugging and foul play became so intense that he ordered both teams off the field, which caused the Notre Dame players and their rooters to rush the field and surround him. They begged him to let the game go on, but he refused. Said he'd given them plenty of warnings, which they ignored, and he wasn't about to change his mind.

But the matter didn't end there.

When Logan was walking to the locker room, he had to pass through a mob of students who pelted him with mud and stones. He didn't get hurt, but we couldn't believe their lack of manners. Coach Machesney was so put off that he wrote a letter to the *Benton Harbor Evening News*. Part of it read as follows:

> Personally I have attended and taken part in scores of games, both baseball and football, in nearly all of the preparatory schools and universities, and many athletic clubs in the west in the past seven years, and have never met a lot of men who were so utterly lacking in qualities that belong to gentlemen. They haven't the first sense of fairness and are determined to win when their own mob is back of them even if they have to steal the game and stone the other official.

It meant nothing to Notre Dame that we forfeited the 1902 game, at least if the rumors were true. The 1903 game was rescheduled for Thursday, November 5, and we heard they were coming for revenge and planned to wipe up the field with us. For that reason, the game was expected to be damn hot. The word about town was that we'd have to fight hard to save our scalps.

The Notre Dame team we played against each year came from the ranks of the teams representing the various halls. Brownson Hall was the top dog in those days, at least the way we heard it. They were also our big adversaries. The Brownson players were underclassmen, but there were always a lot of them and they were well coached and experienced. That's because they were potential recruits for the varsity team, whom they scrimmaged against on a weekly basis. In fact, in Benton Harbor it was rumored they might bring some of the varsity players with them. But even if they didn't, there was no question in our minds we'd be facing a tough, hard-hitting bunch.

We, on the other hand, were going into the game with a very crippled team. Bridgman was not playing because of his sprained knee. Dice Baushke and the Iron Man were still out, and there was no possibility I would be back on the field for at least another week.

Because we were knee deep in halfbacks, the fellows seemed to be alright with the loss of Bridgman and Baushke, but they were uneasy about losing Lathe and me. Wadsworth had a lot of confidence and he looked good against Muskegon, but by the time he went in the game, it was already in the bag. He had yet to prove himself—the fellows knew it and so did I—but in my mind I was afraid it was only a matter of time before he learned the plays. And once that happened I might never get another shot. Worried my mind like a swarm of bees. I was half praying he'd get sick with something lethal—typhoid or yellow fever would have been nice.

While I was stewing over Wadsworth, the rest of the fellows were worried we'd get a small turnout for the game. They wanted a large crowd for support but also for protection. The board members felt the same way. When Burger was interviewed by the *Evening News*, he mentioned that if a large crowd hadn't accompanied the team to Kalamazoo, we might not have won because the opposing crowd would have rushed the field and prevented us from scoring. And he was probably right. It was fairly common back then.

In an editorial that week, the *Evening News* encouraged the rooters to come to the Notre Dame game to help protect us. A fair crowd did show up.

And it was a good thing.

Thursday afternoon, November 5th, was cold and wet from three days of steady drizzle. Most of the leaves had been pulled down by the moisture, leaving the outline of the trees etched against a sky that looked like dirty cotton. The wind pounded from the northwest like a pestle. It was disagreeable—no other way to describe it. To prepare myself, I wore a heavy shirt, turtleneck sweater, and a pair of wool knickers and thick wool socks.

I met the fellows at the Pastime Club and chatted with them while they changed into their togs. The banter was lively, but it was also guarded. Not too much bragging. When everyone was ready, Teetzel led us through the club room and out the front door where we found a platform wagon waiting to take us to Eastman Springs. A couple of scrub volunteers had already loaded our gear. Caully came out while we were climbing up the back step and stacking ourselves along the benches that lined either side.

"Luck be with ya now," he said while wiping his hands on a towel. "And promise me ya won't be bangin the daylights outta me boys," he added, referring to his Catholic brethren.

"We're football players, Mr. Bourke," Teetzel said as he pulled himself up into the wagon, "not Roundheads."

"And thank the good Lord for that, Mr. Teetzel."

"Save some hot water for us!" Mit hollered as the teamster snapped the reins and the horses pulled us into motion.

"Hot water it is!" he hollered back, "and the best rubbers ta ease yer achin limbs!"

When we got to the park we found a small crowd in place—couple hundred at most. They were huddled in groups along the sideline talking and stamping their feet to keep warm. Most of the men were nipping from pocket flasks—I don't remember seeing one single woman. Even Ma, a true blue supporter, begged off because of the gloomy weather, but not without wishing me well and tying an orange ribbon through the lapel of my coat.

The fellows took to the field for warm-up practice looking cold and sluggish. But soon they had the stiffness worked out of their bones and were snapping along at a good pace. It was nearly game time when Notre Dame arrived, which is when we got our first look at them. They were big in size and big in number, and it was plain by the whiskers on their faces that some of them were well into their twenties.

Wadsworth ran the team through a signal practice while Jacob negotiated with the Notre Dame team captain. They agreed the game would be quick, with halves of twenty and fifteen minutes—

Teetzel told Jacob to negotiate it that way to prevent the fellows from getting unduly tired. He also expected the fast playing to minimize the potential for fighting.

The game was played and it was a bare-knuckles scrap from beginning to end. The college boys played rough from the first blowing of the whistle and were anything but shy about slugging. We were less than three minutes into the playing when it virtually exploded.

The fireworks began when Arthur Baushke was carrying the ball on an off-guard play and was tackled. He was still lying on the ground when a Notre Dame player pulled him up by the sweater and slugged him three times in the face. Jacob immediately grabbed the fellow by the hair and kneed him in the gut, which dropped him like a load of gravel, but it also caused every player on the field to begin fighting. Then the Notre Dame bench emptied, but before they could reach the brawl, more than a hundred men and boys from our crowd swarmed over the fence, met them on the field, and forced them to back off. Some of them joined in the fighting, but Teetzel and the Notre Dame coaches and game officials got in the middle and broke it up.

If the fight hadn't been stopped as fast as it was, someone might have been hurt or even killed. As it was, there were lots of skinned knuckles and bloody noses but no serious injuries. No penalty was called and the crowd booed, but the game continued and the preps did no more slugging that day. They must have figured it wasn't a healthy way to play in Bungtown.

As far as the playing went, Wadsworth's work was slow in the beginning, which was only one of our problems. The linemen didn't charge fast enough and the backs played too deep to get into the plays the way they should. Everyone seemed timid. But toward the end of the first half, they started showing some spark and almost got into the end zone before time ran out.

At the half, Teetzel gave the fellows a brisk talking, and then he singled out Wadsworth and explained some possible strategies for him to try in the second half. It surprised me to see Wadsworth become the focus of Teetzel's attention. I knew it would happen, I just didn't think much about how I would react. It stung to see it brought home like that. But in an effort to be helpful I talked with Jacob about some of the Notre Dame weaknesses I'd noticed and also about a few plays he might suggest to Wadsworth.

During the second half, the fellows showed some bursts of quickness on defense, and they even tackled the Notre Dame backs a few times behind the line of scrimmage. The crowd really went wild when Fred Handy made a flying tackle and downed the ball carrier for a three-yard loss after chasing him halfway across the field.

The only touchdown came with three minutes left to play and was set up when Arthur Baushke broke away from the pack and made a run to the ten-yard line. Jacob then made two successive line smashes that finally planted the ball on the three. Wadsworth then scored the touchdown on a mass play up the center. Busby kicked the goal to put us ahead 6 to 0. Wadsworth wasn't as good as me when it came to selecting plays, or as fast at getting the fellows back into action, but he was a scrappy bastard. I had to give him that.

The ball was in our possession when the game ended. We were on the Notre Dame twelve-yard line and probably would have scored again given a little more time. If you ask me, I would have moved the fellows down there quicker and made the score. But in the final analysis, it was still one hell of a good game. For sheer aggressiveness and hard playing, I don't think Eastman Springs had ever hosted a better football game.

Most of the rooters I talked with said they had a great time. Some of them even bragged we wouldn't have won if they hadn't intervened to stop the Notre Dame players from slugging. The rooters felt good about helping us, and in the end they harbored no ill feelings either. The serious Benton Harbor enthusiast typically liked any team that played us hard, even when the playing was rough, which is why they praised the Catholic footballers. But the game wasn't without its disappointments.

Although the total playing time was only thirty-five minutes, it was thirty-five minutes of pure blood-and-guts football. Most of the fellows were cut or branded with fresh bruises, and I noticed a lot of limping when they walked from the field. They were caked with the usual mud and grass stains, but more than the usual amount of blood was flecked on their faces and uniforms from cuts, gashes, split lips, and bloody noses. Lee had to leave the game early with a twisted knee and Jacob got a black eye in the fight that was already swelling up like a steamed sausage.

The victory over Notre Dame was sweet, but it was also costly. And Wadsworth was more confident than ever, cocky as hell about scoring the only touchdown.

Chapter 21

The fellows were satisfied with their showing against Notre Dame, but they were even more happy that Saturday would be a free day—we weren't scheduled to play. Our scrubs would be playing against the South Side Sluggers from St. Joseph, and the fellows felt it would be a real treat to join the rooters along the sidelines. Besides, they desperately wanted the two extra days to heal their injuries. Attitudes were decidedly positive among the fellows who gathered together during Friday's lunch period.

We ate our lunch in a space that doubled as a gym and an auditorium. There was an elevated stage built into one end complete with a proscenium arch. Walls were made of plaster painted a dull mustard color while the trim was dark-stained oak—maplewood covered the floor, and three large, double-hung windows along one wall flooded the room with natural light. Everyone brought their own lunches back then and sat in folding wood chairs or on the floor.

"Hey Jacob," Jones said during a lull in the banter—there were probably ten of us players sitting in a group—"you talk to Doc about that eye ornament of yours?"

Jacob stopped chewing his sandwich and stared at him while gently touching the swollen area around his black eye. "Naw," he finally answered. "There's nothin to be done about it."

"Yes there is," Ossignac said. "My grandfather swears on a poultice made from the mashed roots of slippery elm."

"Slippery elm?" Jacob said with a puzzled look.

"Yep. Says it works every time."

"Won't work," Jacob replied as he put his sandwich to his mouth and prepared to take a bite. We were all chuckling.

"You fooled if you be thinkin that," Busby interrupted.

Jacob put the sandwich down and said, "Who you callin a fool?" We immediately quieted to whispers.

"Maybe you."

"Better watch out, Bus," Ludwig said, "What all's said and done you may be the only fool here." That brought a renewal smiles and some additional guffaws from the fellows.

"I don't mean you is a fool, Jacob. Not in a stupid kind of way. I mean you been fooled into thinkin there ain't a rem'dy for a black eye," he said.

"Alright," Jacob said, yet to crack even the hint of a smile. "I suppose your Aunt Sadie's got something too."

"That's right," he said. "She swears on a poultice made of wormwood sawdust mixed with the yoke of an egg. Says it will hardly fail."

"Never work!" Bridgman cried out. "Not with Jacob's appetite. Before that poultice ever got to his eye he'd have it slapped between two pieces of sourdough bread."

Damn we laughed. The entire table of us howled, including Busby and Jacob, and we didn't stop until Principal McClelland came in the door and walked toward us quick as a man with his pants on fire. We thought he was set to scold us for making too much noise, but we were wrong. We were in for much worse than a scolding.

"I just got wind of a rumor that should make you boys very happy." By the tone of his voice, I couldn't tell if he was being serious or sarcastic. "I was downtown at a meeting and ran into Eugene Wilson. He said Manager Burger has scheduled a game for you tomorrow in Indiana."

That announcement was greeted with dead silence. Not one of the fellows spoke. McClelland chatted briefly about the difficulty we would have getting tickets for the train and then excused himself, which is when the talk around the table turned ugly. Some of the fellows were spitting mad, but they calmed a bit when I reminded them that Fossil was the board member who had no responsibility because of his age and hearing problems. That's when we agreed someone should talk with Teetzel or Burger as soon as possible to determine the legitimacy of the rumor. There was still forty minutes of lunchtime left, so I volunteered. I gulped the remainder of my sandwich, walked out to Pipestone, and hopped a streetcar heading downtown.

"You heard right, Fletch," Burger said as we stood at the end of the Bird's lunch counter. "Tomorrow we're heading south to play the team from Goshen High School."

"You know they won the Indiana state championship last year, don't you?" I said with surprise.

"Of course I do. That's why the coach wanted me to jump at the opportunity. They were supposed to play Wabash, but at the last minute the game was canceled. Seems the parents of the Wabash players didn't want their boys getting hurt."

Goshen was the 1902 Indiana state champ and a contender for the same honor in 1903. They'd defeated Wabash once already that year and insisted Wabash was afraid to go another round with them. I don't know if that was true or not, but I do know it was the parents who stopped the game.

I wouldn't say the fellows are scared of Goshen," I said. "It's just that they're beat up and tired. Two games in three days is a lot of football."

I was about to remind him of how Frank Busby died from an injury he received at the end of the season, when the players were in poor shape, but thankfully didn't get the chance.

"Coach Teetzel received a telegraph Sunday night from the Detroit Athletic Club asking for a game Saturday," he interrupted. "And they were willing to play on our grounds. It was either them or Goshen."

"Alright," I said incredulously. "I guess we'll be taking a whack at the Goshen meat grinder."

"Yes we will, and I hope our aim is true. We're leaving at first light."

I went back to school, spread the news, and was greeted with a bucketful of complaints. Cunningham argued that Teetzel was working us too hard, then Lester started in and was followed by

Ludwig and most of the others. Jacob and I tried to stay positive by reminding them it would be good training for the games yet to be played, but we didn't make much headway. Wadsworth never said a word one way or the other, which didn't surprise me, but I felt sure he was delighted at having another opportunity to show off.

Because the game with Goshen was scheduled at the last minute, there was no time to book a charter. Burger made arrangements for us to take a regular scheduled run on the Big Four Railroad and got fifty tickets. Whatever was left would be immediately gobbled up by our diehard supporters and gamblers.

We boarded the train at 7:15 Saturday morning. The entire team was there with the exception of Cunningham—no one had seen him or knew where he was. Some of the fellows were suspicious he missed the train on purpose, and there may have been something to it. He was one of those who complained the loudest about playing two games in one week.

"Don't jump to conclusions," I said. "He's got five more minutes to show himself."

With each passing day, the fellows were growing more and more bitter over the hard way Teetzel was working them, but I didn't know it had reached the point where a player would purposely miss a game. That's when I found myself beginning to worry about our ability to stick together as a team during the tough weeks ahead. As the train eased out of the station, I had a premonition something terrible was infecting the team, but at the time I couldn't put my finger on it.

We were settled into our seats and the engineer was working up a good head of steam when the train suddenly jolted, which was followed by a continual slackening of speed until it stopped altogether. The train sat there, the engine hissing and growling, while I strained to look out my window at the tracks ahead. I expected to see an escaped horse or cow but saw nothing.

Finally, the door opened and a man appeared. Before I could see who it was, he shouted, "Well, here I am, boys!"

It was Deputy Pearl. Wearing a wide, toothy grin, he climbed aboard and strode down the isle shaking hands as he went. He was talking, but I couldn't hear him because we were all laughing so damn hard. By the time he took a seat, the clatter had calmed enough for me to hear the men pelt him with questions, which he tried his best not to answer, at least until he realized they wouldn't let it rest until he did. That's when he finally stood up and told us what happened. The train was moving again, and he had to hold the back of the seat to steady himself.

"I overslept!" he bellowed. "Can you believe it?"

"Who ever heard of a lawman oversleeping?" someone hollered from the back of the coach. We all clapped and cheered.

"Boys!" he said as he held his hands in the air to quiet us down. He leaned hard against the seat to steady himself. "It was all I could do to get my clothes on! And the missus was squawking the whole time about how I'd never make it to the depot. But I had my ticket…and a plan."

"Hey Irv!" Shorty hollered. "Did you miss your bacon and eggs and your morning shot of Red-Eye?"

"Yep, I missed it, all right!" he said while wiping the sweat off his brow with a gingham handkerchief. "But let me finish my story. I got dressed, ran down Brunson Avenue to the tracks, and slid down the embankment. The engine was just rumblin round the bend when I started wavin my arms."

"He probably thought you were a premeditated suicide!" Ben Curry shouted.

"But I didn't care! I just wanted him to stop!"

And so he did. The deputy said he had a word with the engineer, gave his ticket to the conductor, and everything was fine. Nothing could have done more to brighten my attitude, and that of the fellows in general, than Deputy Pearl's incident with the train. It couldn't have been any better if it was planned.

The train rolled into Goshen early, sometime around ten o'clock as I remember. We disembarked, broke into small groups, and strolled around town looking at the sights while the gamblers searched for the gaming crowd, which proved difficult. Money was scarce. I was with Jacob, Heck, and Butts—Wadsworth was tagging along too.

If the four of us weren't joking or playfully chiding one another, we were pointing out and laughing at anyone we thought looked funny. We were generally trying to ease the tension that preceded our games. But after a while, someone mentioned football and we started talking strategy—couldn't help it. Jacob and I were trying to have a serious discussion about play selections as they related to certain game situations, and instead of joining in, Wadsworth began bragging about how he was going to disassemble Goshen. No particulars. Just general conclusions. His touchdown against Notre Dame had swollen his head. I finally had enough and decided to say something.

"Don't you think you should be planning your play selections?" I knew he had less than half the number of plays memorized as I did.

"Cap it, Van Horne," he shot back. "Or I'll turn you over my knee and fan your biscuits."

Jacob looked at me and shook his head sympathetically. Heck and Butts tried not to laugh, but they finally did, and I felt like a fool.

"Got to make a stop at the drugstore, fellas," I said dejectedly. "I'll catch up with you later." With that, I turned an walked the other way.

"Take it easy on him, Waddie," I heard Jacob say as I was turning the corner.

"To hell with him," he replied. "He'd be more useful if he'd work harder keeping the water buckets filled."

"Bastard," I said under my breath.

I walked down another block before sitting on a bench out front of a furniture store to lick my wounds. I was fuming over Wadsworth's snubs, which by then had become increasingly frequent. Even when he didn't actually speak to me, which was most of the time, his actions betrayed a visceral disdain for any attempt I made to assist him or the team. I'd never faced anyone quite like him. His relentlessness was whittling me down. As a result, I found myself sinking deeper and deeper into a dark pool that threatened to silence me. Of course that's what he wanted.

If I was to play quarterback again, I had to make damn sure the fellows didn't suspect I was feeling heavy-hearted or that Wadsworth's continual badgering was getting under my skin. They must believe I still had the hard bark to lead them. But while I was sitting on that bench in Goshen, I questioned whether my determination to play again was really that solid. After all, being a shadow again would immediately lift the burden. Helping the team with towels and waters buckets would keep me involved without having to deal with the pressure. Yes, it would be very easy. But then I reminded myself of all the training I'd been through, and of all the hours I spent studying rules and play strategies, and I realized the fire was still burning. The more I thought about it, the more I realized some very good things actually favored me.

As the team's leader under fire, I had learned to keep a keen eye on every player's health, attitude, and physical condition. For weeks, I had studied and remembered every shred of information about them, not just their physical abilities but their mental strengths, weaknesses, and idiosyncrasies. That's because those things influenced my play selections. Worrying about them had become habit, and I continued to worry after I was sidelined. Wadsworth may have been physically superior to me, but he wasn't nearly as smart, and I suspected he didn't have the same fire in his gut for getting revenge against Ishpeming on Thanksgiving Day.

And that's why I took his guff. I didn't respond when he slighted me, and I never talked about him behind his back or tried to plant seeds of discontent among the other players. The last thing I wanted was for my resentment to fester up and reveal me, which could very well poison my chances of ever leading the team again. And I certainly didn't want the fellows to choose sides. That could have been disastrous for the team.

I was not happy by any means, but I decided to bite my tongue and keep the hurt and anger to myself.

Sometime close to noon, we gathered at a downtown eatery called the Opera House Restaurant and had a good feed. There were four or five tables of us, and everyone talked near constantly except for me—I was still smarting from Wadsworth's comments. The banter continued after we finished eating, and it was all I could do to stay put and listen. I would have looked foolish leaving anyway. The conversation started out with a discussion about the locals, who were mostly German, or *Deutsche*, which we pronounced "Dutch." Then someone wanted to know what the hell a Hoosier was.

"I've seen em," Monroe said, eager as usual to get in his two cents. "They's the folks who come to St. Joe in the summer…on Sunday afternoons mostly…to picnic with their families on the bluff."

"Yep," said Billy Harper. "I've seen em too. I've seen em sittin on the park benches eatin their lunches from out of their derbies…mostly pork and beans with horseradish and sauerkraut."

The fellows had a good belly laugh and Billy beamed, but that was the closest anyone came to a logical definition of Hoosier. I guess folks have been trying ever since to no avail. The conversation then turned serious.

The men started talking about the game and about us. They knew about our rotten attitudes, which they didn't like and said so. They realized we were physically and mentally beat up, but said it was our duty to finish the job to the best of our ability. They were right and we knew it. It was then that Bridgman and Dice Baushke, who hadn't declared if they'd be dressing for the game, stood up and made brief statements saying they intended to play. Neither of them were fully recovered, but they decided it was the right thing to do because it would be good for the team's morale, which was right on the mark. Everyone gave them a hearty round of applause, including me. It added to the boost the fellows got that morning from the train incident with Deputy Pearl. But Iron Man Lathe was still out and so was I.

It was after two o'clock, and the fellows had already run through a few conditioning routines when the Dutchmen finally arrived. They stampeded onto the field like a herd of cattle—I swear the ground shook. I gave Burger a surprised look and he shrugged his shoulders and said, "Yes, Fletch. They outweigh us by thirty-five pounds a man."

I shook my head in disbelief. Made me wonder if Teetzel knew how big they were when he scheduled the game, and if he did, what the hell he was thinking about and if he had any regrets. I guess he didn't. If he did, he didn't let on. I fetched my pencil and writing pad from my duffel and scribbled: "Coach scheduled game

with herd of hungry cattle." I decided it would be my first observation to be presented at the Pastime Club meeting the following
Monday.

The team captains agreed the game would consist of two
twenty-minute halves, after which the fellows lined up and the referee blew his whistle for the kick. A Goshen player caught it and
advanced ten, maybe twelve yards, and then they made some good
yardage using steady line plunges up the center of the field. There
was still no money in sight, which didn't mean the Goshen rooters weren't behind their team, because they were. In fact, they were
cheering damn hard. Some of them were even shouting to us from
across the field that we were about to be minced, and they kept it
up until the ball changed hands.

We ran a few line bucks before Wadsworth carried the ball from
the fifty-yard line to the ten. It was a great run and I almost sat
down and cried as I watched him dodge through the broken field.
A couple of plays later, Bridgman carried it across for our first
touchdown, which caused the Goshen crowd to lose their steam
altogether. "Sissies," I wrote on my pad.

And from that moment on, the day was ours.

On offense, Goshen did fairly well, much faster than we
expected, but we played low, charged fast, and the heavy
Dutchmen went right over our heads. Before the first half was
called, Jacob and Arthur Baushke scored two more touchdowns
apiece, but the touchdowns didn't come as easily in the second
half. The Goshen boys stiffened and we had to play harder to
maintain our pace, but Wadsworth eventually scored and so did
Bridgman. Both goals were kicked to make the final score 30 to 0.

Even without me and Lathe and Cunningham, and with
Bridgman's knee at half mast, the fellows proved they could still
play winning ball. The plunging of Jacob and Arthur Baushke was
more effective than it had been all season, due in part to the magnificent playing of our linemen. And that was against an opposing
line that averaged more than two-hundred pounds per man. Biffy
Lee especially played a great game opposite of Hoover, the 220-
pound Goshen guard, who never once was able to break through
and do any damage. Heck was another one who showed his hard

bark. He fought like badger and conducted himself as if he were waging his own personal war, in spite of the fact that the game didn't count toward winning the Michigan title. But he paid a high price—by that I mean he got beat up to hell and back. Wadsworth ran the team faster than during the Notre Dame game, and it was clear the fellows were getting their confidence up about him, which was good for the team, bad for me.

The team was winning, and that was good. I was happy about that. But where most of our rooters considered Wadsworth a great quarterback, I did not, and it was more than a personal dislike for him. I simply refused to believe he had the goods to pull the fellows through a tight game. During the Goshen game, I heard some things from Teetzel that confirmed my suspicions.

"Bad call," I heard him mutter more than once.

"I agree," I finally said, and that's when he began to ask for my opinion.

"What would you have called, Fletch?" he'd ask. And if I didn't select the proper play, he'd tell me and then explain why, often in great detail.

After the game, we had to hustle to catch the 5:10 train. The fellows congratulated the Goshen players, washed, changed their clothes, and we made a beeline for the depot, which was already bathed in the long shadows of late afternoon.

On the way back to Benton Harbor, the train made its scheduled stop in Niles where we found a policeman waiting with a prisoner for Deputy Pearl. As I remember it, the prisoner was tall and handsome and in custody for running some kind of scam in Niles. His name was Richardson and he was scheduled for trial in the county courthouse in St. Joe. Pearl and Richardson settled down two seats in front of where I was sitting with Jones, and I saw the deputy unlock the handcuffs after the train was under way.

We were steaming across a lonely stretch of countryside between Niles and Benton Harbor when the conductor came into our coach and asked the deputy for help putting down a fight in one of the other coaches.

"Richardson," he growled as he stood up, "sit tight and I'll be right back."

"Wouldn't have it any other way, deputy." I noticed his reply was polite but laced with sarcasm. At the time, I didn't think too much about it.

As the deputy walked down the aisle I heard him say, "You fellows keep an eye on him for me." He was talking to some of the passengers. But they weren't paying much attention, and he was answered with a series of noncommittal grunts and mumbles. Less than a minute later, Richardson sprang to his feet and ran up the aisle to the door and jumped. I could see him from my side of the car as he tumbled over the weedy gravel bed and then got up and ran into an apple orchard. A short time later, the train jerked to a halt. When we started moving again, the deputy sheriff had already disappeared into the orchard after Richardson, alone and on foot.

It was dark when we rolled into Bungtown. And it wasn't until the next day that I heard the story of Richardson's capture. Deputy Pearl enlisted the aid of a farmer armed with hounds, a team of horses, and a wagon, but they still had to chase him over twenty miles.

The deputy sheriff had a reputation for being a lawman who never missed his man, and he was just as serious when it came to supporting our football team. He had conviction. On game day, I was always glad to see him. And I knew that he, as much as anyone, would enjoy our next game.

Because we wouldn't.

Chapter 22

My first day practicing with the team again was the Monday following our trip to Goshen. That was good news. The bad news was my leg—the damn thing wasn't completely healed and Teetzel knew it. He didn't say as much, but only a blind man would've missed that I was noticeably slower than before. And being slower meant I was favoring my leg, which probably meant I still had a slight limp. Put me in an ornery mood.

To make matters worse, my disdain for Wadsworth continued to fester nicely. I had long stopped trying to befriend him, but as hard as I tried to ignore the bastard, he went out of his way to rub my nose in the dirt. And that's what burned me the most. Taking my position was bad enough, but I could have lived with it had he been the least bit gracious in return. He called me "kid," which he knew I hated, and he derived great pleasure from making wise-cracks about my size.

"Hey kid," he'd say, "keep drinkin your milk and one day you'll be big as me." Then he'd snicker.

At first I wanted to bust him in the mouth. Then I learned to ignore him. Didn't mean my anger wasn't stirred up though, because it was, but I figured it was more positive to stay focused on my continued progress and the team's fight to win the state championship.

If I'd had a normal adolescent mind-set, I would have been whooped-up over our accomplishments. Don't get me wrong, I was very pleased, I just wasn't excited in an overly emotional way. For me, our success was no longer a line-buck proposition as much as a series of exercises in problem solving. I was beginning to see the team's success through the eyes of an engineer. My own story was proof. First I solved the problems that kept me from being a proficient quarterback, and then I did the same thing with my leg. Occasionally, I became my old spirited self again, usually when talking with Jacob or Butts, or most anyone else on the team, about past games, games yet to be played, or potential adversaries.

Ann Arbor happened to be next on our list.

Surprised the hell out of us—Ann Arbor. They defeated Lansing the same day we hammered Goshen, which meant the lower Michigan field had tapered down to us, Mt. Pleasant, and Ann Arbor. All week long we talked and ruminated about the next round of matchups.

Ann Arbor and Mt. Pleasant would slug it out the following Saturday to decide who'd play us for the lower Michigan title. The Mt. Pleasant players were athletic and well coached, and we couldn't see how Ann Arbor had a dog's chance. Burger planned to begin negotiating immediately after the game to entice the winner to play against us at Eastman Springs, and he was already planning for our trip to Ann Arbor on Thanksgiving day.

By that time, the fellows didn't care who we played, Ann Arbor or Lansing, they were confident we could whip either one of them. They were mostly interested in the game between the teams from Ishpeming and Escanaba, and so was I. That was a subject that truly lifted my spirits.

Both of the upper Michigan giants were undefeated going into their game, but we felt confident Ishpeming would win, at least until we heard a rumor that Escanaba was actually the better team. The *Evening News* captured our feelings pretty well when it reported "the local sports enthusiasts were standing on their hind legs yelling for Swede blood," and that we "wanted to hand Ishpeming a bunch of mud like the handful Benton Harbor received last year." And they were right. We were praying Escanaba wouldn't rob us of our opportunity to get revenge. The mere possibility soured us, and then something happened that soured us even more.

Teetzel scheduled Kalamazoo College.

News of the game spread through town like wildfire. The *News* reported the college boys were coming to Bungtown with "blood in their eyes." Through the grapevine, we heard they promised to avenge our hammering of Kalamazoo High by a score of at least 40 to 0. The news wasn't very well received by the team. In fact, it caused us to feel a little uneasy, and it only got worse when we discovered how much it pleased the board members that they'd get to watch us play against a respectable college varsity squad.

Billy Harper told Butts and Mit not to worry, that it would be good experience, challenging, and that we should be happy because the game would guarantee a large crowd and bring in some extra cash for the team fund.

"Have a good time," he said. "Play tough and you can lick that two-bit, over-polished pack of bookworms."

That was easy for him to say. In reality, the Kalamazoo College players were anything but bookworms. They were rawboned football players to the core. That season they won all but one of their games, with their only loss being to the Michigan Agricultural College. The Aggies claimed the championship of Michigan's small colleges, which meant Kalamazoo was number two. That would be an attraction the rooters couldn't resist, even if it was at our expense.

There was a lot of talk around town about why Teetzel would schedule a game with a powerhouse team like Kalamazoo College. According to him it was simple—we needed the practice. In an interview with Al Clark, he said whenever another team pushed us we lost our wind and had to rest. Teetzel agreed that our playing against Kalamazoo College might result in some injuries for us, but overall he believed the game would do more good than harm getting the team ready for the playoffs. Clark asked him if the game would be a slaughter and he said it would not, that we would lose by one touchdown. Seemed like a stretch to me.

Yes, the fellows were damn nervous about Kalamazoo College. None of them talked about it—didn't have to—but I knew. Their doubts were written all over their faces and I could hear it in their voices. Their poor physical condition and natural sense of survival also worked against them, and that's why I was surprised at how well Monday and Tuesday's practices went. Attitudes seemed good. It didn't unravel until midweek.

Wednesday's practice was a disaster. The fellows grumbled and bickered and blamed one another for things like hitting too hard, missing blocks, or moving too slow or too fast. There were even a few shoving matches. Teetzel told us to snap out of it or we'd lose our edge. We didn't and the problem only got worse. It took a while for me to put my finger on the cause, but I finally decided it started with Jacob and Heck and rubbed off on everyone else. I couldn't imagine why. The Grahams lived for football, the tougher the conditions the better. It was in their blood.

The three of us were walking home after our rubdowns at the Pastime Club when Jacob finally leveled with me. All I said to get him started was, "Bad practice today."

"Yeah," he replied, but then paused and kicked a stone that went skittering over the brick street pavers. I could tell he was fumbling with a head full of words. "Got some bad news today," he finally said.

"Serious?"

"The old man's dead...in Oklahoma City."

"*What?*" I said in disbelief.

"D-e-a-d," Heck spelled out slowly, the disgust clear in his voice as he hobbled along beside us. "Struck down with the flu over three weeks ago. Ben Purnell knew about it and didn't tell Ma."

"That stinks," I said. And I thought I had problems.

"Like a dead possum," Jacob replied. "The *News* got a letter from an Oklahoma City lawyer sayin the House of David colony won't pay for the burial. Seems the old man's lyin in the morgue unclaimed."

"That doesn't seem right after all the work he did for them."

"Purnell said the old man wasn't a member...which is a lie."

"Yeah," Heck said. "We know the real reason. They want to wash their hands of the deal because of the bad publicity they got when he left Ma without any means of support."

"So they won't cough up the money for the burial?"

"That's what they say. But Ma wrote a letter that tells the truth and mailed it to the paper."

"What'll you do about your Pa?"

"Someone's got to go down there," Jacob said. "We can't afford to bring him home, so me and Eva's goin down there to put him in the ground. Ma's already scrapin out the cookie jar."

"You have to go?" I said in a calm voice—inside I felt like I'd been struck by a bolt of lightning.

"Yes sir. We're leavin a week from Friday night after Eva gets off work. She'd go it alone…she's a tough one like that…but Ma won't hear of it and I agree. It's somethin I got to do."

"But what about the game?" I pleaded. I couldn't believe this was actually happening. "The following day we play for the lower peninsula championship."

"I know it," he continued. "You fellows will have to play without me. Make sure you win cause I might be back for the state championship game the following Thursday."

"Might be back?"

"Maybe. We got to arrange the burying, and then get a preacher to say a few words before they fold the earth over him."

"What about you, Heck?" I said, knowing damn well they wouldn't let him go because he didn't have the good sense to stay out of trouble.

"I told Ma I'd go, but she said no."

By Thursday, the whole town knew about Hutcheon Graham. The *Evening News* printed the letter from the Oklahoma lawyer and the sympathy was strong. Most folks believed Mr. Graham was a bit off keel for joining the colony in the first place, but they knew him to be a good man and rallied behind the Grahams because of the way Purnell tried to wash his hands of the deal. The response from the board members, players, and the local football enthusiasts was similar. But they were flat out unhappy about Jacob's part in the deal.

They realized the team was severely compromised without him.

Thursday's practice was worse than Wednesday's, mostly because of Jacob's dilemma, but also because of me. After three days of practicing, I had come to the hard realization that my hamstring wasn't completely healed. I was stretching three times a day, just as Doc had said, but my leg was simply too weak to maintain the blistering pace of the practices. And on top of it, I had to put up with Wadsworth calling me things like "pegleg" or "hobble horse." More than once I almost called it quits and walked off the field, telling myself I didn't care that everyone would call me yellow or a quitter. But I did care and I didn't walk off. Instead, I constantly reminded myself I was lucky to be playing again, which was more than the Iron Man—he wasn't practicing at all because of his injured knee. By midweek, Heck was out too.

Heck took his Pa's death harder than Jacob and it showed in practice. He was already in pretty rough shape from the previous two games, but now he was also wearing an attitude that was butt ugly. He missed assignments and got into arguments and shoving matches with the rest of the fellows. Jacob even pulled him aside and talked to him but it didn't help. Teetzel finally told him to get his gear together and go home, which neither he or Jacob were happy about. Jacob argued that Heck would've cooled down given a little more time, but Teetzel refused to talk about it, and for the remainder of the practice Jacob was quiet but fierce. He pounded us without mercy.

Lee took Heck's place at center and did a good job, so good that Teetzel told two reporters observing our practice that he might keep him there for the rest of the season. Lee wasn't happy about that—he knew Heck might have hard feelings.

By week's end, it seemed as though no one was happy about anything. No one was happy about the way Jacob and Heck were affected by their pa's death, and no one was happy about the hard practices Teetzel was putting us through. And our apprehension over the impending game with Kalamazoo College only made it worse. Things were getting so bad, I half expected the fellows to turn in their gear. I think Teetzel was at his wits' end with us.

Without a doubt our attitudes were in the gutter. That's why Burger met us at the Pastime Club late Friday to talk about it while we were getting our rubdowns.

I can still see him pacing among the sheeted tables in his gray suit, eyes watering from the sharp smell of the liniment. He listened patiently to the complaints and grumbling before he made his reply. First, he agreed and sympathized with us that the long practices and the injuries were taking their toll. He also agreed the loss of Jacob was a setback but said it wasn't something we couldn't overcome. Then, as he daubed his tears with a white handkerchief, he talked about responsibility and duty and how our supporters were counting on us to make it to the state championship. He said they would understand if we lost, but the disappointment among them would be immeasurable if we didn't give it our best.

Burger was right. I knew it and I'm sure the fellows did too. I was confident they wanted to be responsible, both to our supporters and to the pact we made with ourselves a year earlier to do what was necessary to win the state championship. But no one said anything—there was total silence except for the dripping of water from a leaky faucet. Before leaving, Burger said we should come down to Billy Harper's cigar factory later that evening for a special presentation.

Said it might help to lift our spirits.

I went home and sat down for an uneventful supper with the folks. I didn't say much. Afterwards, I had to tend the furnace—a daily chore of mine during cold weather. I put on my old work jacket and grabbed a lamp before going outside to the back of the house where the stairway was located. I opened the hatch and went down. The ceiling in our basement was low and the floor was packed earth. A retaining wall of stacked stones was positioned about four feet in from the perimeter of the foundation to make a ledge just below the sill height of the only window. I struck a Lucifer stick match and lit the lamp.

I put on a pair of canvas gloves, opened the firebox door, and shook down the ashes. Then I placed a wad of paper and some wood kindling on the grate before walking over to the wood-slatted bin to scoop out a shovelful of coal. Just as I was kneeling down again in front of the furnace, I heard soft steps padding on the stairs.

"It's just me, Fletch," Ma said. "I need some peaches for a pie I'm making."

"Alright," I replied and she walked to the back of the room and opened the door to the root cellar, which was actually a very small room. She ducked inside and came back out with two jars cradled in her apron. Then she came over and stood behind me.

"So," she began, and I immediately knew something was on her mind. "The ladies at this afternoon's bridge club meeting had a lot to say about the team. They said the boys aren't doing so well."

"You heard right."

"I understand they're feeling a little down?"

"Wish I could say it wasn't so."

"I know they've been working very hard, and I know it must wear on them to be constantly sore or injured."

"I'm living proof."

"Yes dear, you are. And we can thank the Lord your injury was not serious."

"Not serious?" I said. Her seemingly cavalier attitude immediately made the anger boil up inside me. "I'm not playing in the games, Ma. What could be more serious than that?"

"Fletch, I think you know what I mean. I'm very sorry that you're not playing, and I know you are working hard to remedy that. Give it some time and you'll be good as new again."

"But there is no time. And even if there was, that know-it-all potato farmer has pretty much knocked me aside anyway. I don't like it one bit."

"Who?" she replied as she wrinkled her brow.

"Wadsworth."

"Be careful now. Resentment will only hold you back."

"Can't help it. Resentment is the only weapon I have left."

"But resentment doesn't affect the intended as much as it affects the one who resents. And it could have the unexpected result of spilling over and adversely influencing the team in general."

"But I don't let it show."

"You may not think it shows…but believe me when I tell you it does. You may not be leading the fellows on the field, but you can certainly lead them in other ways. By that I mean their attitudes. And now that Jacob is leaving, they'll need all the support they can get."

"There's nothing I can do," I grumbled while arranging chunks of coal around the pile of kindling, "at least that would make a difference."

"You could begin by staying positive. Also look for ways to assist the fellows…compliment them, encourage them, give advice, be a good listener. Even the little things make a difference. Can you do that?"

"Please leave me alone."

"Fletch!"

"Please, Ma. I don't want to talk about it."

She turned and walked to the stairs while I struck a Lucifer and lit the bundled newspaper. Then I turned and said behind her, "I could have brought the peaches up."

She stopped and turned and said, "I know. Now you better get going if you don't want to miss the presentation."

"Piece of pie when I get back?"

"Of course. Now get going."

I walked to the Lester house in the dark and was surprised at the drop in temperature. My hands were cold, and I regretted not wearing my gloves. I found Butts shooting baskets by moonlight.

"Not getting enough exercise from football?" I said sarcastically.

"Don't be stupid," he replied as he took a shot. "After getting out of bed each day it takes a good hour for me to loosen up to the point where I can walk straight."

"What's the deal with the basketball then?"

"Season's just around the corner."

"Sissy game," I replied. "Now let's go. The Grahams are waiting."

Butts tossed the ball up on the front porch and we walked to Lila's house and stood silently in the foyer while Jacob and Heck put on their coats. The house was dimly lit with kerosene lamps, and I watched the flames flicker against the flowers patterned across the light green wallpaper—the smell of fried potatoes and onions hung in the air. Lila was in the parlor clipping articles about our games from a stack of newspapers and putting them in an empty candy box while her husband polished a pair of shoes. Both said hello but offered nothing more.

We left the house and walked without talking to Pipestone Road and waited for a trolley to pass. Lester and I engaged in small talk—Jacob and Heck barely spoke—and within a couple of minutes, a dray rumbled up and stopped. The drayman was a fellow named Elm Sutherland, a football enthusiast, and he hollered for us to climb aboard. The steaming horses stamped impatiently in their traces while we climbed onto the back bed and sat on a stack of wood boxes. Not until the drayman hupped the team into motion again did I breach the subject of Hutcheon Graham.

"I read it in the paper," I said, referring to a letter that Purnell sent to the *News*. I knew Butts had read it too.

There was a pause before Jacob spoke. "You know it's all lies," he said.

"Yeah," Butts replied. "Purnell's a charlatan."

There was more silence before Jacob spoke again. "He said the old man was never a member of the colony, which is why they wouldn't cough up for the burial."

Ben Purnell's letter appeared in that evening's paper and was a reply to Mrs. Graham's letter in which she argued her husband was a member of the colony. She said he worked for Purnell and never sent one penny home to support his family. Purnell wrote that Hutcheon Graham wasn't a member at all because Mrs. Graham never signed the colony waiver that was required of all husbands or wives who didn't join with their spouses. Mrs. Graham said she never knew about such a waiver.

"Doesn't look good for Purnell," I said.

"Damn right it don't," Heck growled. "For a plug nickel I'd whip his ass."

"Someone else might beat you to it," I told him. "My Pa told me some fellows around here are trying to get a mob together to run him out of town."

"Be fine with me," Heck said.

"Me too," Butts added. "And I'd like to be there when they do it."

We continued to talk about Purnell and the colony, which didn't solve anything, other than to give Jacob and Heck a chance to scrub it off their chests. Then we talked about football for the remaining minutes it took to reach Harper's place where we jumped off the wagon and were met by Monroe Morrow.

"Come in, boys!" he bellowed. And then in a much softer voice he said, "And Jacob…sorry as hell to hear about your old man."

"Appreciate it," Jacob replied.

"I read Ben Purnell's letter in tonight's paper…and I know it ain't true."

"It's a strange deal all around," Jacob said and they shook hands.

We went inside and joined Mit Ludwig and Ossignac and a few of the other fellows who were already there and stood in a group and talked. People continued to show up, and by eight o'clock, there was a crowd of forty or fifty, most of them students, but also some parents and the usual contingent of gamblers. Everyone gathered in a work area furnished with stacks of boxes and wooden tables where the buckeyes rolled the cigars—the air was thick with the smell of dust and fresh tobacco leaves. We stood in groups and socialized until Clarence Peck called for our attention. Mr. Peck was an older man with gray hair and beard who resembled General Robert E. Lee. He owned a furniture store and was one of our rock-solid supporters.

Mr. Peck gave a short speech in which he talked about our hard work and how our successes were good for the community. Then, on behalf of Monroe Morrow, he presented each of us with an orange-and-black wool blanket. The blankets were meant to be used at the games to wrap around ourselves when we weren't playing—we didn't have warm-up jackets back then.

After the blankets were passed out, Mr. Peck suggested we show Monroe our appreciation, which we did by giving him a robust round of applause. Suddenly, in the midst of our clapping, Ossignac let out a blood curdling Indian shriek. We players recognized it because he'd done it a few times at practice, but I think the crowd was a little stunned.

Then something really strange happened—we players joined him.

Almost in unison, we threw our fists into the air and shrieked until the rafters rang with the sound of our war cry. But I think we were showing more than gratitude. Ossignac ignited something in us that words can't explain, but I'm sure it had something to do with expelling our pent-up pain and frustration. Each one of us had his own demons to face, but at that moment we came together and committed to everyone present we would face our obstacles with unity. Teetzel probably viewed it as a good oiling for the machine. Even Jacob and Heck seemed happy.

"Be assured!" Bridgman hollered when all had quieted down, "that the Monroe Doctrine is alive and well in Bungtown!"

While everyone was clapping and laughing, Monroe climbed onto a wooden box that had some Spanish words stenciled across the side and held his hands in the air to quiet us. Said he wanted to relay some late-breaking news. When all was calm he told us we might be offered the opportunity to play for the national championship.

"You been drinkin stump water agin, Monroe?" Albert Decker hollered.

Everyone laughed, but Monroe hollered right back at us. "Listen to me, gents!" he said. "And let me say my piece!" The din died down and he was finally allowed to proceed.

Monroe told us we were being talked about among the sports enthusiasts of Michigan. We were well aware of that, but then he told us we were getting some attention in Chicago as well. The reason was Barratt O'Hara, who claimed in one of his articles for the *Chicago American* that Burger was trying to negotiate a game with Hyde Park. Hyde Park was expected to finish the season as the number one high school team in Chicago.

The national high school title was informally decided the previous year by a game between the championship teams from Chicago and New York City. Brooklyn Polytech represented New York. The game was played in Chicago at Marshall Field and Hyde Park put on a stunning display resulting in a 105 to 0 rout. At the time O'Hara's *American* article appeared, Hyde Park was still in the running with Englewood and North Division for the Illinois title.

Monroe explained that Burger denied the validity of the article and said he'd have to wait for a champion to emerge before he could even think about negotiations. He was right to deny it. As it turned out, O'Hara made it up to generate interest in Chicago as well as in Bungtown with an eye toward getting us a shot at the so-called national title. I don't know how it played out across the lake, but it worked here. The possibility of us playing a game against any of the Chicago high school giants was an opportunity the board members could not resist. Monroe said they agreed in secret for Burger to proceed, and on Wednesday he mailed a formal challenge to the Hyde Park team manager.

When Monroe stepped off the box, the room erupted. There was more clapping and cheering, and everyone was shaking our hands and patting our backs. When the commotion eased to a lively banter, the attendees began to file out the door in twos and threes. Jacob's trip to Oklahoma was never mentioned. Before leaving, Teetzel gathered the team together and gave us a little pep talk. Then he said we should go home and get a good night's sleep because we'd need it for Saturday's game.

Boy, was that an understatement.

I went home and ate a piece of still-warm peach pie and then went upstairs to bed. The lamp was burning low, but Charlie was already sleeping and breathing hard. I quietly undressed and then did a couple of my stretching exercises before washing my face in the bowl of water Ma kept for us on the chest of drawers. Then I climbed under the covers.

I laid in bed and watched the lamp flame and the flickering shadows play across the ceiling. As I thought about the day's activities, the shadows jigged and jagged in a nervous back-and-forth motion that both tranced and troubled me. I thought about practice, Monroe's blankets, Hyde Park, and Hutcheon Graham. But for some reason, I thought mostly about what Ma had said to me in the basement. And I wasn't happy with my attitude or with my response to her.

I was resentful, for sure, but that didn't mean I shouldn't listen to the advice of my folks. And it certainly didn't mean I shouldn't help the team in our game against Kalamazoo College. But how best to do that? That was the question. I wanted to help in a way that was truly useful and worthwhile, so I tried to come up with something more than just taking notes and could only come up with one certainty.

I might come up with a better way to help them, but it certainly wouldn't be as the team's quarterback.

Chapter 23

It was shortly after two o'clock Saturday afternoon when our horse-bus pulled into Eastman Springs and we found the opening game in progress. A large crowd already girdled the field. Colorful ribbons whipped in the cold wind while fallen leaves swirled and tumbled across the playing field. People continued to arrive in rigs, on bicycles, and by foot, and the old man in the gatehouse who was selling tickets had trouble keeping up with the pace.

Some of the rooters were there to watch the game between the scrubs and St. Joseph's South Side Sluggers, but not many. Most were there to see us. A lot of folks from Kalamazoo were there too, and a few were boasting their team would pound us off the field. To make it worse, we heard a rumor that the Kalamazoo fullback was a ball carrier of murderous proportions. His name was Wes Clapp. The way we heard it, Clapp started the season with the Michigan Wolverines but joined the Kalamazoo College team after losing his spot on the Michigan squad due to poor grades. Because of him and his team's winning record, the Kalamazoo rooters bragged that the only unanswered question was the size of the score—and they were willing to back their boasting with money.

Many wagers were posted that day. I suppose our gamblers were expecting the worst for us and I couldn't blame them, but at least they were betting against the spread rather than openly against us. We were nervous, I won't lie about that, and the gamblers surely knew it. But they also knew we wouldn't roll over.

We trotted onto the field wrapped in our new wool blankets,

and when we got to our bench and let them drop from our shoulders, the crowd went crazy. Made us feel pretty good in spite of the predictions we were about to be destroyed. We immediately trotted onto the field and began warming up, and very quickly I found myself glancing over to where the Kalamazoo team was running through their routines. The first thing I noticed was their size—compared to us, they were giants. Then I saw Clapp. He wasn't hard to spot because he was the sturdiest and most mature-looking fellow on the field. By sturdy, I mean big, and by mature, I mean bald.

Butts noticed me watching Clapp. "Doesn't have much in the way of head protection does he?"

"Maybe he's starting a new fad…the burnished rutabaga."

"Ha ha," Butts replied sarcastically. Then he added, "So you suppose he shaves his head to unnerve the opposition?"

"You unnerved?"

"Hell no."

"Good. Then this game will be an easy eight ball in the side pocket."

Butts thought about it for a few seconds and then replied, "But you don't have to play against him."

"Never know," I replied. "The leg's feeling better every day. And if Waddie gets hurt, it's me or bust." Lester didn't say anything about that. Instead, he slugged me in the shoulder and we both laughed.

Jacob met with the Kalamazoo College captain for the toss of the coin while the rest of us gathered around Teetzel for some last-minute instructions. That's when my nerves went sky high. And it happened all of a sudden. Struck me as odd—I hadn't been nervous during any game since my injury, and I immediately thought it might be an omen. Jacob came back to the bench and joined us, and then he led the fellows, outweighed by twenty pounds per man, onto the field to do battle. At the same time, my mind raced as I went through plays and signals and began to formulate a game strategy.

I was deep into my scheming when Teetzel hollered my name. "Van Horne!" he said hurriedly while watching the two teams forming up on the field.

"Sir?" I replied, my heart pounding with excitement as I hurried to his side. He'd finally seen the light about Wadsworth and was going to put me in the game even before the kick. At least that's what I wanted to believe.

"Instead of the customary two," he said, "I want you to jot down every mistake you see. Let nothing go by."

The wind immediately went out of my sails. "You mean now?" I asked dejectedly. Our normal routine was to write down our comments after the game and present them Monday at the Pastime Club.

"Yes," he said and then reached into his pocket for a pencil. "Take this...and tear a couple sheets of paper from my notebook and use your eagle eye."

"But you always do that." If I sounded disappointed about his request, I was. I wanted to play, not write.

"I don't see everything, Fletch. You have a good eye for the game, and you may see some things I don't. I need you to do that for me. Can you?

"Yes, I can," I answered without enthusiasm. He never looked at me, such was his concentration on the team.

Our lineup was pretty much the same as it was in the Muskegon game. Wadsworth at quarterback, Jacob playing fullback with Bridgman and Arthur Baushke at the halfback positions. Cunningham was in Lathe's spot at tackle, and to everyone's surprise, Heck was back at center. Jacob must have talked privately to Teetzel about letting his brother play. Heck must have promised to straighten up.

I wrote comments during the game, but not as many as I probably should have. That's because the game was one of the best I'd ever seen, and it was very hard for me to take my eyes from the action long enough to write. I'd be lying if I said every rooter there didn't agree with me. For the most part, it was a grinding defensive battle, with both teams pounding each other unmercifully from beginning to end. But peppered within the playing were some magnificent plays worth the price of the admission alone.

Clapp was the best line bucker we ever played against. He was fast and strong and relentless—practically the entire Kalamazoo offense. When carrying the ball, his knees pumped like piston rods and his heels dug up the sod like a rampaging bull. The Kalamazoo quarterback sent him time after time into our line, but the fellows managed to stop him for short yardage nearly every time until late in the first half when he scored a touchdown around our right end. The rooters groaned, but then cheered as the kick at goal was blown wide by the strong crosswind.

I made certain to record the mistake that led to Kalamazoo's touchdown. Busby was playing too tight to the tackle position and got himself boxed in, which allowed Kalamazoo to sweep his end for the breakaway touchdown.

We took possession and played some hard football ourselves. The backs repeatedly hurled themselves at the Kalamazoo line for solid gains and were stopped only when they threatened to score. Bridgman and Jacob worked like dogs, and we were deep in Kalamazoo territory when the whistle sounded the end of the half—a tough break. Wadsworth was doing a pretty good job. Given a little more time, I think he would've hit paydirt.

"Okay, men," Teetzel said as the team gathered around him at the bench. "Wash your mouths out with water but don't swallow more than it would take to fill a shot glass."

Between their heavy breathing for air and the gulping of water, the fellows tried to talk all at once about the various difficulties they were having.

"Those with injuries over here!" Doc shouted from the bench where he had alcohol and tape and sticks of silver nitrate spread out before him.

"The rest of you sit down," Teetzel commanded while pointing to the grass in front of our team bench. We sat down and wrapped our wool blankets over our shoulders.

One by one, Doc hauled the wounded up to the bench to tend their cuts and scrapes while Teetzel talked to us about the first half. In the beginning, he concentrated on individual mistakes and what had to be done to correct them. Then he talked at great length to Jacob and Wadsworth about play selections and the strategy he wanted them to use during the second half. I sat quietly and listened while reviewing my notes.

Besides my comment about Busby getting boxed in and allowing Clapp to sweep his end, I had other notes. I had Cunningham down for occasionally forgetting to block the inside man when one of the opposing backs took a line position inside their own tackle. I noted Handy was being a bit shy about charging through on defense and consequently not doing as good a job pushing his opponent back or toward the center. I caught Heck snapping the ball a bit too fast or too slow, and although he settled down after a few possessions, I refused to cross it off my list. More than once, both Bridgman and Baushke made the mistake of carrying the ball under their inside arm—not a good policy. It was better to carry the ball under the outside arm and use the free arm to fend off would be tacklers. I wrote that down too. I also had a few things about Wadsworth—mostly related to his signal calling.

"Anything to add, Van Horne?" Teetzel asked. All heads turned my way.

"Nothing you haven't already covered," I said.

By the time the horn sounded, Doc had taped a few ankles, wrists, and even put in a stitch or two. The fellows trotted back onto the field in good spirits.

The second half of the game was filled with the most sensational playing I'd ever seen. The crowd must have thought so too, judging from the way they jumped up and down and howled with delight. Blistering line bucks, dazzling end runs, and pulverizing mass plays followed one another in rapid succession, all made possible by linemen who tore into each other without mercy. The college boys had anything but an easy time of it, and sometimes they seemed to be just as beat up and tired as we. They paid a heavy price every time their runs were stopped by Jacob, Bridgman, or Baushke. And on offense, Jacob, in particular, hit the line with a fierceness unrivaled even by him. More than one Kalamazoo player came away with a bloody nose or split lip, and I even saw a few of them spit loose or broken teeth onto the field. And remember, they bragged they would win by at least forty points. It must have been a rude awakening to have been roughed up by a bunch of high schoolers.

Toward the end of the game, the playing ground away for a long time between the two twenty-five-yard lines with nothing much happening. But then Jacob broke through the line, stiff-armed a would-be tackler out of the way, and made a great thirty-yard run.

He was tackled, but as he was going down the ball was jerked from his hands by a Kalamazoo player and the possession went over to them. Teetzel protested, but the call stood.

I wrote that Jacob should have immediately grasped the ball with both arms when he realized he was going down. The ball became vulnerable when he threw out his free arm in an effort to regain balance. Holding the ball with both arms also decreased the risk of fracture to both arms whenever the runner went down beneath a wave of tacklers.

On their first play, the Kalamazoo backs were charging around the left end when Busby belted the ball carrier and caused him to fumble. The ball was bounding along the grass when Wadsworth knifed through the line and scooped it up without breaking stride, which caused our crowd to explode into a thunderous roar as he dug up the field with his heels. A Kalamazoo runner came up from behind, straining every muscle to make the tackle, and the crowd grew even more feverish. The women screamed and slashed the air with their orange and black ribbons while the men howled and whistled and climbed the wire fence—all of them waving their hats. There were cries of "Waddie, Waddie!" urging him to run faster, and he did—never slowed down until he crossed the goal line.

Where eight hundred silent, heartsore rooters had prayed for the tide to turn, now stood eight hundred frantic, cheering, stomping, arm-waving football fanatics. We missed the goal but no one cared. Waddie was the hero. In spite of my elation at our touchdown, I was sickened to see him showered with so much adulation. I had to remind myself that we were back in the game, and that's what mattered.

The Kalamazoo players were surprised, frustrated, and wild-eyed with anger. With each play, they furiously ripped through our line, and soon the fellows were so exhausted they could barely stand. But Jacob managed to rally them and they bravely fought on. The playing was tough, and they held Kalamazoo until the final minutes of the game, when Clapp broke through our line.

Clapp quickly made open ground and was flying down the field, no one near enough to catch him, when out of nowhere a drunk spectator jumped over the pig-wire fence and tried to make the tackle. The crowd cheered him on, but he was no match. Clapp hit him with a stiff arm that spun him around twice before he fell to the ground, knocked out colder than a block of ice. A few seconds later Clapp crossed the goal line, and the Kalamazoo rooters cheered. Two fellows came out and dragged the drunk fellow off the field and our crowd cheered him again. The goal was kicked to make the score 11 to 5.

Kalamazoo kicked to Butts and he was downed at our own thirty-five. The fellows took the ball into play with everything they had left, and on the third down, Bridgman broke free for one of his open-field runs, sprinting with all his might for the end zone with the crowd cheering him forward. I thought he might make it, but then Clapp appeared. The rooters let out a collective groan as he cut diagonally across the field and brought Bridgman down with a textbook flying tackle. On the next play we got nowhere, and then it was over.

Our fellows limped from the field to a hearty round of applause from the entire crowd, friend and foe alike. The players and coaches congratulated one another, and then the coach and captain of the Kalamazoo team gave praiseworthy statements.

"Why you have a splendid team here, a splendid team," said the Kalamazoo coach. "I tell you, we expected to win 40 to 0, and to say we were surprised is putting it mildly. Your boys fought every minute and died game. I hope, and expect, that you will win the state championship."

Died game? I couldn't believe he said that. I thought he should have been embarrassed by the low score and by the fact that we almost beat them. Everyone agreed it was anything but a walkaway. And just as Teetzel predicted, we lost by one touchdown.

I was green with envy, at least until Teetzel had a word with me.

"I noticed you took some notes," he said.

"Yes sir, that I did."

"That pleases me. Let's plan to review them at the Pastime Club after Monday's practice."

"Some are not very complimentary."

"Uncomplimentary is what we are after, Fletch. Our goal is to identify and correct problems."

I was peeved at not getting in the game, but I suppose Teetzel's compliment about my note-taking was the next best thing. If not, it certainly offered me the opportunity to feel useful.

For days after the game, hardly anything else was talked about in Benton Harbor. It was discussed on the street corners and in the drug stores, and in the *Evening News* it was reported that we played with "nary a yellow streak." Teetzel and the board members intended for us to gain some good experience before the championship series, which it did, and it also boosted our morale. The team's sour attitude melted away with their tough performance.

But, as usual, there were more injuries to deal with.

Arthur Baushke and Heck especially got more than they bargained for, which worked to Kalamazoo's advantage and may be the reason we lost. I say that because both of them had to leave the game. Baushke twisted his knee and was carried from the field while Heck had to make an emergency visit to the sideline for stitching. His injury was not quite as serious as Baushke's, but it was definitely more noticeable—a kick in the head with a sizeable gash over his left eye that spilled rivers of blood. When Heck was finally turned loose, the top of his head was wrapped in bandages with little more than his nose showing.

"You look bad," I said with true concern, as he came up and stood next to me on the sideline.

"Shut up," he replied, glaring out from under his bandages.

"I know how you feel." I was trying to sympathize.

"Maybe so…but I'm like a singed cat."

"What the hell does that mean?"

"It means I feel better than I look. And I'll likely be playing again next week."

He was right. He was lashing out at me for losing my place in the lineup and for having little prospect of returning. I knew he was mad as hell about being put out of the game, and probably about his old man and also about Jacob having to go to Oklahoma to bury him. I should've kept my mouth shut.

The loss of Arthur Baushke and Heck was not good. We were already hurting without the Iron Man, and Wilbur Cunningham was trying to play with a bad knee while Dice Baushke was dressing for the games but not yet strong enough to see much action. That made our dilemma potentially serious. The fact that Jacob would be leaving us at week's end was a problem of catastrophic proportions—insurmountable, at least in my opinion.

We were beat up, undermanned, and our future was uncertain, but we had one thing going for us—our reputation. I'd have to say every high school football enthusiast in the state knew about us, mostly by word of mouth or through articles printed in newspapers from Detroit to Marquette.

Teetzel's Machine was something to be reckoned with, in spite of it's damaged parts.

As the last two weeks of the season loomed before us, we would continue to live football. We would practice hard, eat large meals, and sleep like the dead. During practice, we would throw ourselves recklessly into our work—hitting, blocking, running back punts, and learning new plays—while the remaining hours of the day would find us coddling our ravaged bodies. We were determined to move forward regardless of the obstacles.

Escanaba

Chapter 24

"Ishpeming loses!"

It was early Sunday morning, and when the newsboy shouted those two words from the street below I bolted upright from a deep sleep. I immediately swung my legs over the edge of the bed, but as soon as my feet hit the floor, my leg buckled and I fell down. It wasn't serious, although it was a cruel reminder that I was not yet fully healed. Within seconds, I was hobbling down the stairs cursing and fuming and wondering what the hell was going on. I opened the front door, grabbed the paper, and there it was, printed above the fold across the front page—ESCANABA DEFEATS ISHPEMING!

I took the paper into the parlor and sat in my old man's stuffed chair. There wasn't much to read, just a headline and a line that gave the score, which was 35 to 2, but that was more than enough to send me reeling. I couldn't have been more shocked if a bucket of cold water had been poured down the back of my night shirt. I went into the kitchen nearly teary-eyed and found Ma cooking breakfast and gave her the news.

"Oh, Fletch," she said as she selected a fat piece of bacon that had been draining on a piece of newspaper and handed it to me. "Don't take it so hard. It's not the end of the world you know."

"Might as well be," I snarled between bites.

"Well it's not. You and your father and just about everyone else in town refuse to drop this idea that revenge against Ishpeming is the only legitimate measure for success. Everything is different now."

"No it's not."

"Yes it is," she argued while removing a pan of hot biscuits from the oven. "And what's done is final."

"But we were humiliated," I moaned.

"Fletch. That game is over. You're a different team now with a different coach, and it's time to rid yourself of that demon. It would be better for you and the other boys to concentrate on the job at hand, which is winning all of this year's games regardless of who you play against."

I walked out of the kitchen without answering her although I knew in my heart she was right—that's exactly what Teetzel would tell us. But at that moment, it wasn't within my capability to imagine Ishpeming's defeat as anything but a backhanded slap across the face. I wanted to know more about the game, but that simply wasn't possible. It would be a couple of days before we'd get our hands on an Upper Peninsula newspaper, and by then, the season would be almost over.

Counting down from the Kalamazoo game, there were just twelve days left. Thursday, November 26, was the game for the state title, with the semifinal championship game being held the preceding Saturday afternoon. You'd expect the team to have been concerned about the remaining games, which they were, but the memory of Ishpeming would not die an easy death. Those who played against the Swedes the previous year were spitting mad we wouldn't be meeting them again, and it quickly became apparent to me they were more concerned about Ishpeming—a team we had no chance of playing against—than they were about Ann Arbor or Escanaba.

"Chicken is what they are," Lee said Monday morning amidst a half dozen of us players gathered in the hall outside of Mr. Righter's science room.

"Bastards," Butts replied.

"I bet they lost on purpose," he added, "because they were afraid to play us." He was immediately answered with a chorus of "yeah"s and "you betcha"s.

It was then Bridgman joined us flaunting a lusty smile that betrayed sure mischief. "I don't know where I've ever seen a more sorrow-eyed bunch of pigskin gladiators."

"Damn right, Bridget," Mit growled. "And what are you so cheerful about?"

"Cabbage," he said while holding up a wad of dollar bills as thick as a deck of playing cards. "Sustenance to the weak and self-ish creatures that we are."

"The hell?" Mit said as we all stood there with our mouths open. Excepting the farm kids, who sold their crops at market, most of us never carried more than fifty cents at any one time.

"Upon the arrival of certain news yesterday, I was able to make this noteworthy harvest."

"Damn you," I said. "You bet against Ishpeming didn't you?"

"Right you are my little featherweight. The odds were too good to resist."

Bridgman wasn't a big gambler, but some of the local games-men were so sure Ishpeming would win that they freely offered huge odds to anyone willing to take a risk on Escanaba. He simply took a chance. But the fellows didn't see it that way.

"What's wrong with you?" Mit fumed. "Where's your sense of loyalty?"

"Yeah," Lee said angrily. "How could you bet against us?"

"Listen to yourselves," Bridgman shot back, the smile suddenly gone from his face. "I bet against Ishpeming for the money, not because I'm against us. I wanted revenge just as much as you, but it won't happen and no amount of bellyaching will ever change it now. You're wasting your time whining over it."

Bridgman's harsh reply was met with faces of stone, mine included. No one said anything. He waited until he was satisfied his words had made their intended impact, and then he broke into a wide grin while fanning his wad of bills.

"He's right," I said, breaking the silence. "We should be think-ing about Ann Arbor." Still no one said anything.

"Think about it, fellas," Bridgman added as we broke for class. "And I'll see you at practice this afternoon."

Along with every football enthusiast in town, we were still anx-ious to find out what happened in the Ishpeming–Escanaba game, and all through Monday and Tuesday's practices there was an air of tension caused by the vacuum. Finally, on Wednesday, our curiosity was satisfied when we got the story from a copy of the *Marquette Mining Journal.*

Escanaba apparently protested six Ishpeming players before the game even started and had them removed from the lineup, which forced the Swedes to play with ten men. But the article also said the game was free from bickering and fighting, which surprised us. Apparently, the only sign of trouble came when some of the Ishpeming rooters gibed an Escanaba player for faking an injury. They claimed he was laying down for wind, which meant he was buying time for his teammates to catch their breath. The Escanaba coach argued the fellow was knocked out from hitting the ground, which may have been true. The article said the field was frozen hard as iron.

We were disappointed we wouldn't be playing Ishpeming, but by Wednesday afternoon the fellows had accepted it and were beginning to focus on Ann Arbor and Escanaba. Wasn't so with our rooters. They were sick about Ishpeming's loss, and the talk about town that week reflected their sentiments. I walked into Hoadley's barbershop after Wednesday's practice, which usually buzzed with colorful conversations and ribald storytelling, and was treated instead to a barrage of dead-serious questions about the defeat. Hoadley's partner, Mr. Annis, was especially inquisitive until I assured him it wasn't a rumor, which is not what he or any of the patrons wanted to hear. Some of them looked at me with stunned silence while some flat-out refused to believe Ishpeming was even capable of losing. Others argued that Ishpeming must have intentionally thrown the game so they wouldn't have to play us. One fellow just sat there and cussed. Later that afternoon, some of the other players told me they ran into similar situations practically everywhere they went where people gathered. It was obvious Ishpeming's defeat shook Bungtown to its very foundations and I knew why. We were denied our revenge.

I told our supporters that the team was staying fixed on Ann Arbor and advised them to do the same. I told them we were hungry for any news, scouting reports, or rumors about Escanaba, and would appreciate it very much if they would pass it on should something come their way. We didn't have long to wait.

Through the grapevine, we learned that Escanaba was being championed by the Upper Peninsula press as the state's strongest team. Even Ishpeming's coach, Dr. Sweetland, the Wizard himself, praised them. Said they were probably the best high school team in the country and would have little trouble winning the state title, which was also the opinion of many football enthusiasts in lower Michigan.

Some of the information about Escanaba was useful and some was meaningless, like a description we got from a traveling salesman about their crappy training facilities. Told us they used an abandoned fire station for a locker room and a wash tub and garden hose for a shower. They also had second-rate uniforms, which was no big deal. So did we. It didn't effect our playing and it clearly didn't affect theirs either. They destroyed all their opponents by huge scores, beating Marquette 50 to 0, Hancock 60 to 0, and Manistique 72 to 0. It was reported in the *Ishpeming Iron Ore* that Escanaba was probably the top team in the state that year and for good reason. Seems the bastards were also using the best players from Gladstone, which was the next town over from Escanaba. It would've been like us using the best players from St. Joe. We also heard the kid who ran the team was a terror.

That was the kind of news we needed to know about.

Dexter Stephenson was his name, and he played fullback and was a demon of a ball carrier. We heard his personality was subdued—the quiet loner type—but when he stepped onto the gridiron he was transformed into a ruthless, cold-blooded mangler. Apparently he put fifteen players out of games, six of them for the entire season. Broken arms, legs, concussions—you name it, and he made it happen.

That was the kind of news we needed to know about. And there was even more.

We were told that the Escanaba coach, William Jolliffe, was the fellow who coached Ishpeming to their first state championship in 1900. After hearing that bit of information, I decided it might be better to forgo any more scouting reports.

So that's how the chips fell. Providing we beat Ann Arbor, it looked like it was us and Escanaba on Thanksgiving Day. And we didn't expect to have an easy time of it because of our injuries, but more so because Jacob probably wouldn't be there. But we still had a lot of confidence and good support from our supporters, and not just in Bungtown.

The jealousy in lower Michigan aimed at the upper Michigan teams was strong back then, with most of it leveled against Ishpeming and Escanaba. Paul Jones, the Ann Arbor coach, even referred to it in a letter he sent to Burger confirming our game arrangements. He said if his team lost, the Ann Arbor students would root for us in our game against Escanaba.

The Benton Harbor board members knew Paul Jones was probably an honorable man and meant what he said, but they couldn't rule out the possibility it was a trick to make us overconfident. Their suspicions were further fueled by a rumor that the Ann Arbor team was having trouble practicing because of a six-inch snowfall. In the final analysis, we really didn't know what the hell to expect from them. We played against Ann Arbor in the 1902 semifinal championship game and squeaked by 10 to 6, but in 1903 most of their good players were gone, which is why we were so surprised when they beat Mt. Pleasant.

Mt. Pleasant was a proven team, and not many sportswriters had given Ann Arbor a chance against them. But the boys from the university city rose to the occasion and won. Made our own supporters nervous. That's why they wanted the game to be played at Eastman Springs, so they could be there to give support. Besides, most of our rooters said they wouldn't go to Ann Arbor but would save their money for the trip to the championship game instead. The board members agreed. They said we'd have to play at Eastman Springs if we wanted good support.

Burger negotiated by telegraph on Monday with the Ann Arbor team manager, who was adamant about playing in his town. He argued it was only fair since the 1902 semifinal championship game was held in Benton Harbor. Burger then countered and sweetened the deal by offering two hundred dollars. The Ann Arbor manager wired his acceptance on Wednesday, three days before the game was to be played.

To cover the expense of bringing the Ann Arbor team to

Benton Harbor, the price of a general admission ticket was raised to fifty cents. The student tickets still cost twenty-five cents but had to be bought ahead of time at the Red Cross Drug Store. The fifty-cent price was pretty steep, but Burger thought the rooters would pay it, and he was right. Most of them would have paid twice that much.

Ben Curry made up a batch of promotional posters similar to those used in the advertising of boxing matches and the circus. He enlisted a platoon of boys to tack them on telephone poles, the sides of buildings, and anyplace else where someone wasn't likely to tear them down. He also sent them to towns from Benton Harbor to Detroit, and some went as far as Indiana and Illinois.

By Thursday, most of the rooters had forgotten about Ishpeming and were looking forward to the Ann Arbor game. I continued to practice quietly with the team. And as for my feelings toward Wadsworth—I still didn't care for the bastard—but it was no longer so much about resentment or jealousy. It was about his playing.

After Wadsworth scored his touchdown against Kalamazoo College, he treated me with even more contempt, and he bragged to some of the rooters about how much better a quarterback he was than me. He also said he was better than Hub Allen and apparently some bought it. But I knew better. He may have been physically fit and talented, but his growing independence on the field made the team vulnerable—went against Teetzel's theory that the team should operate as a machine. At practice, Teetzel began to focus on Wadsworth's limited knowledge, or refusal, to use a wider variety of plays while I continued to pray he'd break his leg.

Although I continued to fend off bouts of frustration, the attitudes of the players in general made a turn for the better. As for the rooters, the excitement among them had reached a fever pitch, and wherever men and boys gathered—and even some women—the conversation was about the team. It never stopped. They talked about us in school, in the stores, and on the streets. They discussed our skills and weaknesses and made predictions about who was healthy enough to play and who wasn't. Without a doubt, we were the toast of the town.

To celebrate the season's success, Manager Burger and his wife, Grace, threw us an evening dinner party. It was held at their Brunson Avenue home on the Thursday before the Ann Arbor game. The board members and their wives were there along with Doc, Principal McClelland, Bridgman's sister Ida, and Emily Fitzgerald, who arrived in the company of Teetzel. Surprised the hell out of us. There were some raised eyebrows and a few whispers, but for the most part she was welcomed with courteous smiles and handshakes. Everyone was dressed in their Sunday best. For the men and boys, that meant starched white shirts, coats and ties, and black shoes, cleaned and shined. The women wore floor-length wool or linen dresses of various colors trimmed in lace. Some wore pearls. Each guest was given a yellow chrysanthemum, and I pinned mine to my lapel.

We stood and talked for a while, mostly about football and the impending game with Ann Arbor. Then we were asked to sit down at a long table, which was actually a series of tables placed end to end, stretching from the dining room through the open pocket doors into the parlor. The table was set with white linen tablecloths and napkins, china, and silver. Vases of pine boughs and holly composed the three centerpieces, and the entire downstairs was bathed in the amber glow of the gas lamps. Teetzel sat at one end of the table with Miss Fitzgerald to his right, while Burger and his wife anchored the other end.

We were treated to a meal of ham and turkey with potatoes, beans, boiled cabbage, baked apples with cinnamon, fresh bread, pies, and cobblers. As far as I could tell, we ate everything there was, and when we were done, the table was cleared and the brandy and apple cider came out. The brandy was for the men and the cider was for the rest of us.

We talked and laughed and reminisced about past football games, which was a lot of fun, and then someone badgered Walter Banyon into reciting a few verses of poetry. Banyon was an amateur bard of some repute who often recited at parties and other such gatherings. And he wasn't half bad. He began with a number by James Whitcomb Riley and followed up with Ben King's "Bungtown Canal." King was a St. Joe native who'd died a few years earlier but was still remembered for his bucolic poems and fancy piano playing. The poem Banyon recited was about the Benton Harbor ship canal, of which I can remember a few lines.

Oh, them barefooted days an' the spot where I'd lay
An' jest steeped my hide in the glory o' day,
A-hearin' the bulrushes whisper an' sigh,
An' watchin' the shadder-clouds hurryin' by.
How I long to go back there, with some old-timed pal,
N' dive off once agin in the Bungtown Canal.

When he finished, we applauded heartily, and then he said Fossil Wilson had something very important to report, only he respectfully referred to him as Mr. Wilson. Fossil slowly rose from his chair and steadied himself. At first I thought it was a damn joke. Everyone else did too by the looks on their faces.

"The board," Fossil said slowly in his raspy, ancient voice, "has been quietly working behind the scenes to remedy the problem Jacob Graham is facing with regard to his father." He hesitated and cleared his throat.

"Sir," Mrs. Burger politely inquired and Fossil tilted an ear toward her so as to hear better. "Can I get you a glass of water?"

"I didn't know you had a daughter," he said, and we struggled to keep from laughing.

"Water!" she said louder. "Would you like some water!"

"I heard you the first time," he answered while breaking into a wide grin, which caused us to laugh out loud. "But yes, thank you, I would very much like some water."

"Now as I was saying," he continued. "Eva Graham is scheduled to leave on the 6:15 tomorrow evening for Oklahoma City, and she requires the services of a traveling companion." Then he stopped, took a deep breath and smiled. "Because Jacob is needed here, the board has discussed and agreed that Ben Curry should go in his place."

At that instant, the room erupted in pandemonium as everyone clapped and shouted and then began talking all at once.

I noticed Teetzel and the Grahams were not participating in the celebration, and neither was Manager Burger. When the noise softened a bit, Burger said, "Jacob," and the crowd quieted even more, "is that acceptable to you?"

There was silence as Jacob slowly stood to speak. "This is not as easy for me as you might think," he said. "My going to Oklahoma with Eva seems the right thing to do. I appreciate the offer but will have to talk with my sister and then sleep on it before I can give an honest answer."

"If you should decide to stay," Burger went on, "I want you to know Mr. Wilson has offered to donate the necessary funds to cover both Eva and Ben's transportation and hotel costs."

Jacob and Heck both looked at Fossil, the disbelief clearly written all over their faces. That's because it was probably the greatest gesture ever offered them.

"We both thank you," Jacob said sincerely.

Fossil pondered him for a long minute and then nodded. "The pleasure's mine," he said.

Jacob sat down and Fossil closed his speech by thanking us players for being such a great source of community pride. Everyone who wasn't a team member clapped again, but this time I noticed Emily Fitzgerald did not. Billy Harper noticed.

"So," Billy growled while glaring fiercely, first at her and then Teetzel. "The lady refuses to applaud with the rest of us?" His bile was rising fast, and I'd be lying if I said every single person in that room couldn't smell it. The silence that followed was unnerving.

"She doesn't mean to be disrespectful, Billy," Teetzel replied with an iciness that told me he was fully prepared to stand his ground, or hers.

"Then why the hell is she here?" The alcohol haze in Billy's eyes was suddenly burning hotter than hell's furnace.

"Please Billy," Mrs. Burger pleaded, "Miss Fitzgerald is our guest."

"She's against us!" he raged while banging his fist on the table. "And you all know it!" Then, in one swift motion, he shoved his chair back and stood up to point an accusatory finger at her. Tension gripped the room as he held it on her like a revolver. You'd expect a man in such an agitated state to shake some, but not Billy. He was steady as iron. "If she had her way," he raged, "the boys would be sewing damn quilts instead of playing football!"

Billy was out of bounds and everyone knew it, but the knowing of it didn't mean they were against him. No sir. In fact, I detected a few heads nodding ever so slightly in agreement. We knew Billy's feelings, and it was obvious he was prepared to continue his attack against Miss Fitzgerald. But it was equally clear that Teetzel, who was watching Billy like a terrier about to pounce on a rat, would not let that happen. That's when Miss Fitzgerald came to her own defense.

"May I say something?" she said.

"Please, Emily," Teetzel said, his eyes still locked onto Billy's.

"I'll be polite about this," she continued. "There is something I'd like to say in my defense."

"Of course you may speak," Mrs. Burger said. "We are all friends here, and all opinions are welcomed. Mr. Harper?"

Billy and Teetzel continued to glare until Billy pulled his chair back into position and sat down.

"Thank you," Miss Fitzgerald said. She glanced nervously around the table trying to gauge the temperament of the guests. Then she stood up.

Chairs creaked and men cleared their throats or fidgeted and prepared to listen as she took a sip of tea. I think I speak for everyone there when I say we were all feeling damn uneasy. Billy was red as coal-fire, but he at least he was quiet.

"First of all," she said, "I would like to say I am still an advocate for banning football as an organized sport, but that doesn't mean I am not behind our high school team, because I am. I am very proud of you all." She then paused to cast her sea-green eyes over us players.

"Hear, hear," Monroe said obligingly to break the silence. There was a smattering of applause.

"With that being said," she continued. "I must say I am still troubled by the number of terrible injuries. And we have to look no further than this table to see what I mean."

She was right about that. Cuts and bruises and bandages were evident all around. Stitches too. Gaping holes appeared in our teeth every time we laughed, and I swear half the noses in that room were red and swollen from the repeated bashings. Even those with face protectors weren't safe. Arthur Baushke had a nicely formed devil's halo below his bottom lip, which is what we called the crescent-shaped bruises that resulted from having our nose guards jammed into our faces. The effect of our condition was further heightened by the sight of Arthur's crutches leaning against the wall behind us.

"As a teacher to these boys, I feel partly responsible for their well-being. But as I sit at my desk and watch them march in and out of class, day after day, bruised and limping and exhausted, I feel helpless. I want to help them but cannot."

It was then her voice began to shake ever so slightly, which made me uncomfortable. "I'm sure you read in the newspaper last week about the boy from Indianapolis who was killed playing football. I don't want that to happen to one of my students."

"And we don't either, Miss Fitzgerald," Burger said calmly. "But we try to make sure our players our properly trained before they get into a game."

"Yes," Principal McClelland said. "Injuries do occur, but they almost always look worse than they really are."

"I'm not here to argue with you," she said as she wiped a tear from the corner of her eye. "This has been a lovely evening and I don't want to spoil any part of it. But I just can't help being baffled at how a community composed of good mothers, fathers, teachers, and church leaders like those in Benton Harbor could allow their children to take such risks. There is probably more football knowledge sitting in this room right now than anywhere in the county. I would be grateful if someone could tell me why this is allowed to go on."

"I think I can answer that," Teetzel said, anxious to bail Miss Fitzgerald out of her teary-eyed predicament. "If you will allow me?"

"Of course." She said as she wiped her eyes and sat down. Teetzel stood up.

"First of all, I would like to thank the ladies for a wonderful meal." We all clapped and muttered our approvals. "And I would like to thank everyone here for their unwavering support of the team. We could not have done it without you."

I was on the edge of my seat along with everyone else. It was so quiet you could've heard the soft padding of a mouse over a Turkish rug. All eyes in the room were fixed on Teetzel as he took a drink of water.

"The United States has just entered a new era," he began, "and the primary reason is the growth of manufacturing. People are leaving the farms by the tens of thousands and moving to the cities to work in factories. Right now, there are an equal number of Americans living in cities as there are on farms. That is a first. Until now, we have been an agrarian society, which gets right to the heart of the matter."

Teetzel was a great speaker. He paused in all the right places and spoke loud or soft, depending on the point he was trying to make. While he was taking another drink of water, I watched as Burger adjusted his starched collar. Then I looked at Miss Fitzgerald and noticed her gaze was locked on Teetzel.

"America has never been an easy place in which to live," he continued. "Life has been hard. Anyone here who was raised on a farm, or has worked on a farm in the summer, can attest to that. For most of our history, this lifestyle has been the great training ground for our youth, with hard work, often from sunrise to sunset, setting the standard for their success. Young men and women became strong. They learned how to work together, help one another, and how to survive in the most difficult situations. Most of our great politicians, judges, industrialists, and military leaders came from the ranks of these common people."

"Don't forget about us teachers," Principal McClelland said as he gave Miss Fitzgerald a warm glance. We all laughed.

"And teachers," Teetzel added with a smile and a nod. He took another drink of water as everyone shifted positions, straightened their jackets or dresses. There was some whispering, but in a few seconds everyone was quiet again.

"Boys who live in the city get very little physical exercise. In fact, before the introduction of the bicycle ten years ago and the recent growth of football, there was next to nothing for them to do. They were in such bad physical condition that most of them could barely run one block without falling down from exhaustion."

"Are you saying that football is a replacement for the country life?" Ida Bridgman asked.

"Yes."

"Then why not institute an exercise program," she continued. "One that is free from dangerous physical contact that may lead to serious injury or even death?"

"Ida!" Bridgman said as he looked at her with a wrinkled brow. "Whose side are you on?" We all laughed again, but it was obvious he was stunned by her comment.

"Just asking," she said while flashing her own version of the famous Bridgman smile.

"Because exercise alone is not enough," Teetzel continued. "Athletics in its rougher forms teaches young men to think fast, to react to unexpected situations, and to work together under adverse conditions. It is precisely these conditions that build the character our nation needs to survive."

"To survive?" asked Miss Fitzgerald.

"Yes," Teetzel said, locking his blue eyes on hers. "We are not a world power. While it is true that our standing among the great nations of Europe went up considerably after our recent war with Spain, our sovereignty is not assured by any means. We have a very small navy, a small army, and a huge land mass rich with resources that is the world's envy. Our people need to be strong."

"So," Miss Fitzgerald said. And she was still very calm, the perfect lady. "Football is the answer?"

Teetzel paused for a few seconds, glanced around the table, and then continued without answering directly. He wasn't about to drop his train of thought until he got it all out.

"I will admit there is some risk associated with playing football, but it is precisely this risk that serves a greater purpose. It sharpens the senses, clears the mind of all that is useless, and forces the thinking processes to focus on problem solving, and again, survival. But most of all it encourages a true democratic spirit by building courage. And all good citizens must have physical courage no less than moral courage. It is courage that fights against the evil foes of the soul and body, against corruption and tyranny. To answer your question about community, Miss Fitzgerald, I would prefer the entire community be involved in supporting their high school football team, whether directly with funds or coaching or by ensuring that all the rules of sportsmanship and integrity are strictly followed. As for your question regarding football being the answer to the training needs of our young men, I would have to say yes, football is the answer."

We burst into clapping and cheering while Billy shook his drunken head and quietly said, "Amen." He didn't say anymore, satisfied, I suppose, that Teetzel said the right thing.

I don't know if Miss Fitzgerald was satisfied with Teetzel's argument or not, because she never responded. Never got the chance. Our loud enthusiasm for Teetzel's argument continued until we were distracted by a loud knock at the front door. It was John Poundstone, the photographer.

"All right, everyone!" Burger said after he ushered the cameraman into the parlor. "I want the team members to gather in the corner here so we can get some flashlights." That's what we called photographs back then, because of the flash powder.

Teetzel's great oration was momentarily forgotten as we herded ourselves into the far end of the parlor where we jostled and rubbed shoulders and laughed while Poundstone unpacked and unfolded his equipment. Some of the fellows sat on chairs at the back while the rest of us kneeled or sat on the floor in front forming ourselves into a loose pile. Billy Harper even got into the photo along with Principal McClelland, Monroe Morrow, Fossil Wilson, and Teetzel. A second before the shot was made, Bridgman hollered, "Smile you sissies!" and Jacob and Mit, who were sitting on the floor, fell back into the laps of some of the other fellows. Lester and Bridgman were the only ones who smiled. They were the only ones who had all of their front teeth.

The party broke up after the pictures were taken, and Bert and Mrs. Burger stood at the door and shook each of our hands as we left. Lester and I walked with the Baushkes to their house on Britain Avenue. We walked slow, not only because Arthur was walking on crutches, but because all of us were stiff and limping.

"She's not as bad as I thought," I said to Lester after we'd left the Baushke place.

"What?"

"Miss Fitzgerald."

"Come on, Fletch," he said, shaking his head in bewilderment. "She's against us."

"Maybe…but she's also for us."

"The hell does that mean?"

"She may be against football," I went on, "but I'll betcha she feels better knowing Teetzel is coaching us because of his concern for our safety."

"I might believe you if she shows up to see us play Saturday."

"Bet fifty cents," I said.

"You're on."

Chapter 25

I went to the privy Saturday morning and found a cold wind blowing from the northwest. Heavy, gray clouds had rolled in during
the night, and the air felt thick as oil from an early-morning rain.
The weather didn't help my attitude, which was already sour in spite
of the publicity and the attention our supporters had showered on
us. I practiced every afternoon with the fellows and planned to dress
for the game, but I wouldn't be playing—Teetzel didn't have to tell
me. Throughout the week, Wadsworth led the team during every
drill while I struggled just to keep up with the scrubs.

After breakfast, I put on my wool overcoat, hitched Matty to
the rig, and took a ride through town thinking it might make me
feel better. The moisture crept into my bones to make them feel
like cold steel, but I forged ahead.

The streets were puddled with ice and water, but the students
were undeterred in their mission to decorate the town. On
Pipestone, in the area surrounding Four Corners, I found a sea of
orange and black bunting and ribbons hanging from most of the
store fronts. I turned onto Water and drove north past the turning
basin and warehouses where I heard the crashing of crates and
palates as they were swung on booms from moored steamships or
the occasional scow schooner. Gulls floated and cackled high in
the fast air while pigeons darted from turret to gable to rooftop.
Drays rumbled along in both directions, and a railroad engine
huffed from somewhere in the distance.

As I was passing back through town, I came upon the Ann
Arbor team riding in a huge wagon from the depot to the Eastland

Hotel. They were laughing and having a good time, and I nodded to a couple of them as Matty trotted past. They'd just arrived from Niles, where on Friday they practiced and then spent the night. Niles was less than a thirty-minute ride from Benton Harbor.

After leaving the downtown area, I drove to Eastman Springs where I found two old men, employees of the Colonel's, working on the field. I pulled Matty to a halt and one of them waved. I bundled my overcoat tightly around me and huddled against the stiff northwester whistling through the bare branches above me. More than once I looked up to see their wet outlines etched black against a sky that looked like soiled muslin, and the way they swayed and creaked and moaned made me feel uneasy. I knew that kind of weather. It was the kind that came to no good—snow one minute, rain or sleet the next.

The two workers had already raked the leaves into large, berm-like piles away from the field and had trimmed the grass where it was overgrown, mostly along the edges. When I got there, they were filling some of the field's bigger mud holes, after which they remeasured the field markings and put down a fresh dose of chalk. They did this by dipping a broom into a bucket of powdered lime-stone and dragging it sideways along a string that was staked out as a guide. When they finished, they gathered up their tools and left, leaving me all alone to contemplate my unhealed leg, which pained me all the more because of the cold.

The empty park was a stark contrast to the approaching sounds of the band and the cheering of the rooters, not to mention the banging together of muscled bodies on the gridiron. The wind would likely prohibit the postgame fireworks, but it wouldn't stop the match itself.

We were going against Ann Arbor from a position of weakness. Arthur Baushke was out while Leo Baushke and Bridgman were wounded and not at full strength, but at least they were playing. Iron Man Lathe would be playing too, but he was still question-able. Maybe, with a little luck, I would get my chance. On the drive home, my mind raced with the game plan I'd been mulling over and over for the past few days.

The stakes for the team were huge. The winner would play for the state championship.

The fellows and I rode from the Pastime Club to the playing grounds in a horse bus owned by a fellow named Fred Hannah. We arrived at two o'clock and were stunned, every last one of us, by the huge crowd. People were standing around in groups talking, lots of them stamping their feet and moving their hands in and out of their pockets to keep warm. Most everyone was wearing long wool coats buttoned to their chins and collars folded up to keep the wind out.

A strong contingent of high school students were there, along with a mob of local businessmen, which we really appreciated—most of them had to close their stores to come see us. And our families were there too, all in great spirits. Pa told me later how Judge Bridgman put up with some playful chiding from a group of enthusiasts because of the way he acted during the Muskegon game. Seems he got so excited he grabbed a section of the pigwire fence surrounding the field and accidentally pulled it out of the ground. Like his son, the judge was a colorful character, but not the most colorful that afternoon. That honor went to Colonel Eastman.

The Colonel was wearing a long fur coat he recently bought in Grand Rapids from a vender at Buffalo Bill's Wild West Show. Said the man guaranteed it was made from a buffalo shot by the old frontiersmen himself, which was a great story even if we didn't believe him. The Colonel was selling water, and for those who wanted something warmer, he offered a toddy of whiskey and honey. The water didn't move well, but as I looked around, I noticed lots of folks holding steaming cups of toddy. I heard a fellow tell his wife he needed one to help with a sore throat that was coming on. She complained, but then she gave in and let him have one. Then she got one for herself.

The gamblers were busy calling out the odds, which were nearly even until shortly before the game when one of them yelled through his megaphone, "Two-to-one for any amount on Benton Harbor!" There was a brief flurry of wagering and then it stopped altogether. Most of the Ann Arbor supporters didn't participate— said they didn't believe in gambling. I noticed there weren't any colony men at the park that day, which was unusual. I figured they stayed away because of the controversy surrounding Hutcheon Graham.

The crowd erupted as we ran onto the field, gathered in a large circle, and began our conditioning routines by rapidly tossing a football around. Other routines followed in rapid succession, and when we were almost finished, Teetzel and Jacob walked around the playing field inspecting the ground for areas of bad footing. Yes, Jacob had decided to let Ben Curry accompany his sister to Oklahoma City. When he told Eva of Fossil's offer, she immediately agreed Jacob should stay in Benton Harbor and play. Said their father would have wanted it that way.

After we finished with our routines, Jacob went with the referee to the center of the field and met Wessinger, the Ann Arbor captain. They agreed on halves of twenty and twenty-five minutes and then the coin was tossed. Wessinger won and chose to receive the second half.

Ann Arbor started the game with a wide kick, which Butts caught and advanced eight yards before being tackled. Wadsworth then ran a series of plays where he and Jacob alternated as ball carriers. I jotted that down on my note pad as mistake number one: "Quarterback not spreading duties among the backs." But before I knew it, we had the ball planted on the Ann Arbor fifteen-yard line, and on the next play Jacob took the ball and ripped through the line to score the first touchdown of the day. The crowd was going wild, as I erased comment number one.

"Don't erase that," Teetzel said. "I want you put it back down."

"Yes sir," I replied, writing as Wadsworth kicked the goal.

Jacob kicked to Ann Arbor and they ran three plays, failed to make their yardage, and punted. The crowd was hard at it, cheering and waving their orange and black ribbons, and they got louder as the fellows took possession and went to work with a vengeance. They played cool, methodical, and without fault. The backs ran low when they carried the ball and the linemen charged with a determination beyond their normal nature. And they seemed to get better with each successive play, coming off the line fast and in perfect unison. The way Wadsworth grabbed Jacob's strap and was hauled along for twenty- and twenty-five–yard gains brought cheer after cheer from the crowd. It was magnificent. At that moment, I was both excited and proud to be a member of such a fine machine, but inside I was fighting a hard case of jealousy. And I was still nagged by the thought that Wadsworth didn't have what it took.

The second touchdown was set up when we had the ball on the fifteen-yard line and Wadsworth called for a tackle-back formation with Cunningham as the ball carrier. Lathe would have been the ideal choice, but Teetzel had already removed him from the game because his leg was paining him. The play was run, but Ann Arbor somehow stopped us at the one-yard line. Jacob carried it over on the next play and Baushke kicked the goal to make the score 12 to 0.

On Ann Arbor's next possession, they again failed to make their downs and had to punt. Their line was already demoralized, which is why Wadsworth called for a sequence play—one signal for three predetermined plays in rapid succession. The crowd was cheering so loudly it was hard for the fellows to hear Wadsworth's commands anyway. The plays were run so fast that Ann Arbor was swept completely off their feet. We took the ball again and made our first downs until Dice Baushke carried it to the twelve-yard line. Bridgman made the touchdown. The point was kicked to make the score 18 to 0.

During the half, we huddled beneath a tree with our blankets wrapped tightly around us. Teetzel went through his usual list of mistakes and he talked to Wadsworth about using a wider variety of plays. In my opinion, he didn't dwell on it enough.

In the second half, Baushke twisted his ankle and was replaced by Lester, whose end position was filled by Mit Ludwig. Handy got busted in the head and was so disoriented, Teetzel took him out and put Jones in his place, which meant I'd be going in the game if one more player was injured. Either me or we'd be playing with ten men. But even with ten, we would've killed Ann Arbor. Mit scored the fourth touchdown of the game, and Wadsworth carried it over three more times before it ended. Busby kicked all the goals.

Our playing that day was powerful. And I have to admit that

Wadsworth did a fine job overall, even though he made some calls I wouldn't have. Sequence plays, for instance, were risky because the quarterback couldn't predict the results from any one play, and the sequence may include plays that would not fit the situation at hand. The other play I rarely called for was the double pass, which he used five or six times that afternoon.

The double pass was actually two laterals—the ball couldn't be tossed forward back then, just backward. The quarterback would take the snap and toss it to one of the backs who would begin running and then toss it off to another back, often a split second before he was to be tackled. It was good for spreading out the defense. However, the only time it was successful that afternoon was the first time. Bridgman took the second pass and made a hair-raising line hurdle and almost broke loose. After that, Ann Arbor watched for it. Wadsworth should have known they would.

The successful execution of a double pass was damn exciting, but the old-timer enthusiasts still liked the push-and-pull strategies best. And they always liked it when the ball carrier grabbed Jacob's strap and was dragged along, usually with two or more players pushing from behind. It was exciting, I agree, but dangerous as hell. Trying to tackle a ball carrier who was being pushed was like trying to tackle a steer. But the rooters liked it that way because it was rougher and could lead to more slugging, which also meant more blood.

Probably the most valuable skill in evidence that day, next to our speed, was our ability to shift into other positions on a moment's notice. As Lathe was injured, followed by Baushke and then Handy, other players substituted or shifted into their positions with perfect ease. With less than fifteen players on the squad and a high injury rate, it was essential for all championship-caliber teams to have players who could play all positions. We were well-oiled with those skills, and it showed against Ann Arbor. Ann Arbor's coach, Paul Jones, said after the game that we were superior to any team in Detroit. He was especially impressed with Jacob and Wadsworth.

Wadsworth did everything that day, and part of the reason he looked so good was because he carried the ball more than normal for a quarterback back then. It went against Teetzel's philosophy of the machine, of all parts being equal, but to the rooters and press he looked damn good, and it was hard to argue with that. Teetzel continued to help him with his strategies and so did Jacob, but he never seemed to see the entire picture.

"What's your opinion of the play calling, Fletch?" Jacob said when we were standing around the bench after the team had congratulated the Ann Arbor boys.

"You tired?" I asked.

"Legs feel like rope."

"It shouldn't be that way," I said.

"Amen."

I didn't get in the game, but at least I reaped some satisfaction knowing that Jacob was aware of Wadsworth's shortcomings. I didn't know to what degree he felt it affected the team, or whether he believed as I did that Wadsworth's meager knowledge of our play selections and his inability to construct a viable game strategy was a disaster waiting to happen. He wasn't given to speaking his mind that way. But in my gut I was sure he knew, and that was bolstering. It also angered me. Wadsworth's eagerness to show off left the team vulnerable. Sure, the fellows were so talented and conditioned to perfection that they may never get into a tight situation, but what happened if they did? Could he extricate them? I feared not. The bastard was leading my team to glory over very unstable ground.

As the spectators were leaving the field, Teetzel was surrounded by a group of reporters, one of them being Barratt O'Hara, who asked most of the questions. "Coach," he began, "how do you feel about the playing of your team today?"

"I thought the boys did a fair job," he said while combing his fingers through his hair, brushing it from his forehead. "They've come a long way and seem to be faster now, faster than they were against Muskegon. But they fell flat on the basics, particularly their punt catching."

He was right. Punt catching was one that I can remember. The fellows either got too far under the ball and it went over their heads, which caused them to use their arms instead of hands and body. We bobbled quite a few that way and flat-out dropped a couple others. We'd been working so hard on speed that we neglected the things that should've been second nature.

"What are your predictions for the game with Escanaba?" O'Hara asked without looking up. He was furiously scratching on his pad with the remaining stub of a brown pencil.

"I'd say our odds are about even…Escanaba has a powerful machine. There's a lot at stake here and the game will be anything but a pushover."

Teetzel may not have been satisfied with us, but the rooters certainly were. And they gave Teetzel the credit, even those who were initially skeptical about his "scientific" philosophy. Folks were impressed with his discipline and teamwork strategies, not to mention the way he'd brought us to one game shy of the state championship. They called him the best football coach in the state and began to compare him to coaches like Hurry-up Yost, Alonzo Stagg, and Wallie McCornack.

The reporters talked to Jacob after they finished with Teetzel. "We are satisfied," he said. "The boys played well and we had an easier time than we expected. We're goin after Escanaba now."

That said it all.

Of course we'd rather have been playing against Ishpeming, but since we weren't, we decided the only way we could get back at them was by hammering Escanaba. And in the end, that was fine with us. In our minds, we were the best team in the state, probably the nation, Hyde Park included. We felt invincible. And though I was damn disappointed I couldn't be on the field leading the fellows, it didn't mean I wasn't excited.

While the fellows continued talking with rooters and family members, I busied myself gathering up towels and wraps and other pieces of equipment. I was thinking about the fifty cents I owed Butts after Miss Fitzgerald didn't show up to see us play.

"Hey kid," someone said from behind me. The voice was strangely familiar, but I couldn't place it. I cautiously turned around and saw a tall fellow wearing a long gray wool coat, buttoned up tight, with a matching newsboy's cap cocked sideways on his head. His dark hair was thick and shaggy and sticking out around his ears.

"Hub?" I said, not sure if it was him—I hadn't seen him in over a year. I was in junior high during the season of '02 and never saw him again after football was over.

"How are you kid?"

"Real good," I replied calmly, though inside I was so thrilled to see him that I barely noticed he called me "kid." Besides, he'd never been anything but good to me. Hub was a true gentleman. "How are things at the university?"

"School's a bear. But other than that I'm having a great time following Yost's whirlwinds. Fine team."

"I read about them in the paper."

"I saw the Kalamazoo and Muskegon games."

"Yeah?" I was surprised about that. I didn't see him at either one, and no one told me he was there.

"I rode the train in with some fellows from school. Didn't stay either time…left right afterwards…but I shouldn't have."

"Why not?"

"I should've congratulated you."

Damn. I couldn't believe he said that. For a greenhorn quarterback like myself, a compliment from Hub Allen was almost like getting a compliment from God. "Appreciate that, Hub."

"I should've given you some pointers too, at least after the Kalamazoo game. You didn't need any during the Muskegon game, except maybe to be careful carrying the ball."

"Don't I know that."

Then, as if out of nowhere, he said, "You know Wadsworth's a fool." I just looked at him and he looked back, as if to let it sink in, and I didn't say a word. "He's physically gifted," he went on, "but his head is in the wrong place. He doesn't understand Teetzel's concept of the machine."

"You know about the machine?"

"Come on kid, I live in Ann Arbor, remember? Football is in the air I breathe. That's how I know what you've been going through."

"What?" I said incredulously.

"I know how hard you've worked. I also know how seriously you study your playbook, probably at night by the flame of your bedroom lamp. I know how you pain from the hard playing, and

I certainly know how you worry."

"Worry?" I said, not being sure of his meaning.

"Yes, worry. The good quarterback worries about his players. He worries about the linemen who struggle unselfishly and tirelessly in the trenches only to get beat to bloody pulps. He worries about sending his running backs into situations where they get twisted and mangled limbs, sometimes so bad that they'll suffer with them for the rest of their lives. And then, to top it off, he must use his men in the best way possible to win the game. I know…I've been there."

"Yes. But if I'd have known all that going in," I replied. "I probably wouldn't have asked to play quarterback."

"Yes you would," Hub said. He seemed irritated with me for saying that but his reply was calm, like he was talking to a spooked horse. "Because you've got what it takes."

"Wadsworth…" I started to say but he cut me off.

"Wadsworth doesn't have it," he said. "He's only in the game for the glory. That's why you need to hang in there. Keep up with the training and continue to study the plays and strategies. And listen to Teetzel. He's a good man."

I turned my head and looked across the cold field to where a handful of kids were kicking a football. "Yes…" I muttered. "But his being a good man isn't getting me back in the game."

"You may not get back on the field again this season," he said. "But you will next season. Mark my words." He stuck out his hand and we shook. "You'll see."

I finished gathering up the equipment and joined the fellows in the horse bus for the ride back to the Pastime Club. There was a lot of loud talking and celebration, but I didn't say much. I continued thinking about what Hub had said.

"Damn good to see you Hub," I said under my breath.

"What?" Mit asked amidst the din. He was sharing a seat with me.

"Nothing. Just talking to myself."

I went home and was met in the foyer by a very excited little brother. "You will not believe what's in the *Evening News!*" Charlie said.

"And why should I care?" I replied.

"It's about Teetzel's Machine!" He thrust the paper into my hands and there it was, splashed across the entire front page, articles and photographs about the team.

The board members had arranged a photograph session for us the day before. We met just after lunch at Poundstone's downtown gallery, which was a spacious room with a maplewood floor, a bank of high, north-facing windows, and almost no furniture. We arrived wearing our school clothes but had our uniforms with us in canvas duffel bags.

"Okay boys," Poundstone hollered out as he scurried among his equipment making adjustments. He was wearing a pair of dark wool slacks along with a white shirt and tie, all of it covered with a dingy white artist's smock, which protected him from the developing chemicals. "Get into your playing togs. There's a small changing room in the back, but I suggest you change where you stand to save time."

"You heard him," Teetzel commanded. "Let's put some snap into it." Burger was also there along with Billy and Doc.

We began dropping our trousers and soon there were small piles of clothes scattered about the floor. We suited up, and I remember the strange sound our cleats made on the wood floor as we milled around the room talking. Finally, Poundstone called for us to move to the front of the camera where he had a row of chairs and a bearskin rug positioned in front of a canvas backdrop painted up to look like a stage. When all was right, he arranged us for a team picture and then for individual shots.

Some of the photographs appeared in the two-page collection of articles Charlie had thrust into my hand, headlined GRIDIRON WARRIORS OF BENTON HARBOR. But it was the sub-headline that really told the story. It read "From the Days of the Pioneers in the Game Down to Coach Teetzel's Scientific Aggregation of Punters." There were articles about the history of the game in Benton Harbor, an article written by Barratt O'Hara and one by Coach Teetzel. The paper also included pictures of the teams of 1899 and 1902, as well as individual shots of Jacob and Hub Allen. There was also a photo of the three running backs, Bridgman,

Jacob, and Arthur Baushke.

If a stranger to Benton Harbor had picked up a copy of that paper, he'd have thought the town was football crazy. And he would've been right.

After I'd read the paper, I dozed in the parlor until dinnertime. While eating, my folks talked a lot about the game. Said they had a grand time but couldn't understand why Teetzel didn't allow me to play, especially once the score was run up. I didn't say much about that. Instead I told them I'd run into Hub Allen and they were pleased. They knew how I respected him. After the table was cleared, I walked to Butts's house and together we went to the depot and met the rest of the fellows for the Ann Arbor team sendoff.

The Ann Arbor players were gentlemen about their defeat. We chatted with them a bit on the deck and then cheered loudly when they boarded. We were still celebrating them when something happened to make us stop, and that was the sight of Teetzel walking up to one of the cars farther down and boarding with an apparent sense of urgency. He was carrying a suitcase, and he never turned to look at us.

"Hey fellas!" a lone voice called out from down the way. It was Barratt O'Hara, and he was waving his scratch pad at us trying to get our attention. "Did you hear?"

"Hear what?" Jacob hollered as O'Hara trotted over to where we were standing.

"Bad news."

No one said anything. We just looked at him with blank stares until Jacob finally said, "Give it to us."

"The championship game is off."

"What?"

"You've been disqualified."

One Last Fight

Chapter 26

Conkey's Billiard Parlor was long and narrow, and everything from the planked floor to the pressed tin ceiling was covered in layers of filth. Heavy wood pool tables with laced leather pockets were arrayed along its length, and against each side wall were small sitting tables, most of them cluttered with ashtrays, glasses, and plates of half-eaten food—some had pool cues leaned up against their chipped edges. On the wall behind the service counter, just above the wood-fired cookstove, was a large tin sign advertising Grand Rapids Silver Foam Beer. The air was heavy with the stench of overcooked meat and the sweaty smell of unwashed bodies. The usual Saturday night contingent of gamblers and hustlers was there along with some of the roughest, whiskey-soaked toughs I'd ever seen. Through the dull, smoldering glow of the gas lamps and the clouds of blue cigar smoke, I saw Jacob. He was standing in the middle of the room. Alone.

By the time I arrived, the patrons were already backed out of the way. Even the handful of delinquents who'd been playing the slots had turned to watch. But like vultures they hovered in the shadows along with everyone else waiting patiently for the fighting to begin. Some even talked odds. Jacob was facing the Gill, who ominously fingered a pool cue while two rangy dockhands stood behind him, friends I figured.

The confrontation started less than an hour earlier when the neighborhood paper boy went to Lila's house and told Jacob the Gill was at Conkey's. Without saying a word, Jacob went into the front hallway and sat down to put his shoes on while Lila stood over him trying to reason with him. She knew his mind, but she also knew he probably wouldn't listen. And she was right. He had his coat on and was out the door without so much as an acknowledgment. That's when she told Heck to get a couple of us fellows together and watch after him. I lived closest. We stopped at Ossignac's house on the way and he said he'd be along in a few minutes.

"I heard you told them about Baushke," Jacob growled. He was standing stiff, both arms at his sides with fists balled tight.

"Yeah...what of it?" The Gill replied with a sneer loud enough for all to hear.

"We're disqualified...that's what," Jacob said, eyes boring hard into the Gill.

"Well ain't that just too bad."

"Yeah...it is too bad. I should've expected you'd have somethin to do with it."

"Why don't you go home and cry on your mama's shoulder." It was then I heard the door open and turned around to see Ossignac ease himself in and stand behind us. The heavy smoke below the ceiling swirled in the dim lights from the sudden breath of outside air.

"No." Jacob said as he carefully eyed the two thugs. I knew he was sizing them up. "I have a better idea."

"I suppose you'd rather cry on your baby brother's shoulder," the Gill said sarcastically, which is when Heck couldn't stand it any longer and exploded.

"Come on, shitbucket!" he said. "Put up your fists...now!"

Encouraged by Heck's outburst, along with the realization that the Gill was Muskegon's spy, some of the men in the crowd started to shout. Others quickly joined them and soon there was so much yelling and shaking of fists that my heart began to beat a furious pace. The fellow working behind the counter never made a move to control the situation—in fact, he seemed rather amused. The kid working with him slipped quietly out the door. I was so scared I almost left with him.

"Stand to," Ossignac whispered as he put his hand on Heck's shoulder to calm him.

"Tell you what I'm gonna do," Jacob said after the noise slackened. "I'm gonna whip you like the mangy dog you are."

The men started yelling again and it was obvious they wanted blood. That's when the Gill and the two thugs made their move. Jacob put up his balled fists and crouched while Ossignac pushed his way through the crowd and stood beside Jacob. "Let's have a fair fight here!" he shouted over the din.

That brought more shouting, most of it in favor of Ossignac, who grabbed one of the two thugs and began to wrestle him out of the way. Some men from the crowd immediately grabbed the other one, and that's when the Gill smashed his cue on the edge of a pool table, splitting it in two. He lunged at Jacob with the splintered end but missed. The crowd jeered him. The Gill jabbed again and Jacob sidestepped, but this time he grabbed the cue and jerked it from the Gill's hands. Then, with a quick, sideways snap of his arm, he spun it high over the crowd and everyone stood in silence until it clattered against the back wall. Then the crowd erupted in raucous cheering, creating a moment so infectious I couldn't resist joining them.

"Now let's see what you can do!" Jacob yelled so everyone could hear.

"Wipe the floor with him," someone yelled.

"Kill the bloody traitor," said another.

When the two combatants raised their fists, greasy wads of bills appeared and the men began to make their wagers. Whiskey, gambling, and gaming—it's what they lived for—and who among them would have guessed they'd be standing witness on that cold Saturday night to the resolution of a simmering grudge match?

The Gill got in a couple of good blows, and then it was Jacob's turn. It went back and forth for two or three minutes before Jacob began to get the upper hand. Finally, when the Gill's stamina was running short, Jacob went to work with both fists, first one and then the other, and he kept it up until the Gill went down on his knees. Without hesitation, Jacob kicked him in the gut and knocked him sideways onto the greasy plank floor. By that time, the Gill's lips were split and swollen and blood was running from his nose. His cheeks were already turning black and blue and he was heaving. I knew Jacob was good with his fists, but I didn't realize he was that good.

We all cheered again and then some of the men started to jeer the Gill. They shook their fists and spit on him while others began shoving the two thugs, which is when Ossignac whispered that we'd better get out of there.

"Hey, Jacob!" one of the gamblers yelled before we could get to the door. "How bout I buy you a beer!"

"Naw!" he yelled back. "But thanks the same."

Outside we were met by the kid who'd been behind the counter, and he had a burly police officer in tow. "There's one of them!" he said pointing at Jacob.

"That one?" the officer said, pointing his nightstick at Jacob's chest.

"Yeah. That's him alright, he started it."

"But that's Jacob Graham," the officer said, "captain of the football team." The kid stood there with a stunned look on his face. "What's the problem, Jacob?" the officer went on.

"Had a little mix-up, officer. Got into a tussle with the fellow who ratted us out about Art Baushke."

"Now that's one hell of a rotten deal, ain't it," he said as he nudged his hat up with the tip of his nightstick.

"Damn right it is," Heck interrupted.

"The troublemaker still inside?"

"Yeah," Jacob answered. "But he's having some difficulty standing up." We were chuckling by then.

"You boys go on home and I'll take care of it."

As we turned to walk away I saw the officer pull the door open, and the smoke and noise and the stink of unwashed men came roiling out. Then he entered with the kid trailing behind.

As soon as we were a block away, we started to recount blow by blow the way Jacob hammered the Gill. We also talked about how the fellows in the pool parlor turned on the Gill once they discovered he was Muskegon's spy. I think he was lucky to get off so easy. Some of those fellows were mad and drunk enough that they might have killed him.

As dejected as we were about the news of our disqualification,

Jacob's revenge felt damn good that night.

By Sunday morning, news of the team's disqualification and Jacob's fight with the Gill was all over town. And it seemed everyone wanted to talk about it, even in church, which didn't make Pastor Hoffman too happy. But the story of our disqualification gripped Benton Harbor like a plague, and everyone wanted to know what the deal was and what was being done to get it resolved. At the time, we didn't know the story ourselves. It took a few days for us to piece the thing together, and as I remember it went something like this.

On the day of the Ann Arbor game, an investigation was conducted by the State Athletic Committee's three-man Board of Appeals into Muskegon's charge that we were using illegal players. We didn't know it at the time but it was the Gill who tipped off Muskegon in the first place, and the man doing the investigation was a member of the appeals board named Durand Springer.

Springer came to Benton Harbor with the Ann Arbor team, and before the game was played, he arranged to get into the courthouse to search through the birth records. That's how he discovered Arthur Baushke was twenty-one. By late afternoon, Barratt O'Hara had sniffed out a rumor that something was up and conducted a quick interview with Springer. O'Hara then reported the facts to Teetzel, including Springer's claim that he would recommend the team be disqualified. It was O'Hara who told us about the Gill.

Teetzel and O'Hara met with Burger, who in turn scheduled a meeting with the board members. Burger presented the facts as he understood them and then proposed Teetzel go to Ann Arbor to plead our case. That seemed the logical thing to do, in fact the only thing. But Teetzel flat-out refused. He was still unhappy over the way he had been forced to let Baushke and Wadsworth join the team after the October 1 cut-off date, and the fact that no one told him Baushke was over the legal age limit only infuriated him further. He told the board members he'd never have let Baushke stay on the team had he known he was over twenty-one.

Billy Harper responded to Teetzel's refusal by arguing that Baushke had, in fact, only recently turned twenty-one—said he couldn't see what difference a few months made. Teetzel replied that the difference was our disqualification from playing for the state title. He told the board members he wouldn't go to Ann Arbor to spread more lies, and that they should accept our punishment fair and square.

Teetzel's refusal was some hard medicine, but he was holding all the cards. That's because he knew the system and how it worked.

The five-member State Athletic Committee established the overall rules for team eligibility, and through their appeals board, they investigated teams suspected of using fraudulent players. It was the Athletic Committee who in 1899 initiated the first formal Thanksgiving Day state championship game, although they didn't have the manpower or the financial resources to actually conduct the contest. That was done by a student organization within the University of Michigan's Athletic Department called the Interscholastic Committee.

The Interscholastic Committee was comprised of twenty students elected by the university's student body. The committee organized intramural sports at the school, but they also promoted high school athletics by conducting baseball round-robins, invitational track meets, and the yearly football state championship. The chief officer of the committee was called the interscholastic manager, who also filled one of the three positions on the board of appeals—the other two were filled by Athletic Committee members. In 1903, the interscholastic manager was James Carpenter. Teetzel knew Springer would have to enlist his cooperation in stopping us from playing the game. And that gets to the heart of the matter of why Burger and the board members wanted Teetzel to go to Ann Arbor. Teetzel, you see, was a former member of the Interscholastic Committee.

In the end, the board members offered Teetzel a hundred bucks to go to Ann Arbor and argue our case. He refused the money but finally agreed to go. O'Hara said Teetzel did it to fulfill his promise to us. That may have been true, but I think he also did it for the same reason he fought Muskegon—to fight for his own reputation.

All day Sunday we waited to hear from Teetzel but got nothing. Rumors were flying everywhere, some good, but most bad.

Burger and the board members got tired of waiting and began making their own plans to arrange a game between us and Escanaba. They put the word out that we might need money to offer them for a sanctioned game and immediately collected over a thousand dollars in pledges. It was Ishpeming all over again.

Around eight o'clock that evening, Burger finally received a telegraph from Teetzel explaining that the appeals board would meet Monday morning to hear Springer's case against us and then vote on our disqualification. It also said Escanaba would be given the state championship title by default if the decision went against us. He promised to telegraph the results to Burger immediately after the verdict was announced.

Monday arrived, and by lunchtime there was no word from Teetzel, which told us there must have been a meeting delay or a problem. Either way, it didn't look promising. But at 3:30, Burger came to the practice field to tell us Teetzel's telegraph had arrived at three o'clock. It simply said the game was on and that he would report the particulars upon his arrival. We immediately rejoiced. It was truly one of the happiest moments of my life. We continued with our practice, and every last player, whether a varsity player or scrub, played with a snap in his step that I hadn't seen in weeks.

Teetzel returned Monday evening on the seven o'clock train and was met at the station by Doc, who drove him straight to the Columbian Cigar Company. Butts and I had arrived a good half hour earlier, just as the lamplighter was working his way along Pipestone, to meet up with the rest of the team. Doc and Teetzel burst through the front door at nearly half past seven, and without saying anything more than a cursory hello they disappeared into Billy Harper's office while the rest of us waited in the work area. Other men were there too, gamblers mostly, but also serious enthusiasts, students, and a few fathers.

The work room where we gathered was dimly lit. It was cold and drafty and smelled of dust and dried tobacco leaves. Some of us sat and fidgeted, while others paced—most of the men smoked cigars. After half an hour or so, the board members emerged and Burger did the talking.

"I have some bad news," he said. "The appeals board voted to disqualify us."

The response was immediate, like someone had flicked a switch. No one said anything, but every single eye, cheek muscle, and jaw in the crowd dropped in bewilderment. The silence was unnerving.

"Could you repeat that?" Shorty Blake finally called out.

"You heard right, Shorty," Burger said. "They voted to disqualify us. Durand Springer led the attack and the vote was two to one. The board member from Kalamazoo sided with us."

"But what about that interscholastic manager fellow?" he continued.

"Carpenter? He's from Iron Mountain, need I say any more about that?" Iron Mountain was located in the upper peninsula.

"Then what about the telegram saying the game was on?" someone else shouted.

"I'll let Coach Teetzel tell you about that."

"I met with the board first thing this morning," Teetzel said, "and argued that Baushke played illegally in one game…the one against Muskegon…and that he was now off the team and we were legal without him. We discussed that for a few minutes and they agreed we would have won the game anyway without him, but in the end they said we still broke the rules. Then I pointed out that technically we didn't break the rules at all according to the way they were written. The rule in question stated a player could not be over twenty-one, which Arthur was not. To be over twenty-one, he had to be twenty-two."

"Good thinkin, Coach!" Bridgman yelled.

"Not good enough though," Burger added.

"He's right, men," Teetzel said. "I'm afraid it didn't matter. They changed the rules on the spot to read that a player had to be under twenty-one to play. After that, they met in private for twenty minutes before Jim Carpenter came out and told me their decision. He said we were disqualified."

The crowd rumbled. But then they stopped when Bridgman asked, "How about we arrange the game ourselves?"

"I asked him how the committee would view it if we went ahead with the game anyway and he said it wouldn't matter if we played or not. The game would not count for the state championship."

"What about the appeal?" Caully shouted from the bowels of the crowd.

"Yes, I asked for an appeal and it was granted for one o'clock that afternoon. I met with them and we had a serious discussion, which I won't go into here, and then they met in secret for twenty minutes before Carpenter delivered their decision. He said the disqualification still stood. There was to be no championship game this year."

The room echoed with boos and hisses and angry oaths. Burger held his hands in the air to quiet them, and when they did, he said, "There's more. Let Coach Teetzel continue."

"Yes, he did say there would be no championship game, but then he said the Interscholastic Committee wanted us and Escanaba to play an exhibition game."

"The hell?" someone behind me growled. Then the crowd erupted into a cacophony of hoots and catcalls.

"Can't be so!" Roscoe Farmer's voice rang out above the din.

Then Burger moved forward and held his hands in the air to again quiet the crowd. "The board will be meeting in a few minutes with me and Doc and Coach Teetzel to discuss the proposal. But I can tell you right now it doesn't look good. The board already feels it's a setup, that if we send the team they'll be duped like last year and made to look like fools."

I didn't know what to think, none of us did. Me and the fellows were all of the same mind. Of course we wanted to play, but we weren't keen to the idea of subjecting ourselves to a public hanging by dishonest game officials. As the men were leaving the building, Teetzel gathered us around him and asked whether we wanted to play the game or not. No one could say one way or the other until we hashed it out among ourselves, which he understood. He said to meet him at the Pastime Club at seven the following morning to talk it through. Said Caully would be there to unlock the doors.

After Teetzel finished with us, he and Burger and the board members disappeared into Billy's office. Doc, Caully, and Roscoe Farmer all grabbed chairs and went in behind them and closed the door. Through the frosted glass above the doorknob, I could see shadowy silhouettes of men moving around the room and hear their muffled conversations as they dragged chairs across the plank floor. Then there was quiet. The crowd continued to talk among themselves for another few minutes, but very soon they began trickling toward the door, and we players went with them.

Once outside, I noticed some of the men were heading toward Bird's Drug Store. Out of curiosity, me, Butts, and the Grahams followed. Inside we found some empty stools and sat with our backs to the lunch counter, elbows up, and watched as supporters continued to stream in the door. Many of them hadn't been at the meeting but had heard the rumors and wanted to get the facts.

Very soon the room was filled with men talking and arguing in loud voices. The meeting was not official and there was almost no order until Shorty Blake took charge. He was standing in the middle of the lunch area with his shirt sleeves rolled up and a derby cocked sideways on his head. A half-smoked cigar jutted from the corner of his mouth.

"I can't figure out why this happened!" he hollered. Some of the men immediately began to quiet down, and while waiting for the remainder he spit into a brass spittoon that was on the floor next to his feet. "The committee knows that every damn team to win the championship has used at least one player over twenty-one."

"They're agin us!" an old sod-buster farmer yelled. "And we ain't done nothin wrong!"

A chorus of voices erupted in agreement and then everyone tried to get their two cents in at once. That's when it became obvious to me that these men were not considering an exhibition game.

"And even..." Shorty interrupted and then stopped to let the crowd settle down. "And even this year there were teams who used illegal players that weren't penalized. Kalamazoo played at least three ineligible men, and remember how South Haven borrowed those two fellas from Allegan, one of them being the Gill. Muskegon used an illegal man too. And in the Upper Peninsula, seven of Ironwood's players were ruled out, as were six of Ishpeming's, and the loss of those men cost them the game with

Escanaba!"

"You betcha!" someone yelled. "And what about Escanaba using the best players from Gladstone?" That comment elicited a chorus of boos and cursing. The men were getting madder by the minute.

"Jacob!" Shorty called. "What's the word among the players?" The crowd quieted to a whisper, all eyes turning to the four of us.

"Well…" he said as he stood up. "We're pretty hurt about the whole thing…and we feel Springer and his board of appeals are wrong. We don't know why they jumped on us…and we sure as hell don't know why the university's Interscholastic Committee suddenly put their nose in the pie and called for us to play an exhibition contest. The only way we'll go to Ann Arbor is if Manager Burger can fix it for us to play a sanctioned game."

The crowd murmured its approval.

"But I can tell you one more thing," he continued. "I've talked to lots of fellas around here about this deal…and I feel it'll be a cold day in hell before anyone from Bungtown plays football for the Wolverines."

That proclamation was like throwing a match into a puddle of gasoline. The crowd went crazy, hollering and clapping their approval. After Jacob's quip about the Interscholastic Committee, the crowd turned its anger back to Durand Springer.

Besides being a professor at Ann Arbor High, Springer was a founding member of the original 1895 State Athletic Committee. Except for him, the committee members were and had always been high school principals. I supposed you could say he was a visionary, and without a doubt he was a tireless supporter of high school athletics, but the men at Bird's that night suspected his investigation into the Baushke affair was conducted out of prejudice.

"Come up here, Roscoe!" Shorty yelled. "Tell us about the problems we had with Springer last year."

Roscoe Farmer, who was standing with Alvah Cady off to the side up by the front of the store, was the county game warden and a strong team supporter. He eased his way through the crowd and stood next to Shorty.

"As some of you know," he said, "the team went to Ann Arbor

last year to play against Ann Arbor High for the championship of lower Michigan. Springer, in addition to being a member of the State Athletic Committee and appeals board, is also a member of their team's Board of Control."

"Isn't that a conflictin interest?" Strawbags shouted.

"I'd say so. But what bothered us was that one of their players, a fellow named Butler, was in his sixth year on the team. The rules say that no player can be on a team for more than four years, so we protested. They removed him and everything was fine. But then they substituted a fellow we knew to be a former college player."

"Why those stinkin cheats!" the old sod-buster hollered.

"Yeah!" a few others yelled in unison and the room erupted again.

"But!…" Roscoe called out as he held up his hands to quiet the crowd. "But we played the game anyway and won."

"Serves em right!" sang a lone voice from the crowd I didn't recognize.

"And that's one reason we think Springer's prejudiced against us," Roscoe said. "Because we beat his team."

"Men," Alvah Cady said as he walked to the center of the room. "Roscoe is right. He cheats when the occasion suits him…and I can personally attest to that."

Cady was the founding father of Benton Harbor football. For that reason his word carried a lot of weight around town, but also because he was college educated and a good man. The fact that he was a lawyer didn't seem to hurt his reputation either. The room quieted respectfully as he continued.

"I was on the Olivet College track team in the early '90s," he said, "when Springer was a professor at Albion College. As many of you know, Olivet and Albion are blood rivals. Springer was also in charge of field sports at Albion, and at the time he had no fast runners or decent jumpers so he induced a professional athlete, last name of Gale, to attend school during the track season. In doing so, he broke the rules. The only class Gale took was a writing class."

"Hypocrite!" someone yelled.

"Yes," Cady responded. "But I can honestly say we especially treasured the medals we won against Springer and his ringer!" The crowd exploded into laughing mixed with more boos and catcalls.

That's how the meeting went. A group of men and boys talking, arguing, swapping stories, and trying to make some sense of our misfortune. They took our disqualification hard, and down to the last man they felt we'd been cheated for the second time in two years. The meeting broke up with nothing resolved, but at least they'd found someone to blame.

As I think back on that night, I'm sure those men were on to something. I do believe Springer acted out of jealousy and prejudice, even though he claimed our disqualification was intended to make an example of Benton Harbor. But why us? That was the question. Why not Ishpeming or South Haven or Muskegon or any other team? They all used illegal players. The men at Bird's that night maintained that if we hadn't beat his team those two years in a row nothing would have been said about Baushke. But we won, and it seemed Springer was holding it against us. For that reason, he became the target of our wrath.

As the meeting was dying down, I said good-bye to the fellows and went home where I found my folks waiting for me.

"Piece of pie, Fletch?" Ma asked.

"Alright." I took the plate she offered me and sat down at the kitchen table.

Pa came in and sat down with us. "What is the verdict, son?"

"Looks bad," I replied between bites. "The appeals board voted to disqualify us, but then the university's Interscholastic Committee demanded we play an exhibition game."

Ma wrinkled her nose and said, "Sounds very confusing."

"It is. We don't know what to think. Most everyone downtown seems to think it's a setup."

"What do you think?" Pa asked.

"I think we're about to be shut out of our chance to prove we're the best."

"I know it looks bad now," he said as he and Ma glanced at one another. "Just remain hopeful and perhaps it'll work out."

I didn't answer. All the talking in the world wouldn't have made me feel any better, and they could tell. Mercifully, they left me alone. When I finished with the pie, I put my plate in the sink and went to the basement to stoke the furnace. Then I went upstairs to bed.

I washed my face and climbed under the covers but couldn't get to sleep. I tossed and turned until finally I got up, dressed, and went back to the basement. The firebox was stoked and burning fine so I pulled up a wood-slatted crate and sat in front of the open door and watched the blue flames. Soon I was deep in thought about the team. I thought about how hard we'd worked and how far we'd come since our loss to Ishpeming, only to be shut out of the opportunity to avenge ourselves. I thought about the things that were right about the season and those that weren't, and how most of those that weren't were unfairly overblown.

That night was the worst night of my short life. I was being strangled by things over which I had no control, but I couldn't help myself. My only hope was for the problem to be whittled down by my own despair until it became so small it would disappear altogether.

"Fat chance," I said out loud to myself.

Chapter 27

I gathered up my books and stepped out the back door to find the morning air cold and filled with frost. The eastern sky was showing the first smudges of light, and I paused only long enough to feed and water Mattie. Then I hustled down the alley to Catalpa Avenue where I said a quick hello to the iceman, Mr. Wills, as he hefted out a block of ice from the back of his wagon. His nag stomped and snorted while he grunted something equally as indecipherable. I cut a quick path over to Broadway, passed the high school, and arrived at the Pastime Club ten minutes later where I found Caully sweeping the sidewalk. "How ya doin, boyo?" he asked.

"Good as can be expected," I answered. I was about to open the door but then stopped and asked, "How did it go with the board last night?"

"Twas a long session, and not a pretty one at that. Coach Teetzel will be giving you the details shortly."

Caully was a tongue-wagger of tremendous proportions, at least until he was specifically asked to keep something under his hat, and then you could threaten to kill him and he wouldn't divulge the secret. Teetzel must have made such a request. In my mind, that possibility didn't bode well.

I went into the clubroom and found Ossignac, Bridgman, Arthur Baushke, and the Grahams sitting around a table wearing their overcoats. The coal stove had been fired and was burning nicely, but the room still wasn't warm enough to eliminate the chill. I left my coat on too. The fellows were quietly throwing dice for pennies, and Bridgman was the only one who acknowledged me.

"Welcome to the opera," he muttered as I pulled up a chair and sat down.

"Feels like a damn wake in here," Heck complained as he rolled a pair of boxcars.

"It's all my fault," Arthur muttered under his breath, "and I'm damn sorry about that. You fellows are only in this mess because of me."

His comment was met with silence. No one moved and no one said anything. The dice lay untouched on the table as if they were too hot to handle.

"You don't have to apologize," Jacob finally replied, the bitterness clear in his voice. He was bitter about our predicament, not at Baushke.

"Yeah," Ossignac added. "It wasn't your fault. You were pressured by Billy and the Board."

"But I should have known better than to lie to the coach and Principal McClelland about my age, especially after all that crap we went through with Ishpeming."

"Stop it!" Jacob said as he slapped his big hand on the table. One of the dice flew into my lap, and like a hot nail I quickly tossed it back onto the table where it came to rest beside its mate. "You know damn well that no team has ever been bumped for using a player who's slightly over the legal age limit…and every team uses em." Each one of us responded with a word or nod expressing our agreement.

It was obvious Jacob was irritated at Baushke for blaming himself. That's because the blame wasn't his to bear, at least in the opinion of the team, and most everyone else in Bungtown. And if anyone blamed Teetzel or the board members I never heard about that either. As far as we were concerned, the blame fell squarely on Springer for disqualifying us and on the Interscholastic Committee for demanding we play an exhibition game. Everyone I talked with thought the committee members should have stood up to Springer and allowed a sanctioned game.

The craps game started up again and Bridgman began wise-cracking, which we ignored. But he didn't stop until the sound of shod hooves and iron-rimmed wheels grating over the brick pavers caught our attention. I turned and looked out the window just in time to see Teetzel spring from Doc's rig. A few seconds later, he and Doc burst through the door followed by Lee, Mit, Busby, and Jones, all of them having arrived about the same time. Doc went behind the counter and poured himself a shot of whiskey while the rest of them joined us.

"Good morning, men," Teetzel said. There were some replies, but damn few. "We'll get started just as soon as the rest of the team gets here."

Caully came in and joined Teetzel and Doc at the counter where they chatted quietly. Five minutes later, the entire team was sitting loosely around a group of tables clustered in the middle of the room. Teetzel walked over and positioned himself in the center.

"Last evening's meeting ran for three hours," he began. "And every member of the board was against sending the team to Ann Arbor. So was Doc, Roscoe, and Deputy Pearl. And all of them were vehement about it. Manager Burger and myself were the only ones in favor of playing the game."

"Jesus, Mary, and Joseph," Caully said under his breath from behind the counter where he was standing with Doc. I think he said it because of the pale, hang-dog looks rutted across our faces.

"The men were very concerned that you were being duped and setup for a fall just like last year, and I can't blame them for thinking that way. But I felt confident our situation was different. I told them nearly every member of the university athletic department, including most members of the Interscholastic Committee, were in favor of us and Escanaba playing a clean game."

He was right. But so too were our board members for being cautious. To understand the dilemma they faced, I should take some time here to explain exactly what happened when Teetzel went to Ann Arbor. The story composed a confusing chain of events, and it was only much later that we were able to put everything into proper perspective.

We hadn't known it at the time, but a sizeable number of the Ann Arbor university students were anxiously awaiting the Thanksgiving Day high school championship game. The student population in general was absolutely crazy about Fielding Yost and his football teams, but for some of them their interest in football didn't begin and end with the Wolverines. They also followed the progress of the state's high schools, encouraged to do so by the university's Athletic Department.

We were told the students had been pulling hard for us throughout the season, which surprised the hell out of me. I knew a large number of them were rooting for a lower peninsula team to win the state championship, but I didn't realize we were their great hope.

Teetzel told us the students were so angry over our disqualification that a large crowd of them marched to the university athletic offices Monday during the lunch hour and demanded the game be allowed to proceed. James Carpenter met with them and was forced to explain why he voted for our disqualification. Said Springer's case against us was iron-clad and he couldn't very well go against him.

Springer's three-man Board of Appeals held its afternoon meeting and Teetzel again made a plea for our reinstatement. He told the committee Baushke had lied about his age, that he participated illegally during one game, but that we would have won whether he played or not. He also reiterated that we were legal without him. After the meeting, James Carpenter made a statement regarding their decision. It appeared in the *Michigan Daily* as follows:

> The state interscholastic championship game is declared off because of Benton Harbor's disqualification. But owing to the fact that the Escanaba team is already on its way to Ann Arbor, and that the game scheduled for Thanksgiving Day has been advertised, and is generally expected, there will be an exhibition game. Said game will indicate the relative strength of representative teams from the Upper and Lower Peninsulas.

Exactly why the game was allowed to proceed is a mystery to this day. Teetzel never told us what happened, in fact he claimed he didn't know himself. But through the grapevine, we heard it was the higher ups in the athletic department, including Yost himself, who pushed for the game to go forward. Apparently, Teetzel's lobbying behind the scenes made the difference. I heard he told them if the game was not allowed, they might as well cross Benton Harbor off the list as a potential feeder school for their athletic teams. Was a brilliant move—and true.

An exhibition game wasn't the perfect solution, but it did allow all parties to walk a very fine line. The game was probably called an "exhibition game" to lessen the embarrassment to the State Athletic Committee and their appeals board. But without a doubt the game itself, regardless of how it was billed, would determine the state's true champions. Under the circumstances, it was the best deal we were going to get, Springer too. Since the game was actually conducted by the Interscholastic Committee, which was controlled by the university's athletic department, there was no way he and his appeals board could stop it if they had wanted.

"For the remainder of the meeting," Teetzel continued, "the board members discussed and argued until they were blue in the face. For three long hours, the talk went back and forth until they finally voted in favor of our playing the game. There was only one no vote…Monroe's."

"Does that mean we play, Coach?" Mit asked.

"Gentlemen, the decision is yours. I propose we take a formal vote to decide if we go to Ann Arbor on Thanksgiving Day to play the game or not."

We voted and it was unanimous—all favored going.

"And may God's good graces shine upon you all," Caully said as he and Doc each saluted us by holding up a shot glass filled with whiskey. Then they threw back their heads and tossed them down in unison.

The meeting broke up and we went to school feeling confident the matter had been put to rest. All our classmates wanted to hear about it, and even Miss Fitzgerald cornered me just before lunch and asked about the latest news. I told her the game was on.

I couldn't have been more wrong.

While we were sitting in class, the streets of Bungtown were burning with discontent. Word of the board's decision, and ours too, streaked across town like lightning, and most of the football enthusiasts flat-out rejected our decision to play.

Knots of men argued throughout Tuesday morning and into

the lunch hour, mostly on the downtown street corners and in the Star Drug Store. I got word of the brewing controversy from Principal McClelland just as the lunch hour was beginning, and I quick-hopped a trolley downtown. I found the Star packed to the doors, and the conversation was very hot indeed. Monroe was standing in the middle of the room with Tom Logan, who was acting as moderator, and for a solid hour, the talk went back and forth with no change in attitude. I should have gone back to class but didn't.

Five major reasons emerged as to why the enthusiasts felt we shouldn't play the game.

The first reason had to do with the unfair treatment we received from Springer and the appeals board. We'd been slighted. The men agreed no one should have to put up with that. The second had to do with the game being billed as an exhibition and not a true championship. The third was fear. Many were of the mind we'd get a dirty deal by the game officials if we played. The fourth was the belief that the Interscholastic Committee would weaken and allow a sanctioned game if we held to our guns. The fifth and final reason had to do with rooter participation. The possibility was strong that few rooters would travel to Ann Arbor to support us unless the staunchest among them could be convinced we were doing the right thing.

At half past one, an employee of Burger's from the Red Cross Drug Store, a fellow named Bert Spaulding, burst through the door and wiggled his way to the middle of the room.

"What is it, Spaulding?" Logan said as the crowd quieted.

"Burger knows bout your objections and has called for a two o'clock meetin at the Armory! All interested parties should attend!" The men immediately began talking among themselves.

"Do we go or don't we?" Logan said to the crowd in a voice loud enough for all to hear.

"We've got to let him say his piece." Monroe answered, and everyone seemed to agree it was only fair.

I looked at the big brass clock on the wall behind the counter and realized again I should get back to class. I almost did go, at least until I convinced myself the team members and teachers would be disappointed if I couldn't report the entire story of what happened. Within ten minutes, the crowd of men was moving toward the Armory, and I was walking front and center next to Monroe and Tom Logan. When we filed into the drill room, we found a number of people already there. And more arrived after us. When all was said and done, the entire crowd was probably a hundred or so strong. Most were men, but there were some boys and even a few women.

"Yes men," Burger said from the stage positioned at the end of the room, "we have not been judged fairly by the Board of Appeals, particularly when we consider the number of other schools that acted illegally."

"That goes without saying," said Shorty Blake. "But why should we send our boys to play in a game that is not really for the state championship?"

"But it is. The board admitted that except for Baushke our team is a legal high school team. And because Escanaba and we are both undisputed champions in our regions of the state, the winning team would be universally accepted as state champion."

"But even if we play," a voice I immediately recognized as Albert Decker's rang out from the back of the crowd, "who's to say we're not bein set up...like last year?"

"I've been given the names of the officials," said Teetzel, who was standing next to Burger, "and I know them to be fair and honest men."

"Besides," Burger added, "if we don't play Escanaba, Kalamazoo High School will be given the opportunity, and Benton Harbor could be out of the interscholastic schedule for all time."

The crowd murmured darkly—not a good sign and Burger knew it. That's when Teetzel stepped forward and the crowd quieted.

"Gentlemen," he said and then paused to scan their faces. "I came to Benton Harbor for one reason, and that reason was to build your boys into the best football team in Michigan. Together you and I have done that. They are the best...I know it and so do you. But there are doubters all across the state. And there are others who believe Benton Harbor's complaining last season over the Ishpeming defeat was bad sportsmanship...and many of those are newspaper sportswriters."

"Who gives a damn what was said last year?" someone yelled from the crowd.

"I do," Teetzel said calmly, "and you should too. Because it will influence what they say about us this year if we don't play Escanaba. Will they say we didn't play because we were afraid of them? Will they call us bad sportsmen? Gentlemen, is that a risk we want to take? Think hard about it."

Teetzel was greeted with an uneasy silence.

"Coach Teetzel is right," Burger quickly added. "The boys want to play, to prove themselves, so I beg you to let them finish the job. And let Coach Teetzel finish the job he came here to do."

No one said anything. Instead, the crowd moved and shifted and finally reformed into small groups—I'd never seen anything like it. Some of the men stood in silence, deep into their own thoughts, while others talked. Soon the room was filled with the dull sound of low murmuring, and it was then I truly realized how important this issue was for them, and that they weren't about to make their decision lightly. They hashed over everything, every angle, looked at the pros and cons and argued the what-ifs. After about ten minutes, Monroe decided it was time to let the world know what he was thinking.

"Yep!" he hollered, and the room quieted. "I think I'll let Stone do the work!" He was referring to his partner in the grocery store business, who didn't care a whit for football. "Just think of a back-woods town like Ann Arbor telling Benton Harbor where to get off! We'll see if they can shove their feet into our vest pocket!"

"He's right," rang a voice from the crowd.

"Amen," said another. "I vote we play!"

"We'll show em just like we did Muskegon and Ann Arbor!" someone else shouted.

I could feel the tide turning. The talk became more feverish, and within a minute the armory erupted in yelling and cheering as the enthusiasts started coming over to our side. There were a few holdouts, but damn few of them.

"And you can count me in too," I heard Deputy Pearl say after the crowd quieted down again. "If I stay home and see those bulletins go up, Benton Harbor six, Escanaba zero, I'll kick myself clear around the block. And if the report comes in Escanaba six, Benton Harbor zero, I'll cuss myself for not being there to yell for Bridgman to make a touchdown." The deputy sheriff was referring to the telegrams that were sent to Benton Harbor throughout our away games and posted in the window of the Star Drug Store. "You won't see Irving Pearl eating turkey in Bungtown this Thanksgiving."

The meeting broke up and I went back to school to report the good news. And by the time football practice started, I'd have bet a dollar that everyone in town but the shut-ins knew the game was on. Teetzel briefly mentioned the meeting with the enthusiasts and then he put us to work. We had a light load with no scrimmage work, which was intended to make us enter Thursday's game filled with energy and good spirits. Later, at the Pastime Club, Burger told us the Rooter Special Number Three had been secured and the rooters were digging into their pockets for the $3.20 round-trip tickets to Ann Arbor.

That evening, we met again at the Pastime Club to discuss our schedule for the trip to Ann Arbor. The fellows were still feeling some anger that we'd be playing an exhibition game, but they were gradually warming to the idea. I could tell by the increase in their friendly gibing of one another. I, on the other hand, was becoming more withdrawn. I was beginning to realize how difficult it would for me to sit on the sideline watching Wadsworth at the helm of my machine.

When the meeting was over, those of us who lived to the south of downtown walked home in a group. It was cold and dark, and as we strolled down the middle of Broadway, the fellows talked and joked with each other. Coal smoke was settling over the town like a fog, but it was still light enough that we could see the stars through the bare maplewood branches arrayed above our heads. One by one, the fellows split off as we came to their streets or homes until it was just me and Teetzel. When we got to my house on Columbus, he stopped at the end of our sidewalk.

"I want you to know I appreciate all you've done to help out with the team."

"Thanks. It's the least I could do."

"I know that whenever the fellows get demoralized, you always try to lift their spirits. Your efforts have been good for the team. I'm just sorry your injury has kept you down for so long."

I felt a burst of pride that he recognized my efforts to help the team. It was the part about my leg not being healed that bothered me. "My leg is healed, Coach," I said.

"I wish it were so," he replied. "You are a good, solid quarterback."

Again I felt a burst of pride, but I also couldn't believe he thought I wasn't ready.

"But I am ready to play...tomorrow," I argued. "I may not be as big or strong as Wadsworth, but I know a lot more than he does about..."

"Fletch," he interrupted. "I watch you practice each afternoon. I see how you limp and favor your leg. One wrong move and you could become lame...I don't want to be responsible for a permanent disability. Condition yourself gradually and by next season you will be in fine shape."

"Then I might do better to step aside now and not burden the fellows," I said, my anger beginning to rise.

I was met with silence. That's when I knew I'd said the wrong thing, but by then I didn't care. My frustration was boiling over and I had no regrets. After a few seconds, he finally said, "What do you mean?"

"I mean if I'm not going to play, then why should I even put in the effort?"

"If you even have to pose that question, then your heart is not in the right place. You are not being dedicated and not prepared to make the necessary sacrifices. No one ever makes a success of anything unless his heart is properly aligned."

"But my heart is aligned."

"Then show me, and show the rest of the fellows by being willing do the hard work, even if the hard work is writing down mistakes from the sideline. Be honest with yourself, Fletch. Look forward with enthusiasm and remember, discipline should be adhered to as if it were more important than the mere winning or losing of a game. And for you, discipline means getting healed again."

I nodded in agreement. "But I am willing to do the hard work," I said, "and I do follow all the rules. I am ready to play, but I'm beginning to believe you won't let me because I'm simply too small to lead the team to success."

That's when Teetzel reached up and put his hands on my shoulders and looked me in the eye. "Fletch," he said seriously, "the smallest player on the team can be just as valuable as the largest. There is always a place for the player who makes himself strong and courageous and is not afraid to perform his duties."

"But how would you know?" I replied. "You were a star in high school and college. I weigh 118 pounds." I paused to gather more courage before continuing. "What chance do I really have?"

"You have just as much chance as anyone else."

"But how would you know?" I said again, the tears beginning to form at the corners of my eyes. "You couldn't possibly understand."

Teetzel looked at me hard for a long ten seconds, and then his expression softened and he said, "I do understand. Ten years ago I was just like you."

"What?" I said, confused.

"Ten years ago I weighed about the same as you. I was thin and frail, and our family physician warned my folks I might easily die of consumption if I didn't improve physically. But he was wrong. I began to exercise and eat more. I learned to play baseball, run track, and only then did I pick up a football."

"You can't be serious." I didn't know if I should believe him or not.

"I'm very serious."

"But you played football at Michigan and set track records."

"I set one record. But that doesn't matter. What matters is that my accomplishments were due to dedication, commitment, and a strong belief in myself."

I didn't know what to say. At that moment, I felt like a damn fool. I couldn't believe I'd bemoaned my situation, which was anything but life threatening. I felt so ashamed, I wanted to bolt for the house and hide.

"Can I count on you, Fletch?" he said kindly. "Whether it's playing on the field or standing along the sideline helping me?"

I sniffled once, looked off to the side and said, "You bet."

Chapter 28

O ur breath steamed in the cold air as we stood in small groups talking with friends and family members. For propriety, we were dressed in our Sunday best, but for the cold we wrapped ourselves in wool coats and gloves, hats too. When a Pere Marquette conductor walked past, Heck asked him in a voice edged with impatience when the boarding would begin. Without so much as a nod, the conductor replied, "Directly." We'd been standing on the deck with our suitcases and duffels since before noon—it was nearing 12:30 and we were ready to sit down.

Burger arranged for us to take a regularly scheduled run to Jackson, where we would spend the night and then make our final leg of the journey to Ann Arbor the following morning. Manager Burger was traveling with us, as were Billy, Monroe, and Arthur Baushke.

It was half past twelve when the conductor finally shouted for the boarding to begin and we said our good-byes. As we climbed into one of the coaches, the small crowd cheered, but they were subdued by comparison to past sendoffs—most of them simply waved and hollered good luck.

"See you tomorrow, son!" Pa shouted. Ma waved and I waved back, but then she blew me a kiss. I couldn't believe it…embarrassed the hell out of me. The ribbing from the fellows was fierce, but after thirty seconds or so, they mercifully left me alone.

Butts and I settled into a seat together, and at 12:45 sharp, the big ten-wheeler began easing out of the station amidst blasting clouds of steam and smoke and hot cinders. The coal stove in our coach had been fired and was burning warm. The lanterns were also lit, and I cracked the window for some fresh air to clear away the oily fumes.

The train quickly worked itself up to speed and everything was fine until we hit that damn Hartford-to-Lawton section of the line. That's where the cars banged and rattled so fiercely it was difficult to talk. Some of the passengers propped their windows open with sticks, combs, hair brushes, or anything else they could find to keep from getting sick. Once we made Lawton, the ride smoothed out again, but most of us players continued to sit quietly and think to ourselves or look out the windows. I found myself watching a little boy sitting with his mother in the seat in front of us, his nose pressed against the glass in fascination of the world that was hurtling past. Finally, his mother whispered something in his ear and he turned and caught me looking at him. I had to smile when I noticed the black smudge of coal dust stamped across the tip of his nose.

By then, Butts was sleeping hard, his coat rolled up for a pillow and stuffed in the crook between the window and seat. That's when I shifted around in my seat to ease the pressure on my leg and looked out the window myself.

The landscape was cold and lonely and nearly devoid of color except for a patch of blue sky in the distance and the green of an occasional pine mercifully spared by the lumberman's axe. The last of the fruit had been picked, and the only sign of life was a solitary hawk soaring high above a broad field. A minute later, we passed a grower cutting firewood. From the front of the car came the sounds of laughter, but mostly there was the noise from the rails. Like me, I suspect most of the fellows were thinking about the game.

No other high school championship game in Michigan's history had been advertised like the one we were about to play. Sports reporters from all corners of the state were writing about us, as well as some from Indiana, Illinois, and even Ohio. I don't know how the other fellows felt about it, but I was damned nervous. My stomach held butterflies the size of grackles. And I couldn't stop thinking about Stephenson, Escanaba's fullback, who we'd dubbed the Disemboweled Spirit. Bridgman gave him that name as a wordplay off of Yale's famous end, Frank Hinkey, who Walter Camp had dubbed the Disembodied Spirit. Hinkey was a fearless demon of a player.

So was Stephenson, if the stories were true.

Before our disqualification, we'd laughed a lot about Bridgman's clever labeling of Stephenson as the Disemboweled Spirit, but it was an uneasy laugh as best. That's because he was an unknown, just like his team. Sure there were lots of rumors and eyewitness accounts, but most of them were third or fourth person, and that only opened the door for more confusion and speculation. But we talked about them anyway, and in great detail. I wouldn't say the fellows were struck with fear—they had too much confidence in their abilities for that—but I'd be lying if I said they weren't apprehensive. As I sat on the train that afternoon I wondered how each one of them was dealing with it.

I turned away from the window and cast my gaze around the coach. Jacob was sitting a half dozen rows in front of me, his big neck bulging at the places where his necktie compressed the edges of his starched collar. If he was apprehensive about the game, I imagined he simply told himself it wasn't worth worrying about, that he could do nothing more than play to the best of his ability. Heck was sitting next to him, sleeping with his head slumped back against the seat. I suspected he faced his apprehension with aggression, confronting his demons head on with fists balled. Lee was probably of the same mind. They were two peas in a pod that way.

I glanced out the window again as we passed through a countryside that was heavily cultivated. There were woods in the distance, stark and gray, but on both sides of the tracks were cornfields, harvested and looking like hard-bristled brushes in the places where the ragged cornstalks poked through the light dusting of snow. Then I noticed Ossignac. He was sitting with Jones across the aisle from me, neither of them talking much, but the big Indian was staring into his lap mumbling something. No idea what he was saying—signals I could only hope.

Cunningham was sharing a seat with Mit Ludwig a couple rows behind me. They talked a lot during the ride, mostly about plays and strategies, which I knew was their way of curbing their nervousness. Logical deductions and mental manipulations of skill and past performance were measures they felt could easily tip the scales in their favor. Butts would have fit right in with them.

Teetzel and Burger were together in a seat across the aisle, one back from mine, and they talked for a long time, at least until we passed Kalamazoo. Then they too were quiet. Teetzel sat ramrod straight, arms folded across his chest with his eyes closed. It was obvious he was deep in thought, perhaps trying to pinpoint the weak links in our lineup. Or maybe he was thinking about everything he'd been through with us—no idea. Never could read the man very well.

Then there was Lathe, the Iron Man, who I couldn't miss because he was sitting ahead of me with his sore leg stretched out into the aisle. I watched as he constantly rubbed his knee with his big hand.

Bridgman was way up in the front of the coach sitting with Wadsworth in the vicinity of Monroe and Billy. They were quiet during short intervals of time, but for most of the trip they were loud and boisterous, especially Bridgman. That's how he dealt with everything, including his nervousness. He simply turned the source of his apprehension into a joke, and I admired him for having that ability. For that reason, some called him Smiling George. I, on the other hand, dealt with my apprehension by thinking about everything in terms of what could go wrong.

Potential problems involving play execution and game strategy plagued me. But that's also what encouraged me to mentally work through them ahead of time with an eye toward prevention. I didn't expect to play against Escanaba, but I wanted to be damn sure I'd have a fighting chance if I did get in the game. I was a little unsure, I won't deny that, and for two reasons.

The first was a lack of confidence. I no longer had the same self-assurance as when I led the fellows against Kalamazoo and Muskegon. It's not that I was deficient in my knowledge of our play selections and overall strategies, not at all. In fact, I was right on top of those things. It's that I was afraid the fellows wouldn't believe in my abilities or respond to my commands with the same eagerness they once did. I also feared they might have become enamored of Wadsworth's hip-shooting unpredictability and his loose, rollicking style of generalship and would now view me as dull or inferior.

The second problem I faced was my hamstring. The damn thing was not completely healed. I was still doing my stretching exercises and could walk and run without a noticeable limp, but an uncomfortable tenderness still stirred deep in my thigh that seemed more than eager to flare up again at the slightest provocation.

It was a fear of falling flat on my face that encouraged me to think about all the things that could go wrong. That's why I spent every waking hour of the previous two days repeatedly going over the signals and plays to ensure I wouldn't forget even one.

We were already en route when the Wednesday edition of the *Evening News* came out with an editorial regarding our disqualification. It supported the board's decision to let us play the game based on assurances from the University of Michigan's Athletic Department that the game officials were honest men and would give us a fair calling.

The Wednesday edition of the *Escanaba Record-Herald* also ran an article about the game, which Burger eventually got a copy of and allowed me to read. Without a doubt, the article was a great display of overconfidence. The reporter claimed Escanaba was upper Michigan's best ever high school football team and probably the best in the nation as well. He also reported they were considering an offer to play Indianapolis High School for the championship title of Indiana but were holding off to see if they could arrange a game with this year's Chicago champions, either North Division or Englewood—Hyde Park was out of it. The article barely mentioned Benton Harbor, other than to say they wouldn't have any trouble beating us.

Teetzel didn't seem as sure of success as the Escanaba folks. Or if he was, he didn't boast about it. When asked by an *Evening News* reporter to give a statement, his reply was cautious—said we'd have a fair game with a fifty-fifty chance of winning. But even if he thought we were a shoe-in, he never would've said so. It wasn't his style. He was quiet where other men were boastful. But he was more withdrawn during the final days of the season than I'd ever seen him, and the reason was obvious. He was worn down from Billy Harper's browbeating and from the way the board manipulated him into letting Arthur Baushke on the team, not to mention his maneuvering with the university's Athletic Department.

I felt bad about how Teetzel was used, Baushke too for that matter. But if it had to happen, I wish they'd also have nailed Wadsworth, even though I realized the possibility of his being disqualified was little more than a fairy tale. He was within the legal age limit and no team had ever been penalized for using a player who started school after the October 1 deadline. Teetzel knew that and probably wasn't worried. But to be cautious, he made Burger swear to him that there would be no other surprises, which Burger did, but I think the coach still felt uneasy. And I suspect many of our supporters felt the same way.

First our supporters were humiliated by Ishpeming, then by the Baushke controversy. And to make matters worse, they were criticized in a letter sent to the *Evening News* by a student editor from a University of Michigan newspaper called the *Michigan Daily News*. The editor was a former Benton Harbor student named Stanley Baley, and he wrote his letter before we were disqualified, but the editor ran it anyway. It appeared in Monday's edition.

In the editorial, Baley said the university students supported Benton Harbor, but he also warned that some of them might roast us over our defeat of the year before and that we should take it in good spirits. He also warned our rooters not to get out of hand, which was a polite way of saying they shouldn't taunt and badger and swear at the officials or the Escanaba rooters. Then he got to the real purpose of the letter, which had to do with gambling. He tactfully recommended our gamblers restrain themselves from calling out the odds at the playing grounds. Said the college students and the Ann Arbor rooters in general were against betting and that it wouldn't sit well with them.

Baley's comments were fodder for Benton Harbor's gamblers and the hotheaded among the rooters. Most of them couldn't believe a college kid would have the nerve to preach to them about rooting etiquette and gambling, which after all was still perfectly legal. Burger didn't agree with Baley either, but at least he and most of the board members agreed with the part about our rooters being on their best behavior. It was crucial for the college students to remain on our side, which I figured Burger would explain to our rooters in terms they'd understand. But the request for our gamblers to hold down their betting was a different story altogether.

Gambling was openly embraced as an integral part of Benton Harbor football—had been ever since the first game was played here. It occurred at every high school game including the 1902 game against Ishpeming when the gamblers wagered stacks of money. Stopping it would be a tough sell. But the board, acting on Burger's recommendation, agreed it would be better if the gamblers at least abstained from making bets in the open areas surrounding the playing field. Their wishes were made known via the grapevine, but also in an *Evening News* staff editorial that appeared the day after Baley's letter was published.

It was still dark on Thanksgiving Day morning when more than three hundred Benton Harbor men, women, and a sprinkling of children climbed aboard the Rooter Special Number Three. There were no decorations, no brooms, and the rooters were orderly and quiet. My folks told me about it later. Emily Fitzgerald was also on board, which raised more than a few eyebrows, especially when she was cajoled by Jacob's two sisters into explaining her true motives. Said she felt sorry for us and wanted to lend her support because of the hard work and controversy we'd been through. She never admitted she was sweet on Teetzel, although by then everyone knew she was, and only a fool would've been blind to the fact that he had feelings for her too.

The train steamed through Lawton, Kalamazoo, and finally made Ann Arbor around one o'clock. The rooters disembarked and were met by a group of highly excited university students who were from Benton Harbor—Pa told me later Hub Allen was among them. Quite a few of the rooters left the station on their own, bound for restaurants, stores, pool halls, to visit with friends, or look for bets while the rest gathered together at the sound of the call. A parade line formed up behind Professor Null and the band for the march to the Cook House.

The Cook House was loaned to us by the university Athletic Department for use as a headquarters. We were already there when the rooters marched up, chanting and singing and waving orange and black ribbons. We had just finished eating a hearty lunch of steak and potatoes.

We socialized with the rooters while they nibbled on cookies and cakes and washed it all down with lemonade or coffee. Most of the men were sipping whiskey from flasks—I could tell from their arguments that a few of them were already drunk. Supporters continued to arrive, and by 1:30 the house was so full that people spilled out onto the porches and into the yard where a group of men were smoking cigars. It was cold and gray, and the yard was filled with mounds of wet leaves, but no one seemed to mind. Shortly after that, we climbed into a four-horse brake for the ride to the playing grounds, and the rooters who'd followed us outside shouted and cheered when the driver snapped the team into motion. We were taken to the locker rooms adjacent to Ferry Field. That's where we suited up in nervous silence.

At two o'clock, the rooters formed up again and walked behind the band to the playing grounds, which was less than a mile away. When they arrived, there were nearly five hundred students already in place, along with about two hundred Escanaba rooters sitting in the south bleachers. We heard later that a number of college students said they passed on the trip to Illinois for the University of Chicago–Michigan game just to see us play, if you can believe that—that contest was one of the country's most anticipated college games.

It was just after 2:30 when we trotted onto Ferry Field wearing our standard black jerseys, black sweaters, and orange socks. The Escanaba boys came out a minute later also wearing black sweaters, but their sleeves were ringed with orange stripes. Both sides were fitted with tan moleskin or canvas trousers and most wore head harnesses or at least carried them. The Escanaba boys were about the same size as us, maybe a midge heavier, and they appeared to be alert and well muscled.

The Iron Man and Dice Baushke were back in the lineup, along with Heck, which should have put the team in good spirits. Maybe it did, maybe it didn't—I couldn't tell. But when we began our conditioning routines, I noticed the fellows were more sluggish than normal, which I reasoned was due either to the cold or else Teetzel's intensive last-minute practices followed by nearly two days of sitting. Riding trains didn't sit well with muscles conditioned to constant activity. But I also prayed it wasn't due to the wear and tear caused by our disqualification and the subsequent effects of not sleeping well. I too was sluggish, but I was also eager in spite of my bum leg being stiff as a wooden peg.

Busby and Lester were punting to us when Jacob broke away and joined Teetzel on the sideline. Together, the two of them paced up and down the field inspecting the conditions, testing the ground with their toes for loose sod and generally searching out and making mental notes of any overly wet areas. They didn't have to worry about the sun, but they certainly observed the direction of the wind. When they finished, Jacob rejoined us on the field for a quick signal practice before Teetzel waved us over to the sideline.

"Stay loose, men," he said as we milled in front of the bench. "And Jones, stand up here! I don't want anyone sitting down—even you subs need to be loose and ready to play on a moment's notice."

Jacob walked to the center of the field to meet the Disemboweled Spirit for the coin toss, while Teetzel gathered us around him in a semicircle for his last-minute instructions.

"First thing to remember," he said, "is that you are as good as any football team in America. Do not be nervous. Do not be intimidated. Your opponents are made of the same flesh and blood as you, and nothing they throw at you today will be any different from that which you have already faced this season."

I was listening to Teetzel while at the same time watching the Spirit, sizing him up. He had thick, pitch-black hair and a crop of heavy whiskers, which made me wonder about his age. He was taller than Jacob but leaner, with a face that looked like it had been chiseled from tree bark.

"The field," Teetzel continued, "is in fair condition. The sod is loose and clumped in the center, which means your footing will be unstable there...so pay attention. And there are soft, wet spots at the east end of the field between the ten- and fifteen-yard lines. Watch for them too." Then he looked directly at Wadsworth and said, "Got that Waddie?"

"Amen, coach. Won't be no dirt clod trippin me up."

"You might be able to negotiate the obstacles just fine," Teetzel shot back. "But make sure you don't unnecessarily send any of your running backs over bad ground."

"Yes sir," he said, his voice betraying sarcasm. I could smell his overconfidence.

"Escanaba won the toss and there was no negotiation," Jacob interrupted as he rejoined us. "Two thirty-minute halves…the rest are straight Spalding rules. They'll be receiving the second half from the west end."

Jacob and Stephenson agreed to full halves without arguing or complaining. That's because the state's two best teams were expected to play the high school limit of sixty minutes. Anything less would have been a sign of bad sportsmanship. Sixty minutes would tell the tale. All the bragging in the world didn't matter now, and neither did the charges of cheating or the money that was wagered. The day of reckoning had arrived and it was anyone's call.

"Okay men," Teetzel continued as the crowd got louder and louder. "That means we'll be protecting the west end during the first half. And remember…do not let up for one minute. Speed, speed, speed is your war cry. Now get out there and show these rooters how we play football in Benton Harbor!"

The fellows clapped and walked onto the field. The crowd erupted, yelling and stomping their feet so hard it sent a chill down my spine. The team arrayed itself in a receiving formation across the field while the Escanaba players assumed their positions behind the fifty-five-yard line. Just as all was ready to begin, Jacob came back to the sideline and tossed his nose guard to me.

"Won't be having it in the way," he said after I'd caught it. I didn't actually hear what he said because of the cheering, but I was able to read his lips.

"Give em hell Jacob!" I hollered back as a tear welled up in the corner of my right eye. He winked and then turned and strode back onto the field.

As Jacob took his position in front of the goalposts, I saw him point and holler instructions to a couple of the fellows to move a little one way or another. Then he bent down and put his hands on his knees and waited. He truly looked liked a gladiator, strong and confident and in complete control of his emotions.

The referee blew his whistle and the game began.

Chapter 29

The clouds momentarily broke apart to reveal a clear patch of sky. The Disemboweled Spirit kicked the football and sent it soaring like a fat bird into the blue hole before it fell back down into Jacob's arms. He was drenched in light as he crouched and began to run behind Handy and Lee, both of whom smashed an effective interference that allowed him to make twenty yards before he was tackled by an Escanaba player named Stonehouse. It was a hard hit. Jacob dropped like a lead weight and fumbled.

The dark clouds roiled back into the hole as our rooters, every last one of them standing tall on their toes, made a painful groan.

The Spirit picked up the football and dodged through the broken field with the nimbleness of a panther, and within seconds he was through our line and in the open. The rooters pleaded for salvation, and it was Butts who cut across the field to intercept him, but when Butts finally made the distance, the Spirit grabbed his face and shoved him to the ground like a rag doll. Seconds later, he thundered into the end zone.

The Escanaba rooters howled like Indians, and as their kicker sent the football through the goalposts, I had a flashback of our disastrous game against Ishpeming. I looked at Teetzel, who was standing next to me, and said, "What is it about these north country teams?"

"It's just the beginning, Fletch," he said. "Let's see what they can do once we get up to speed."

The fellows seemed angry but calm, which reassured me they would likely rise to the occasion and do whatever was necessary to get back into the game. Teetzel appeared confident too, but he was more focused than I'd ever seen him. He had a freshly sharpened pencil and was already scribbling furiously on his notepad.

Escanaba kicked to us again and Wadsworth, playing deep, caught it and ran ten yards before he was stopped. On the next play, Jacob grabbed ten more. Seconds after the referee whistled the ball into play, the fellows were off again, this time with Wadsworth carrying the ball around the right end with Jacob running interference. A matched pair of mules, that's what they reminded me of the way they worked together, pushing, shoving, running over, or dragging any Escanaba player who got in their way. Even the Spirit couldn't stop them. Wadsworth finally went down thirty yards later, which was too bad. Escanaba held us for the rest of the series.

After that, the game turned into a punting match.

The ball changed hands a number of times with neither side gaining much on offense. Our linemen weren't opening holes the way they should, and Escanaba wasn't moving the ball either, partly because Lee was doing a good job breaking through to foul their runners. But that was too good to last. The next time the Spirit carried the ball, he smashed Lee in the jaw with the heel of his left hand and dropped him like a rock. Ten yards later, Handy bull-wrestled him to the ground but the damage was already done.

The umpire pulled Lee up by his sweater and gave him a couple quick slaps to the face but failed to bring him around. That's when the referee called a time-out.

Doc Bastar went on the field to assist and found Lee knocked unconscious. He checked his eyes and then put the smelling salts to his nose, which caused him to wince and half come around. Then Doc called for a couple of fellows from the Athletic Department to carry him off the field. They laid him on the grass behind our bench and threw a blanket over him.

While Doc had been attending to Lee, the rest of the team was gathered in front of our bench listening to Teetzel run through his list of comments. First was Jacob's fumble. He told us for a thousandth time how a single fumble could easily lose a game. He also talked to Wadsworth about plays he might employ to trip up the Escanaba defense. Teetzel recommended using a variety of strategies that would help identify the weak spots in the Escanaba line for further exploitation. He also wanted Waddie to use more ball carriers. Said it would keep the defense guessing and prevent our runners from tiring too quickly.

"Leave it to me, coach," Wadsworth replied.

"I have been, Waddie," he responded. "I have no choice."

The referee blew his whistle and the team ran back onto the field with Cunningham in place of Lee. It was only then that Lee finally came around.

"What the hell?" he moaned. Doc bent down to see about him. "What's your name?" he asked while helping him to sit up.

"Come on, Doc," Lee protested in a voice that was obviously disoriented. "You know damn well who I am."

"Tell me your name."

"Got to get back on the field."

"You're done for today, son. Now what's your name?"

"Got to get back," he mumbled again.

"You've got a minor concussion," Doc shot back, "and you need rest."

I helped Doc get Lee to his feet and up to the bench where we sat him down and draped the blanket over his shoulders. Lee huddled, his hair still wet with sweat, and stared blankly at the field.

"How is he, Doc?" I asked.

"He'll be fine after a few days of rest."

Meanwhile, the game had started up again with neither team progressing until McCune, the Escanaba quarterback, broke out for a gain of twenty yards. Next he ran a mass play off their right tackle and gained ten more. This put them on our twenty-five-yard line. Heck knifed through the line on the following play and downed the Spirit, hitting him so hard the ball was knocked loose. Busby fell on it and our rooters roared.

The main contingent of our rooters were sitting behind us, and I recognized some of the voices. Deputy Pearl was one, along with Monroe Morrow and Judge Bridgman. I turned around at one point and even saw Emily Fitzgerald frantically waving a stick tied up with orange and black ribbons. I jabbed Jones with my elbow so he could see for himself.

After Busby's recovery, the fellows burned with determination, and they played a furious, battling round of football. On the first play, Jacob carried the ball for twenty yards. Two plays later, Wadsworth gained ten more yards to plant the ball on the eight-yard line for the first down. He took the ball again and ran behind Jacob to score our first touchdown of the day. Was a beautiful piece of work. Waddie attempted the try at goal and the ball went wide.

That's the kind of crap that baffled me. Why the hell didn't he let Dice make the kick? He almost never missed. And that wasn't the only fault beginning to surface.

It was clear Wadsworth was getting tired, which didn't surprise me since he and Jacob were doing all the work. And Teetzel wasn't happy about it either. I heard him mutter something under his breath about Waddie not using his head, which told me he still wasn't satisfied with the play calling. I knew if something didn't change, Waddie and Jacob would be spent before the half.

Jacob kicked to Escanaba and their man advanced to the thirty-five-yard line. Then they made a couple of first downs before we got it back on our own forty. Once again Wadsworth gave the ball to Jacob, but the Escanaba boys nailed him before he even reached the line. On the next play Jacob carried the ball again and got nowhere.

"Spread the work, Waddie." Teetzel said. He was talking to himself, but I heard it.

"Careful, Coach," I said in a respectful way. "If the officials hear you they'll throw you off the field for coaching from the sidelines." Of course, Teetzel knew the rules better than I ever would.

"I just can't believe my eyes, Fletch," he said as he unfolded his penknife and began whittling his pencil to a fresh point. "We're not playing our game," he went on. "The fellows are slow...miserably so. This isn't the same team that played against Ann Arbor."

"Escanaba is a lot better than Ann Arbor."

"Maybe...but we're not taking advantage of their weaknesses."

I knew what he meant—Wadsworth wasn't calling a wide enough variety of plays. I'd have bet a stack of money he simply couldn't remember them, and when he did, he couldn't fit them properly into the puzzle. And he only made the situation worse by working himself too hard. On the next down, Wadsworth again carried the ball but this time fumbled as he was tackled. Teetzel and I groaned in unison when Escanaba made the recovery. After a quick series of plays and two first downs, Stephenson scored on a mass play up the center. After the kick through goal, the score climbed to 12 to 5.

I couldn't believe what was happening and neither could Teetzel. And this was after he'd worked so hard with Wadsworth about play selections, and particularly about distributing the ball-carrying duties among all the backs. To make matters worse, the Escanaba players had figured out Waddie's one-two strategy. They were expecting it. Wadsworth was playing right into their hands.

We had the ball when the half ended a few minutes later.

As we walked in a loose group to the locker room I couldn't help but notice how poor the fellows appeared. They were already beat up and tired, and dirt was smeared into their uniforms and on their faces, disguising the bruises and the swellings that were beginning to take shape.

"What the hell's going on out there?" I asked Jacob as we walked along together.

"It's Waddie, Fletch," he said under his breath so no one could hear. "I hate to say it, but he just ain't seeing it."

"I know…and so does Teetzel."

"But he won't touch him," he replied.

"And it's too bad, damnit." I was surprised to hear those words come from my mouth, but my frustration was building to the point where I couldn't keep it contained. "I should be in there with you," I added.

Jacob smiled ruefully at my comment and agreed. "For damn sure," he said. "But the coach won't pull Waddie cause he's afraid your leg won't hold up." I knew Jacob was right, but I didn't care. At that moment, I was so frustrated I wanted to scream.

In the locker room, we sat down on the benches. There was no talking. Instead, the fellows wiped their faces with towels and washed the cotton from their mouths with dippers of cold water. The room echoed with the sounds of hard breathing and the hoarse clearing of throats. Doc began stitching a gash on Handy's face while Teetzel continued to study his notes. But no one spoke, not a word. There was fear in the air, and it wasn't the terror kind of fear. It was the hopeless kind. I could smell it.

The situation was dire and I had no idea how Teetzel planned to get the fellows back on track. He remained calm, I'll have to give him that—there wasn't the slightest hint of desperation in his demeanor. When he finally did speak, it was a steady reading from his list of mistakes, one after another while pointing his pencil at the appropriate players. No one was left out, including me. He said something about my not paying close enough attention to the game, which took me by surprise. And it got me wondering. Was he thinking about putting me in the game?

Then Teetzel began talking to Wadsworth about the game plan. Said Baushke and Bridgman should carry more, but also the Iron Man and even Lester and Busby. The way he said it was more of a command than a request. The fellows may have agreed, but most of them sat there with blank stares—it was clear to me they were physically and mentally exhausted. At that moment, I knew the weight of the entire season had descended upon them, bringing them to the brink of breaking.

Judging from the tenor of Teetzel's talk, it was obvious he was firm in his resolve to inspire the team. But when it was time for the fellows to take the field again, I hadn't detected much of a rise in confidence. I'd never seen such ambivalence in them, and it worried me. The thought that this team, composed of the most talented group of fellows I had ever known, would ever give up was unacceptable. It was especially aggravating because I felt so confident I could do something about it given the chance.

And my confidence was not unfounded.

For the past few weeks, I'd engaged in a careful observation of the team's most intricate workings, their signal practices and games. Then I dissected and reworked play strategies by carefully utilizing the strengths and weaknesses of the individual players. I knew each fellow intimately—had grown up with most of them. When it came to their physical and mental capabilities, I probably knew more about them than their own mothers. And they knew me. Because of what Jacob said during our walk to the locker room, I felt sure the fellows wanted me in there, Teetzel too, but I also understood the risk. He was afraid to pull Wadsworth because once a player was taken out of a game he couldn't go back in. If my leg gave out, it really would be all over.

"Alright fellas!" Jacob blurted out, startling the hell out of me and probably everyone else. "We've worked hard all season for the chance to be here and look at you, acting like a bunch of melancholies." Then he threw his towel on the floor. "We can beat this team!"

That's when I sprung to my feet. Wasn't planned, I just did it out of emotion. "He's right!" I hollered. "They're not invincible...their defensive strategy is peppered with soft spots...offense too."

I paused, and no one said anything. It was so quiet that even the dripping water and the uneasy shuffling of feet stood out above the rising crowd noise. Still no one said a word, neither Teetzel or the fellows, most of whom sat there glaring at me with looks that betrayed hopelessness, or maybe disgust that I would profess to see something they didn't. I would have preferred the latter, although that would mean they were cursing me for daring to lecture them when I hadn't even been in the game.

"It's a meat grinder in there, Fletch," Butts mumbled.

"Then do what we've always done!" I shot back undeterred. Teetzel stood quietly and watched.

"And what might that be?" Ossignac said, looking at me through a rope of long, black hair hanging wet across one side of his face.

"Look," I said, gaining more confidence. "I know you're tired and beat up, but we haven't worked and struggled for three months learning Coach Teetzel's strategy just to give up now. With a little strategic playing, we can pull this out."

"He's right," Jacob added. "Strategic playing combined with guts. No bunch of fellas anywhere is in better condition than we are."

"Hear that, Waddie?" Teetzel said, breaking his silence.

"Yes sir," he replied while glaring at me. "I hear jus fine."

"I want everyone to understand one thing," Teetzel continued, only this time his voice was more impassioned. "Speed is still the key, speed and precision. You men are conditioned, you're tough, and you know the plays and the signals better than your own backyards. Put it together and refuse to give up!"

"I'm game." Jacob said. "I'll be playin to win or bust myself tryin. Are ya with me?" He was answered with a number of enthused "yeah"s and "you betcha"s, as we stood up and prepared to resume the fight.

The two teams jogged onto the field and found a soft, cold rain falling. Undeterred, the rooters erupted. Then our band began playing and everything seemed to be at the beginning again. For me, it felt like a new day. After a quick warm-up routine, the teams lined up for the kick and our rooters chanted even harder while the band played louder and stronger than I'd ever heard them—it was clear they had not given up.

The second half began with Jacob kicking to Escanaba, who ran a quick series of plays and made some good gains. Then, just when it seemed they were about to break the game wide open, Busby ripped into the ball carrier and caused him to fumble. In a rush, our rooters and most of the college students came to their feet cheering. Without breaking stride, Wadsworth scooped it up and skirted the mass of players for a thirty-yard gain before he was finally brought down. On the next play, we were penalized for holding, but then Bridgman ran for twenty-five more yards. Next, Jacob went through the Escanaba line and carried the ball up to the eight-yard line. I felt a surge of exhilaration believing we were about to add five more points to the score, but then we ran two plays and got nowhere. I sat down and put my head in my hands. On the third play, we got two yards and the ball went over to Escanaba. I should have seen it coming.

Jacob was talking to Wadsworth between each play, which was slowing down our offense, but I knew he was trying to establish some control over the plays Wadsworth was calling.

Escanaba took possession but chose to punt rather than risk losing the ball so deep in their own territory. We ran a series of plays, weak selections every one, and the Escanaba players stopped us cold before we could make a first down. It was obvious to me Wadsworth was not paying attention to Jacob. In fact, it appeared they had begun to argue.

Escanaba took the ball and battled hard with each play, steadily pushing us down the field until finally the Spirit scored on a mass play off their left guard, running over five of our players along the way. I wasn't sure if Cunningham and Baushke would even get up.

In spite of our bad fortune, the playing was fierce. In fact, the playing during that second half was some of the roughest football I'd ever seen. Football today is a garden stroll compared to the way those fellows tore at each other. The faces of players from both sides were so cold and scraped and rubbed raw that they looked like peeled beets. Ossignac and Lathe were nursing split lips, while Lester and Bridgman and Cunningham had black eyes, with one of Lester's being so swollen it was nearly closed up. Everyone had scabbed knuckles and banged shins. Handy was limping with a twisted ankle, and his forehead was bleeding from the gash Doc stitched up at the half—the stitches were like a bull's-eye painted across his face. It hadn't taken long for an Escanaba player to rip them open with a slug or the hard brush of an elbow. Heck's forehead also looked like raw hamburger, and I remember seeing a number of players from both sides, Ludwig and Busby among them, spit loose or broken fragments of teeth onto the field or into their hands with intentions of saving them. The only first aid that time would allow was a wad of gauze. Without a doubt, the carnage was horrendous, but not one player was timid. They fought like wolves and the rooters loved it.

The goal was kicked to make the score 18 to 5. I shook my head in disbelief as I watched the cards on the scoreboard change.

As the players were lining up for the kick, Jacob ran over to have a word with Teetzel. I couldn't hear what he said, but when they both looked at me I knew Jacob was asking Teetzel to put me into the game. I felt an immediate explosion of hope, but it was doused just as quickly when Teetzel shook his head no.

"Damn!" I said out loud while slapping my thigh.

Escanaba kicked off and Jacob caught the ball. He ran forward at a low crouch and mauled three, maybe four Escanaba players before he was brought down on about the thirty-eight. On the next play, Wadsworth gave the ball to Bridgman, who made one yard. Our rooters started chanting the Locomotive Yell, but even that failed—on the following play we got nothing. Frustrated and not knowing what to do, Wadsworth took a time-out, which is something I never did. It wasn't part of Teetzel's strategy. He said we should never, ever, under any reasonable circumstance give the opposing team a break. Our goal was to wear them down, break them, turn them into wet dishrags. That's why the quarterback had to know his play strategies like the back of his hand.

Teetzel didn't yell at Wadsworth. Instead he carefully recited the same list of instructions he'd recited during the half, mostly about spreading the ball-carrying duties among the players. Waddie didn't say anything because he was breathing so hard, but he shook his head a number of times implying he understood. Jacob was furious—through the dirt and the exhaustion, I could see it in his expression—but he didn't say a word. His steely eyes were locked on Teetzel, begging him to do something decisive.

The fellows went back out and took their defensive positions.

Escanaba ran a series of plays and we held them. Then the game seesawed back and forth for nearly ten minutes with neither side making any progress. Wadsworth spread the duties better but he still wasn't seeing the entire picture. I wanted to holler the plays at him. For his sake, I wished his disorientation had been caused by a blow to the head. But I knew better. He was simply incapable of performing under that kind of pressure. It was his inexperience, but also his damned cockiness, that placed my team on the brink of disaster.

It was at this point in the game, just when I was sure we'd be traveling home defeated, that I saw Jacob grab the Iron Man by the arm and tell him something. It was fleeting, easy to miss, but I happened to be looking right at them. Two plays later, Bridgman was carrying the ball with the Iron Man and Wadsworth running interference when Waddie got hammered. It happened when they ran into a wall of Escanaba players and he was elbowed in the gut—by the Iron Man. At first I thought Lathe must have been trying to take out an Escanaba player, missed, and hit Waddie instead, but then I thought about Jacob and wasn't so sure. When the heap of bodies was untangled, Wadsworth didn't get up. Then, when Butts and Ossignac pulled him to his feet, I saw the hard grimace pressed across his face. He doubled over and heaved.

I took a deep breath. Then I released the blanket that was draped across my shoulder and let it fall to the ground.

Chapter 30

"Van Horne!"

"Yes sir!" I answered quickly. At that moment I felt like a racehorse, nervous but eager at the gate as I turned to face Teetzel.

He looked me straight in the eye and calmly said, "It's your machine now."

Without saying a word, I made a quick sidestep onto the field and began to run while at the same time pulling my head harness down over my ears. I was tightening the strap as I passed Wadsworth coming the other way, a mud-splattered wreck, soaked with sweat and holding his stomach in pain. His appearance should've unnerved me, or at least clued me into the terrible fight that was taking place on the field, but at the time I didn't think about that.

The thing I remember most about running onto Ferry Field was the crowd noise. Most of it was in my favor, but I'll never forget how the Escanaba rooters laughed when they saw how small I was. It also bothered me the way the university students groaned, I guess because my appearance didn't convey much hope. I ignored the bastards. I'd been laughed at all my life because of my size. I'd been picked on and joked about and pushed around and I'd learned long ago how to take it.

When I got to where the fellows were standing, I found them filthy and hollow-eyed and in much worse shape physically than I had expected. They were gasping hard for air and some of them were coughing and hawking wads of phlegm from their lungs. I was immediately worried they were too far gone to make a stand, but then I looked at the Escanaba players and noticed they didn't look any better.

"Alright Fletch," Jacob said as I tried to shake loose my jitters and think of the first play. "Let's give the bastards hell."

I steeled my courage, looked at the waiting faces gathered around me and said, "Okay, fellows…I want you to hold on just a little longer. It's going to be one helluva fast ride."

The referee blew the whistle for the game to begin and I called for a tackle-over formation, which placed the Iron Man and Ossignac together on the right side of the line. Then I called the play I wanted and the fellows limped to the line and crouched. I barked the signals and handed the ball to Baushke, who ran between the tackles with me and Butts and the rest of the backfield pushing him six yards for a first down. In a matter of seconds, I called the next play and we were off again with Butts carrying the ball on a left-end-around play with the entire backfield running interference. We made ten yards.

The fellows were coming back to life—I didn't know if they would, but they were—I could feel it. A couple plays later, we had the ball planted on the Escanaba twenty-yard line, and I put the fellows into a tackle-back formation. Lathe was to carry. He line-bucked between Ossignac and Busby with me and Butts and the backfield pushing for a pulverizing twelve-yard gain.

By then, I felt confident the fellows were firmly with me, and that's when I began to worry about the clock.

For the next play, I wanted Baushke to carry the ball inside the left tackle position, which was between Lathe and Cunningham. Baushke was the smallest back and he was fresh, but I figured they wouldn't expect him to run the ball into the end zone. At the snap, Ossignac crossed right and I faked a handoff. On his heels was Baushke, who took the ball and ran into the line behind a battering ram composed of Jacob and Busby. I ran interference on the inside and was able to keep their center out of the play.

It was over in a matter of seconds. Baushke tumbled into the end zone for the touchdown, but not before he was hammered hard by Stephenson. It was a late hit if you ask me, and it immediately changed the happy, foot-stomping cheers of our rooters to hoots, catcalls, and cries of foul. Baushke got up limping and could barely walk, and had to leave the game. The crowd howled even harder. Butts was moved to right halfback and Mit Ludwig came in to play end. Busby kicked the goal.

"Hal-le-luja," he muttered as the football sailed through.

"Amen," I said, which was my way of congratulating him. The score was 18 to 11 with six minutes to go.

As we took our places on the field for the kickoff, I glanced to the sideline and Teetzel nodded, which I took as a sign of approval. Wadsworth was slumped on the bench next to Lee, his head buried deep in his hands.

We kicked to Escanaba and Stephenson took the ball and immediately charged forward, which is when I finally got to see him firsthand as he came at me. His long, black hair was slick with sweat, and I was astounded at how compact he made himself. Seemed to defy his height. He held the ball tight to his chest with his right arm and bent forward with knees pumping furiously while stiff-arming players with his left arm. He was like a buzz-saw, a whirling mass of muscle and hellfire, and I could see player's arms and legs, nose guards, and head harnesses literally fill the air around him as he exploded down the field. When I tried to tackle him he belted me in the face and knocked me down as easy as if I'd been hit with a sledgehammer. He broke two more tackles before Busby tackled him around mid field. I stood up dazed and disoriented, and then, before I knew what was happening, Jacob had my shoulder gripped tightly with one hand and was slapping me in the face with the other.

"Snap to, Fletch!" he yelled. "Time's a-wastin!"

I shook my head a few times and called for a new defensive formation. By the time I took my position in the backfield, I was adequately recovered. The fellows remained confident and we held them on the next three plays, which meant we took possession on our own forty-five-yard line.

I noticed some of the Escanaba players were on the edge of breaking physically, and I made mental notes of who they were. One of them, their left tackle, had a fresh wound on his forehead with blood trickling into one of his eyes. I immediately called out our first play, which was a left-tackle around-and-through-right-tackle play. It was risky on a wet field, since the Iron Man would have to leave his position quickly and swing around behind me to take the ball. But I knew they wouldn't expect it.

I called the signals and took the snap. My leg buckled as I turned, but I managed to make the handoff. Ossignac hammered the bloody-eyed fellow, and then Lathe ripped through behind him with Jacob and Bridgman on either side and Mit pushing from behind. He made three yards. I got up and quickly tested my leg, which seemed okay. It hurt, but it was the same nagging pain I'd been living with every afternoon at practice. I was used to it. As I moved toward the line, I put the fellows into a tackle-over formation and then hollered the numbers for a left-end-around play, which called for Mit to cross behind me and take the ball around our right end. He made three yards with the backfield running interference.

I acted as a blocker on that play and ended up beneath the pile. It took me a little longer than normal to get up, and when I did, I was concerned because my leg clearly ached more than it did after the previous play. But I was excited that Mit made three yards for the first down and put it out of my mind.

I was breathing very hard and limping, but I called the play and within ten seconds, we were off and running. Eight seconds later, I took another snap. Another eight seconds passed and again we hit the sod. Jacob, Lathe, and then Butts carried the ball into the line, each one of them hammering, pounding, and muscling their way through for good gains. By then, the Escanaba boys were gasping for air and so were we. But no one was lying down. We were waging war.

We finally made it to the ten-yard line on a wide run by Bridgman, but it was third and four. We didn't have time to run another series, so I called for a drop kick. It was a tough call, but I had to make it. I took the snap and tossed the ball to Busby, who stepped back, dropped the ball, and kicked it just after it bounced back up from the ground. The ball sailed a little to the right but went through beautifully for five points, and the stands erupted. The score was now 18 to 16 in favor of Escanaba.

"Two minutes left to play!" yelled the linesman.

In spite of their poor condition, the fellows were fueled with a determination I never imagined possible. Never had I seen them more focused, more eager to throw themselves into the fray while at the same time executing their duties with such precision and skill. Their every nerve and muscle was focused on one single objective, and that objective was victory. We may have been bruised and bloody, but we were Teetzel's Machine and no one was going to take that away from us. We understood it and so did Escanaba—that's why they were equally as determined to stop us.

I prayed the good Lord would allow my leg just two more minutes. And then he could do with it whatever he saw fit.

Jacob kicked off to Escanaba. On their first play, they gained two yards through Cunningham, and on their second play they tried an end run but Mit stopped the runner at the line. By then the crowd was again on its feet screaming like fanatics for us to hold them. Escanaba punted the ball and Busby caught it and advanced to our thirty-yard line before being tackled.

Jacob hollered at the linesman for the time. The team captain could ask for the time whenever he wanted during a game except for the final five minutes of play, and then he could only ask for it three times. The linesman hollered back through a megaphone that there was one minute left.

"Alright, Fletch," Lathe gasped in his steady, country way. "Why don't we get this thing over with so we can put the horses back in the barn."

"Yeah," Bridgman added, breaking into a guarded grin. "It's time to limber up this machine."

I called out the first play and the fellows crouched. As I walked up to the line to take the snap, I thought about the enormous responsibility hanging on my shoulders, which should have frightened me but didn't. In fact, I embraced it. I'd worked all season for that moment, and I'd rather have died on that field than fail. Sixty seconds was all the time I had left to make it happen. I barked the signals and we were off.

Bridgman ran for thirty yards, and the crowd was still going wild when we were off again, this time with Jacob smashing interference for Butts. Together, the two of them made a magnificent run of twenty-five yards.

We were really pouring on the coal, both us and Escanaba, and I can't begin to describe what it was like to be on that field. The fierceness of the playing went far beyond anything I'd ever seen. Every player was gulping for air and exhausted to the point of collapse. My nose was filled with the pungent smells of sweat and dirt and rotted grass, and my lungs burned so hot they felt as though they'd been scraped raw. The taste of fresh blood was in my mouth.

On the next play, the crowd was so loud I tried to bark the signals and had a hard time of it because my voice was almost gone. Bridgman took the ball and skirted around the end for a brilliant thirteen-yard romp to plant the ball on the nine-yard line.

Jacob called for the time and the linesman yelled, "Twelve seconds!"

There was only time for one more play. As I frantically sorted through my mental play list, one call—and only one—emerged. It was me into the line. I figured they wouldn't expect the quarterback, especially a featherweight, to run within the twenty-five-yard line. In that area, most teams used their most powerful muscle plays, which told me they'd be looking for Lathe or Jacob.

The team was already in a tackle-back formation when I called the play. The fellows scrambled into position without hesitation as our rooters started the Locomotive Yell. I glanced around at the backfield and Jacob nodded while Bridgman took a long, deep breath as he crouched and put his hands on his knees. God they looked terrible, both of them, Busby too. Their sweaters were ripped and caked with mud, their faces and knuckles scraped raw and smeared with a sweaty, bloody sludge. I quickly turned back and inspected the line, where I saw Ossignac and Handy poised like granite statues, waiting for me to unleash their fury, while Lathe stood a few paces behind them. He was wound up like a strand of barbed wire, jaw muscles working hard and fast. I bent down to take the snap, and above the crowd noise I heard Mit snarl across the line at his opponent, like an animal preparing to attack. At the same time, the Escanaba players tried to trip me up by jabbering their own numbers.

I took the snap and Bridgman crossed to the right. I spun around, faked a handoff, and a split second later, Lathe and Jacob stampeded past me to the left. Mit and Cunningham opened a hole and Lathe went through first. The Escanaba backfield was there and he managed to shove one of them out of the way. Then Jacob went through with me close behind. Butts was on my right hip.

Immediately after crossing the scrimmage line, we were hit by two Escanaba players, who we battered through only to find the Disemboweled Spirit front and center and charging fast. By this time, I was supposed to be hanging onto the strap at the back of Jacob's belt but couldn't reach it—the pushing and shoving was too intense for me to grab hold. But there was no turning back. Jacob went right at him with his left arm out to clear the way, but the Spirit cleverly fended it off and then fiercely belted him in the face with his forearm, the force of the hit breaking Jacob's nose. I knew it was broken when blood splattered across my face.

Jacob continued to move forward, but he staggered, and in that split second, the entire season flashed before my eyes—the hard training, the injuries, the suffering, and also the happy parties and rallies and especially the accolades. And then I saw myself, a small boy made of flesh and blood, about to be mangled by the terror of upper Michigan. The season's success or failure was about to be determined, and there I was, mere yards from redemption with nearly all hope of success vanishing like wheat chaff blowing in the wind. I gripped the ball tighter and forged ahead, resigned to give it my all or die trying.

That's when I saw Jacob recover. Somehow he regained his footing, sprung forward like an angry bull, and belted Stephenson right back, knocking him off balance enough to send him stumbling sideways. Then Jacob reached back with his right hand and I grabbed it. He pulled me forward before the Spirit could recover enough to grab my legs. But by this time, all the other Escanaba players were closing in on us and we'd only made three yards. There were six more to go.

In the next second, there were bodies whirling all around us, the air filled with flying fists and elbows. Each time I thought I was going down, Jacob would jerk harder and pull me forward while

Butts propped me up from the side. Some of the Escanaba boys were jumping on top of us trying to knock me down, and at one point two of them were on top of Jacob. We were running through a meat grinder, but he kept going.

I couldn't see the goal line, but I knew we crossed it when the screaming from the stands instantly doubled. From the corner of my eye, I saw the gray sky suddenly fill up with hats spinning toward the heavens in celebration. The fellows were jumping all over the three of us, and then they started slapping us on the back and shaking my and Bridgman's hands. But not Jacob's. He was holding one hand over his nose, blood streaming through his fingers, while holding a tooth in the other hand. That was number four for him—poor bastard. All of them were front teeth, too.

There were only five seconds left to play when Jacob walked off the field to a great roar of applause. Jones came in to replace him. We lined up and Busby kicked the goal to make the score 22 to 18.

Ossignac kicked to Escanaba and their man caught the ball and made it to the forty-yard line before we brought him down. At that point, our rooters ran screaming onto the field and hoisted us onto their shoulders. Hundreds of them were jumping up and down while shaking orange and black ribbons. Some of them were so happy they cried. I saw Emily Fitzgerald run into the crowd and throw her arms around Teetzel, who hugged her so hard her feet left the ground.

Back in the locker room, there was much congratulating between team members. The board members circulated among us smiling and shaking our hands in gratitude. All of them made a financial kill that day, and some of the players too.

"Damnit, Fletch," Bridgman hollered from across the room. "If you didn't give my cookie jar a scare when you decided to carry the ball on that last play!"

"Amen to that!" Monroe answered. "I was afraid I'd be goin home with moths in my wallet like last year! The missus would've whupped me a good one!"

"Yes sir." Billy mumbled in his alcoholic haze. "And we would've had to do some whupping ourselves." He was referring to us players, jesting I could only hope.

No one talked about Ishpeming and the fact that we'd avenged ourselves. Instead, there was a lot talk about the game and the good plays we ran, especially during the time I was leading the team. No one mentioned Waddie, who was sitting alone on one of the benches slowly removing his uniform. Periodically, one of the fellows would walk over and chat with him, but they never stayed long and he never joined in with our celebrating. I didn't speak to him—didn't intend to either.

The room didn't calm down until Teetzel called for our attention. "Just a few words," he said while holding his hands in the air to quiet us.

"I want to thank the board members for bringing me to Benton Harbor, and especially I want to thank the team. It's been a tough season with a number of surprises, not the least of which was my training schedule and football philosophy." He quieted to let us have our laugh. "It wasn't easy for you," he continued, "but it could not have been any other way. Building a first-rate football machine is not an easy job. All the pieces must work together, as you certainly did, and sometimes the machine must flex itself to accommodate unforeseen situations."

I'd never heard that from him before—the part about flexing. I assumed he was referring to Jacob's conspiracy to remove Wadsworth from the game. At first I wasn't sure Teetzel realized it was intentional, but that was stupid. He knew us better than we knew ourselves.

"I have something to say," Burger said and we quieted. "I've already talked to Coach Teetzel about leading the team again next season and he's agreed to have a discussion."

"No discussions allowed!" Butts yelped as we all cheered our approval.

"Say yes now!" Mit hollered.

"Now boys," Burger continued. "Discussion is just a delicate way of saying we must talk about his fee. But I don't think I'll have much of a problem convincing the board members to sweeten the pot, do you?" We all cheered again.

After Burger finished, Jacob gave a small speech, followed by Bridgman and then Mit. After taking showers, we daubed copious

amounts of iodine on our cuts and scrapes before rubbing ourselves with Doc's tincture of raw quinine and alcohol. Finally,
bandages were applied before we coaxed our stiff bodies back into
our street clothes.

After leaving the locker room, we stood outside talking with
students and other supporters who'd waited to congratulate us.
Everyone agreed that Escanaba played hard and straight football,
but it was also agreed they couldn't cope with us once I was in the
game. I was told that not a single person in the stands denied we
were the true champions of Michigan, unless they were from
Escanaba.

Newspaper men interviewed both coaches and Coach Jolliffe
was plainly disappointed. He didn't have much to say, and what he
did say was sour grapes.

"We cannot acknowledge Benton Harbor as state champions,"
he declared. "That was merely an exhibition game."

An exhibition game? I couldn't imagine he actually believed
that. If that was an exhibition game, I wondered what the hell a
real game would've been like. Wholesale slaughter was the only
thing I could imagine. Teetzel, on the other hand, was pleased with
our playing. When asked to give his opinion, his reply was short
and to the point.

"Our boys did great work and are certainly the champions of
the state."

For him, that said it all. I think he was satisfied, even without
the formal championship title. It was good enough for him that
we'd beaten the best Michigan had to offer, but the best was yet to
come. At the depot, Burger told us there was a good chance we'd
formally get claim to the championship title anyway. Dr. May of
the University Athletic Department told him after the game that
he was certain the Interscholastic Committee would vote in our
favor.

It was well after midnight, cold with a light snow sifting
through the air, when we approached Bungtown. I thought it
would be quiet at the depot but I was wrong. They were waiting
for us. Word of our victory was sent over the wire just after the
game's conclusion, and as we neared town, the people were roused

from their sleep by the sounding of the fire station alarm, which brought hundreds of them streaming to the depot. As we approached the station, the soft, amber glow of the street lamps illuminated the wagons and buggies overflowing with cheering people, many of them still pulling in to join the crowd already there.

The train rumbled to a stop, and the sounds of blasting steam and grinding metal mixed with waves of cheering. From my window, I could see directly into the faces of the people surging beneath the depot overhang, clapping and waving orange and black ribbons. Then a group of boys shot off some flares and Roman candles while the crowd chanted "Three rahs and a tiger for Teetzel's Machine!" And they said it over and over and wouldn't stop. We got off the train and each one of us was hoisted on the shoulders of the rooters and carried around the depot.

The crowd spilled out onto the street, still chanting, with us riding on their shoulders, and my eyes misted. I got a feeling that I'd never have again, not in my lifetime. The last thing I remember about that night was looking over at Teetzel and waiting for him to notice me.

When he did, I threw my fists into the air and yelled, "Three rahs and a tiger for Clayton Teetzel!"

Epilogue

Teetzel left for Chicago two days after the Escanaba game, and most of us players met at the depot for the send-off. Burger put him on notice that he might be called upon to coach us one more time if a game could be arranged with the Chicago champions, North Division, or any other of the big Chicago teams. Teetzel agreed, but it never happened. Even Barratt O'Hara's article about us in the *Chicago American* failed to drum up interest.

In the end, we were given the "sorry, but we don't know you" treatment.

The University's Interscholastic Committee formally awarded us the championship title of Michigan, and in the January issue of *Boys Own Sport*, Jacob was named to the 1903 All-American High School Eleven. The editor singled him out by praising his line bucking abilities and by saying "...the greatest honor that is due Graham is the honor of playing the highest class ball of any member of what might justly be called an all-star eleven."

Jacob's award was the last gasp of the 1903 season. Many of my teammates would never play organized football again. Bridgman was finished, as were Art Baushke, Lee, Lathe, Ossignac, Busby, and the Grahams. Jacob was contacted by a number of colleges and universities, but in the end he declined all offers. Said he was needed at home.

The following season, Teetzel coached us again. Me and Butts and Cunningham were the top dogs, but Handy was the true shining star—he filled the breach left by Jacob's departure and the rooters loved him. They affectionately dubbed him "Elephant

Handy, the Breakfast Food Baby." We slaughtered everyone we met and were undefeated going into the semi-championship game against Mt. Pleasant, which, to our disappointment, we lost 11 to 0. Most of us played with the mumps, but we probably would have won anyway if Mt. Pleasant hadn't used three ineligible players, which Springer knew about but in the end did nothing to remedy. Escanaba defeated Mt. Pleasant for the state title. I was damn happy for them.

Teetzel coached us again in 1905 and for this, my senior year, Butts, Cunningham, and Jones were the stars. We surely would have won the state championship if any of the schools in our district would've had the guts to compete against us. We played a total of twelve games, but only four of them were against high school teams from Michigan. The one game we lost was to the University of Chicago Freshmen, which is where Handy was playing. When it was time to play the winning teams from the other districts we found ourselves disqualified. The Interscholastic Board of Control acted against us for using an illegal player in a practice game with an outside team. Ishpeming won the state championship, and they did it without the 'Wizard. He left to coach at the University of North Dakota. That was Teetzel's final year in Benton Harbor.

In 1906, we almost went independent because of the lousy treatment we were getting from the State Athletic Committee. There were few returning players and no coach, which is why at the last minute the job was offered to Butts. He accepted and coached the team using Teetzel's training methods to win the unofficial state championship by defeating Escanaba 50 to 0!

The final game of the 1906 season was played against a pickup team sponsored by the Miami Club of Benton Harbor. I played for the Miamis along with Jacob, Mit, Art Baushke, and other Benton Harbor enthusiasts and alumni. Playing at Teetzel's characteristic breakneck speed, the high school boys handily defeated us. The score was 14 to 0. The hurry-up style hurt us, but not as much as the new rules that had been adapted that season in response to the public outcry against football's brutality.

The new rules were designed to spread out the playing. This was done by adding a neutral zone at the line of scrimmage and by extending the distance required for a first down from five to ten yards. Hurdling was also abolished, but the most devastating change, at least for us old-timers, was the addition of the forward pass. That was a trick we couldn't accommodate.

The next great rule changes occurred in the year 1910. That's when the mass play was eliminated altogether by outlawing inter-locked interference, pushing and pulling the runner, and by requir-ing seven men to be on the offensive line of scrimmage at all times. I never played under those rules, but I consider myself fortunate to have played at least once under the 1906 changes, for I believe that's when football became the game we recognize today. It was also the year that football as I knew it drew its final breath.

What happened to the fellows who played on Teetzel's Machine of 1903? Some of them I never saw again after high school and some I did, or at least heard about. Most of us married and settled into normal lives. Lester, who continued to be a good friend, went into the gravel business and became quite successful in spite of loos-ing a leg when a pile of gravel rolled over him. Ossignac became a foundry mold maker while Busby moved to St. Paul and I never heard much about him again. Fred Handy went to the University of Chicago and played football for Alonzo Stagg before returning to work the family farm. Wilbur Cunningham became a lawyer and Bridgman a druggist and then a politician. His first position was an alderman, and then during the early years of prohibition he was elected county sheriff. In 1922, he gained brief national recognition when he led a raid on a secret convention of communists. Many historians have called that meeting the founding moment of the American Communist Party.

The Grahams, true to their upbringing and personalities, led lives that continued to be anything but routine. Heck went back to work as a carpenter, and although he could have legally played two more years on the high school team, he never again wore a Benton Harbor high school football uniform. A few years later, he joined the Marines and satisfied his urge to travel.

Jacob Graham went to work as a clerk at Kidd, Dater, and Price wholesale grocery in Benton Harbor. Then he worked construc-tion along with a number of other odd jobs. For a number of years, he seemed destined for a life of mediocrity, his greatest moments having already passed him by on the gridiron. But even after he married and had children he continued to please the public with his physical strength and athletic ability. He good-naturedly played the part of an acrobat and wrestler in Hindpaw's Circus, which was a local fundraiser named in jest after Adam Forepaugh's real circus. When the Benton Harbor Elk's Club held their annual carnival for children in the hall above Conkey's Grocery Store, he of course was the strong man. He wrestled a man dressed in a bear costume, tore telephone books in half, and bent twenty-penny nails with his hands. I found it rather sad to watch this tough, talented athlete and leader of men relegated to such an ignominious end, but that wasn't to be the end.

In 1914, Jacob joined the Benton Harbor police force and two years later became a deputy fire marshal for the State of Michigan. By the end of the First World War, he was solving some of the strangest arson cases in the Midwest. Then, in 1918, he was invited to join the newly formed Michigan State Police as a detective, and in 1929 he was appointed by the governor to the position of Deputy Commissioner of the Michigan Department of Public Safety. It was his work as a detective during the prohibition era that earned him accolades enough for ten men.

Barratt O'Hara had an even greater public career. He eventually left the newspaper business and went to law school and then into politics, finally ending his career as a U.S. Congressmen from Illinois. During his speech at the great 1964 Congressional Integration hearings, he stood at the podium and held up a large photograph of his high school football team, the Benton Harbor team of 1899. There were two colored fellows on that team, which he made reference to when he said that he came from a town where the races once lived together in harmony. It was his contention that people could and should live that way everywhere.

After the season of 1905, I never saw Teetzel again. I heard some things about him, but I can't say if they're true or not. I know for the season of 1908 he was an assistant coach for Yost, and from 1909 until 1915 he coached football at Utah State Agricultural College. Then I never heard another word about him until one hot July morning in

1948 when I ran into Jacob at the grocery store just after I'd retired from the trust department at the bank. Told me Teetzel died the day before in South Haven while visiting from Chicago.

"He saw a lot of changes in the old game, didn't he?" I said sadly.

"Yes sir, we all did," Jacob replied. "But we were damn lucky to have been there."

"Amen to that," I said as a young mother with two kids in tow squeezed past us.

"Excuse me!" she snapped as we shuffled out of the way. It was obvious she was perturbed that we had nothing better to do than to block the aisle while reminiscing about a long-forgotten football season.

I shook my head and shared a smile with Jacob.

"Things have changed, Fletch," he said as he squinted to look after her. "It's not the same as when we were young."

He was right about that. Things had changed, in a big way, and it wasn't just the people. One by one, the old Benton Harbor buildings disappeared, then the canal was filled in and the street cars sold for scrap iron. Eastman Springs was bought up piecemeal by the House of David and the old football field turned into a potato patch. And now it was Teetzel's turn. Everything that had meant so much to us was leaving.

Most of the fellows that played football with me and Jacob are gone now, and so are the memories. I can't believe the season of 1903, as big and broad and as exciting as it was, could ever be forgotten. But it has been and I suppose that's alright. Makes me glad to have written about it. I may be long gone before anyone reads this, and that's alright too, but someday someone will read it and mutter, "I never knew."

And then it'll have all been worthwhile.

Sources:
A Note from the Author

I found this story in an old stationery box, literally. For eighty years, it was the safe refuge for a collection of newspaper articles relating to the football seasons of 1902 through 1904, collected by my grandmother while a teenager in Benton Harbor. Long after my grandmother's passing, I was searching for something in my folk's storage closet when I had the luck to uncover her little treasure chest of clippings. It was a discovery that led to the eventual writing of *The Way We Played the Game*.

In 1903, Benton Harbor had three major newspapers—the *Daily Post*, the *Daily Palladium*, and the *Evening News*. My grandmother's clippings, nearly all of them undated and without sources, seem to have come primarily from the *Daily Post*, while the articles I subsequently obtained from the microfilm archives of the Benton Harbor Public Library were from the *Evening News*. I used all three newspapers to write the story. Quotes came from all three, but for the sake of simplicity I attribute them all to the *Evening News*.

Other sources used in writing *The Way We Played the Game* were team photographs and yearbooks from Benton Harbor and the other schools represented in the story. I read books that gave me a feel for old-time football, among them Allison Danzig's *Oh, How They Played the Game*, Alonzo Stagg's *Touchdown!*, and Alexander Weyland's *The Saga of American Football*. I also researched popular periodicals of the day for information relating to the great public debate that swirled around football during the early years of the twentieth century. Those included *The Nation*, *The Outlook*, and

The North American Review.

Most of my information regarding the beginnings of high school football in Michigan and the seven experimental state championships came from a book published in 1950 by a former Ann Arbor High School principal named Lewis Forsythe. The book was titled *Athletics in Michigan High Schools: The First Hundred Years.* Within its pages, I also found detailed accounts of the Benton Harbor–Ishpeming game of 1902 and the resulting grudge match that developed between them.

Interviews with relatives and acquaintances of the story's characters added to my body of information, and Bob Pruter's article, "The Greatest High School Football Rivalry in Illinois," added much to the scant background data I had about Teetzel's high school sports career. But it was Dick Kishpaugh, sportswriter and long-time historian for the Michigan High School Athletic Association, who from the very beginning put me on the path to success. His support was crucial, and he gave it unselfishly.

Dick offered advice, lent photographs, and he read and reviewed the manuscript in its early, nonfiction format. In response to my more detailed questions about the rules, he put me in contact with David Nelson, former secretary of the NCAA Rules Committee. When David discovered Teetzel's coaching style was patterned after that of Fielding Yost, he suggested I read Yost's 1905 book, *Football for Player and Spectator.* Another invaluable book was suggested by Dick himself—Spalding's *Official Foot Ball Guide*—which also included a detailed catalog of football uniforms, equipment, and their prices. Cleve Lester's stepdaughter, Mona Eastman, graciously loaned me his 1905 copy of Spalding. Imagine my surprise when I discovered the name "Butts" scribbled across the inside of the back cover. My understanding of the "hurry-up" strategy was further enhanced by reviewing a seven-minute film clip taken of the 1904 football game between the Universities of Michigan and Chicago.

All the pieces eventually fell into place except for the most intricate details of the disqualification controversy. Forsythe didn't mention it and neither was there anything in Durand Springer's minute book from his years as secretary of the State Athletic

Committee, which along with the aforementioned film resides at the University of Michigan's Bentley Library. The event as I describe it was primarily taken from the Benton Harbor papers.

My goal in writing *The Way We Played the Game* was to present the material in a way that would accurately portray early high school football. The game's rules, playing strategies, and uniforms along with the community participation and the prevalence of gambling were meticulously researched. I was especially careful to paint a clear picture of the high injury rate.

Regarding settings and living conditions, I read every book, pamphlet, and newspaper article I could find about Benton Harbor's early years. I even walked the grounds of Eastman Springs, which is now owned by the City of David, where I was able to find the site of the old football field. I visited the lakeside town of Escanaba and then Ishpeming, which is still quietly nestled within the hills and valleys of Michigan's Marquette Iron Range. Details like food, clothes, railroads, horsedrawn vehicles, and medicine were equally researched. Home remedies came from the local newspapers while others were found in Clarence Meyer's book, *American Folk Medicine*.

But there are areas of the story that were tampered with historically, and I feel the reader has a right to know where they are.

The real Fletch never wrote a manuscript, although he probably lived a life very similar to the one I describe. Two game scores were modified. I changed the names of certain characters and created a few others. Miss Fitzgerald is one. She was created to carry the anti-football arguments that were raging across the country at that time—most of her arguments were lifted from George Merrill's 1903 article in *The Outlook* entitled "Is Football Good Sport?" The information contained in Teetzel's Burger party speech was taken from an address given in 1893 by Theodore Roosevelt entitled "The Value of an Athletic Training." The characters of Caully and the Gill were also invented. My research revealed the presence of a so-called Muskegon "spy" living in Benton Harbor, and the Gill was created to give him a face.

Wadsworth's personality was a product of my imagination along with the facts regarding the Disemboweled Spirit, who was based in name only on the Escanaba fullback, Dexter Stephenson. My portrayal of Durand Springer was lifted directly from the Benton Harbor newspapers. Colonel Eastman was already dead, having passed away in 1898 and buried in Green Bay, Wisconsin.

In closing, Benton Harbor truly did have grudges with the teams from Ishpeming, Muskegon, and, to a lesser degree, Notre Dame. Be assured I did not single them, or for that matter, the House of David out for foul treatment. Instead, I remained faithful to the historical record as recorded in the Benton Harbor newspapers, which finds its outlet in Fletch's narrative. In some instances, the bias is clear, but my own personal view, of Ishpeming in particular, is quite different and merits a brief comment.

Ishpeming's three successive state championships were probably won fair and square, at least when measured against the officiating practices of the day, and for that reason I believe they deserve to be placed on the short list of America's all-time great high school football teams. A week after their 1902 game against Benton Harbor, at which Fielding Yost was a spectator, an article appeared in the *Ishpeming Iron Ore* that quoted Yost as saying Ishpeming was the best high school football team he ever saw. He said he was greatly surprised at the variety of play, the smoothness, speed, and the fine spirit displayed.

No greater endorsement could be found anywhere.

John Armstrong
April 2002

Photographs and Illustrations

The 1902 Benton Harbor High School Football Team
(Armstrong Collection)

Coach Clayton Teetzel
*(*Evening News, *Nov. 21, 1903)*

Three Benton Harbor running backs from the 1903 team
(Armstrong Collection)

"Before and after" photos of Van Buren County,
Michigan, high school football players in 1898
(Appleyard Studios)

Two unknown players in their football
uniforms prior to a game, circa 1903
(Courtesy of Lee Worley)

*Teetzel as a collegiate player, in his
University of Michigan yearbook photo
(Michigan Historical Collections, Bentley
Historical Library, University of Michigan)*

*Barratt O'Hara in Benton Harbor,
circa 1903
(St. Joseph Public Library)*

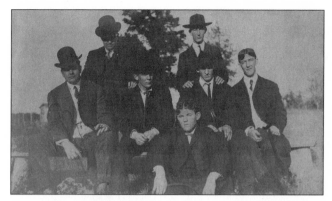

Four 1903 Benton Harbor players surrounded by supporters
(Armstrong Collection)

Hotel Benton with the H.L. Bird Drug Co.
on the main level
(Armstrong Collection)

The Eastman Springs ticket shack
(Armstrong Collection)

GETTINB READY FOR THE GAME TOMORROW.

From the Evening News, *Friday, October 2, 1903*

From the Evening News, *Saturday, September 5, 1903*

From the Evening News, *Tuesday, September 8, 1903*

From the Evening News, *Saturday, September 12, 1903*

From the Evening News, *Saturday, September 19, 1903*

*(Top to bottom) two tickets for Benton Harbor football games,
an advertisement, most likely handed out at games,
a ticket to a Benton Harbor High School football dance
(Armstrong Collection)*

From Spalding's Official Foot Ball Guide, *1905*

From Spalding's Official Foot Ball Guide, *1905*

Group photo taken at the party at Manager Burger's house, November 19, 1903

About the Author

John Armstrong is a writer of essays, short stories, and magazine articles. For inspiration, he draws on the historical past and a diverse background that includes stints as a foundry worker and a songwriter, along with two years of homesteading in Michigan's Upper Peninsula. His interest in writing began while completing a master's degree in architecture. Publishing credits include a short story, "The Quiet Neighbor," and numerous articles for *Michigan History Magazine*. *The Way We Played the Game* is his first book. John and his wife live in west Michigan.